The Sermons of Mark Houseman

In Outline Form

Old Testament
&
New Testament

Josie (Houseman) Blocher

Copyright © 2019 Josephine (Houseman) Blocher, known as Josie Blocher.

First Edition. All rights reserved.

Mark Houseman (1908-1958) is Josie (Houseman) Blocher's father. All sermons are used by permission.

All sermons are in outline form and in chronological order of the books of the Bible in the Old Testament and New Testament.

All scripture quotations used are from the King James Version of the Holy Bible.

These sermon outlines may be used by Pastors or church leaders and church workers in helping their presentation of the gospel.

No part of this book may be reproduced, stored or transmitted by any means, without proper credit and acknowledgment that these sermons are the copyrighted Sermon Outlines of Reverend Mark Houseman, except for brief quotations in review.

Another book written by Mark Houseman is UNDER THE RED STAR. It is his true-life story of how he was born in Russia during the Russian Revolution of 1917, exiled to Siberia, and orphaned at the age of eleven. (The back cover of the Book *Under the Red Star* mistakenly says he was orphaned at the age of 13. The correct age he was orphaned at was 11.) It tells about his daring escape from Communism and reveals God's guiding hand in helping him become an evangelist of the gospel of Jesus Christ.

ISBN: 13:978-1-948118-20-0
Library of Congress Control Number: 2018962235

*Rabboni Book Publishing Company is owned by Josie (Houseman) Blocher, the daughter of Reverend Mark Houseman.

RB Rabboni Book Publishing Company

Foreword

About Mark Houseman

My father, Mark Houseman, (1908-1958) was a Russian Evangelist. He died when I was nine years old, but I still remember many of these sermons being preached. He had a distinct Russian ascent, so much so that other people found him hard to understand, but not me. To me he just sounded like daddy. He was a great story teller and captivated his audience. I remember him walking back and forth on the platform with his Bible in his hand. Many times he told his life story of how he was born in Russia, exiled to Siberia, and orphaned at the age of eleven. He told how the Lord protected him and helped him escape Communism and become an evangelist of the gospel of Jesus Christ.

I was saved under my father's ministry. He was an inspiration to me and to all who heard his preaching. People often said that he had an aurora about him, which was none other than the light of God shining in him. Sometimes we went with daddy on his evangelistic trips and helped minister in song. He and mother would sing a duet; Margaret and mother would sing a duet; and sometimes I would sing. Walter helped with the sound equipment and setting up the slide projector.

Every day, in our home, we had family devotions. Daddy read the Bible and then we would all get down on our knees and pray. Mother would put her arms around me and help me pray. Such was the faith I grew up with. This type of faith shaped my life forever. I thank God of a godly father and a praying mother who taught me about the Lord.

As I type these sermons I often find myself crying and praying, being convicted by what he wrote. His sermons were inspired by God and many souls were saved under his ministry. These sermons were preached from 1944-1958. It is my privilege to present them to you in the exact form that they were written. Since my father was fluent in seven different languages some of his sermons were written in different languages, which I am unable to read, but I have typed what I could read. May God bless these sermons and the reading of God's Word

Josephine (Houseman) Blocher

A sample of Mark Houseman's writing in his own words.

> Messages for 1949
>
> These messages shall be prepared each week as they shall be needed. Prayerfully, thoughtfully under the guidence of the Holy Spirit. Oh, that Mark Houseman may not be seen in these messages but only Christ my Lord. And the faithfullness of the precious Holy Spirit, and God the Father.
> Amen

Introduction

Marzelius Hausmann, known as Mark Houseman, was born in Russia in the year 1908. In the year 1914, the First Great War broke out in Russia under the reign of Czar Nicholas II; and anyone who was not of Russian blood was exiled to Siberia, of which he and his family were among. His autobiography *Under the Red Star* shares his life story of these harrowing accounts. It tells of all the sorrows and hardships he and his family had to endure. During the Russian Revolution of 1917, he was orphaned at the age of eleven. Surviving alone on the ravished streets of Russia, facing death and starvation during the cruel and bloody Russian Revolution is nothing short of a modern day miracle. *Under the Red Star* follows Mark Houseman's daring escape from Communism and reveals God's protective hand on this young man. He came to Canada and attended Prairie Bible Institute, and became an evangelist of the gospel of Jesus Christ. These are the sermons that God gave to Reverend Mark Houseman, the Russian Evangelist. They are a testimony of God's glory, and evidence of His guiding hand on a life totally surrendered to Him.

Old Testament
Contents – Old Testament

	Page
Foreword	3
Introduction	5
The Book of Genesis	14
The Creation and Fall of Man (Genesis 1:1-26)	15
The First Sermon Ever Preached (Genesis 2:15-17)	17
Five Steps - How Men Fall (Genesis 3:1-15)	19
God's Plan of Salvation through Abel (Genesis 4:1-16)	21
The Righteous Judgment of God (Genesis 6:1-22)	23
After the Flood (Genesis 8:1-22)	24
Disobedience (Genesis 11:1-9)	26
The Abrahamic Covenant (Genesis 12:1-5)	28
A Message for Fathers (Genesis 18:17-19)	30
Isaac – A Type of Christ (Genesis 22:1-14)	32
A Bride for Isaac (Genesis 24:1-27)	33
The Deceitfulness of a Human Heart (Genesis 27:1-33)	35
Realizing the Presence of God (Genesis. 28:10-22)	37
His Chosen Man (Genesis 31:3)	39
The Book of Exodus	41
Moses Hid in the Bulrushes (Exodus 2:1-10)	42
Moses and the Burning Bush (Exodus 3:1-12)	43
The Passover in Egypt (Exodus 12:1-13)	45
Christ's Deity (Exodus 6:1-3)	47
Passing Through the Red Sea (Exodus 12:37-38)	49
Manna – A Type of Christ (Exodus 3:7)	51
The Golden Calf (Exodus 32:1-35)	53
The Tabernacle in the Wilderness (Exodus 25:1-9)	54
The Book of Numbers	56
Man's Rebellion and God's Judgment (Numbers 21:5-9)	57
The Book of Deuteronomy	60
City of Refuge (Deuteronomy 19:4-5)	61
The Book of Joshua	63
Be Strong and of Good Courage (Joshua 1:1-9)	64
Seven Kings (Joshua 8:25-29)	65
Joshua's Last Charge (Joshua 24:14-31)	67
The Book of Judges	68
Compromising (Judges 2:1-15)	69
Blessed and Tragic Unconsciousness (Judges 16:20)	71

Contents – Old Testament

Page

The Book of I Samuel 73
Another Year - Another Milestone (I Samuel 7:1-7) 74
Disobedience and Obedience (I Samuel 15:1-23) 75
The Book of II Samuel 78
Humbleness (II Samuel 6:1-24) 79
The Book of I Kings 81
A Man's Knees in the Sand (I Kings 18:42-46) 82
The Book of II Kings 84
Digging Ditches in Faith (II Kings 3:5-24) 85
Seven Dunks (II Kings 5:1-12) 87
Salvation in Time of Great Need (II King 6:9) 88
The High Cost of Doubting (II Kings 19:14-19) 90
Book of I Chronicles 92
Jabez - The Man of Prayer (I Chronicles 4:9-10) 93
Book of II Chronicles 95
Power through Prayer (II Chronicles 16:9) 96
Book of Nehemiah 98
The Fight of a Christian (Nehemiah 4:1-23) 99
Book of Job 101
Satan's Desire (Job 1:1-12) 102
The Manifestation of His Own (Job 1:1-22) 104
The Book of Psalm 106
Temperance (Psalm 1:1-6) 107
God's Hand Upon a Nation (Psalm 2:1) 108
The Frailty of Human Life (Psalm 39:4) 109
A Horrible Pit (Psalm 40:1-3) 110
Revival – Part III (Psalm 42:1-11) 112
Where is Thy God? (Psalm 42:3 & 10) 114
What is Man? (Psalm 90:1-17) 117
The Priestly Service of Christ-Coming Again (Psalm 110) 119
No Hiding Place (Psalm 139:1-24) 121
The Book of Proverbs 122
Father's Day Sermon (Proverbs 14:34) 123
The Gospel in a Proverb (Proverbs 16:1-9) 124
Book of Isaiah 125
The Devil (Isaiah 14:12-17) 126
Satan's Downfall (Isaiah 14:12-17) 128
A Bed Too Short (Isaiah 28:14-21) 130

Contents – Old Testament

Page

Radiant Gems (Isaiah 43:1-11)..131
Revival – Part I (Isaiah 44:22)...133
Book of Ezekiel..136
As God Sees You (Ezekiel 1:8-9)..137
Satan - Part One (Ezekiel 28:11-19)...139
Satan – Part Two (Ezekiel 28:11-19)..141
Book of Daniel..143
The Prophet Daniel – Part One (Daniel 1:1-21)...144
The Prophet Daniel – Part Two (Daniel 2:19-49).......................................147
The Prophet Daniel – Part Three (Daniel 3:1-28).......................................150
The Prophet Daniel – Part Four (Daniel 4:1-37)..152
The Prophet Daniel – Part Five (Daniel 5:1-31)...154
The Prophet Daniel – Part Six (Daniel 6:1-28) 156
The Prophet Daniel – Part Seven (Daniel 7:1-14)......................................159
The Prophet Daniel – Part Eight (Daniel 7:7-28)......................................161
Vision of the Seventy Weeks (Daniel 9:1-19)...162
The Time of the End (Daniel 12:1-13)...164
The Book of Amos..165
God's Longsuffering (Amos 4:12)...166
Book of Jonah..168
As God Sees the World (Jonah 1:1-17)...169
Book of Malachi...171
Will a Man Rob God? (Malachi 3:1-12)...172
Baccalaureate Service..175
Remember Thy Creator...175
Funeral Service...178
Burial Rituals at the Graveside...178
Flannel Graph Board Messages...180
The Creation and Fall of Man (Genesis 1:1-26) 181
Moses Hid in the Bulrushes (Exodus 3:1-12)..183

New Testament

Contents – New Testament

	Page
Book of Matthew	185
Jesus (Matthew 1:18-21)	186
He is a Great God (Matthew 1:18-Chapter 2:1-12)	188
Repentance and Faith (Matthew 4:1-17)	190
Recognizing Jesus (Matthew 14:15-36)	192
The Marriage Feast (Matthew 22:1-14)	194
The Great Paradox (Matthew 17:35-28:1-20)	195
Resurrection (Matthew 28:1-10 & 16-20)	197
What Scripture Says about Baptism (Matthew 28:18-20)	200
Book of Mark	201
Victory Through Love and Unison (Mark 2:1-12)	202
Grain the Whole World (Mark 8:27-38)	203
Not Ministered Unto, But to Minister (Mark 10: 35-45)	205
Broken in the Hands of the Master (Mark 14:1-9)	207
Book of Luke	209
Christ - As a Great King (Luke 2:1-20)	210
The Humanity of Christ (Luke 2:7)	211
Come to the Feet of Jesus (Luke 7:38-48)	213
The Price of a Soul (Luke 8:22-39)	215
Swept and Garnished (Luke 11:14-32)	217
The Test of Discipleship (Luke 12:35-40)	219
The Long Suffering of God (Luke 13:1-9)	221
Earth, Heaven and Hell (Luke 15:3-10)	222
The Parable of the Lost Son (Luke 15:11-24)	223
The Two Distinct Natures of Man (Luke 16:19-31)	225
The Questions about Salvation (Luke 18:18-30)	228
The Facts of Christ's Resurrection (Luke 24:36-53)	230
Book of John	232
What Christ was Made (John 1:14)	233
Christ the Light of the World (John 1:4)	234
The Calls of Christ (John 1:35-51)	236
The Purging of the Temple (John 2:17)	237
Analysis of John 3:16 (John 3:16)	239
New Birth (John 3:1-21)	241

Contents – New Testament

Page

The Samaritan Woman (John 4:1-42) 243
Repentance and Faith (John 5:1-17) 245
The Great Divide (John 7:37-43) 247
The Resurrection of Lazarus (John 11:1-7, 17-44) 248
The Heroic Life of Our Lord (John 12:12-33) 250
The Triumphant Entry (John 12:12-36) 251
Love for His Own (John 13:1-20) 253
God's Promises (John 14:1-6) 254
The Holy Spirit (John 14:13-27) 255
Abiding in Christ (John 15:1-27) 257
The love of God (John 17:1-26) 260
Sanctification (John 17:1-26) 262
It Is Finished (John19:1-42) 265
The Book of Acts 267
The Ascension of Christ (Acts 1:1-14) 268
Revival - Part II (Acts 5:1-16) 271
The First Martyr (Acts 7:44-60) 274
The Conversion of Saul of Tarsus (Acts 9:1-25) 276
Perfect Liberty Gives Perfect Victory (Acts 12:1-19) 278
The Unknown God (Acts 17:1-23) 280
Salvation or Religion (Acts 28:16-37) 283
Book of Romans 285
I am a Debtor (Romans 1:1-16) 286
The Guilty World (Romans 1:18-32) 287
The Fact of Sin (Romans 5:1-21) 288
Justification - Part I (Romans 5:1-21) 290
Baptism (Romans 6:1-23) 292
What the Resurrection Guarantees (Romans 6:1-23) 294
To Conquer the Capital "I" (Romans 7:1-25) 296
The Spirit of Leadership (Romans 8:14-17) 298
Justification –Part II (Romans 8:28-39) 300
The Five Principles of Discipleship (Romans 10:1-15) 302
The Living Sacrifice (Romans 12:1-21) 306
Book of I Corinthians 309
Christians, What Are You Building? (I Corinthians 3:1-23) 310
Purge Out the Old Leaven (I Corinthians 5:1-8) 312
Covet the Best Gifts (I Corinthians 12:1-31) 313

Contents – New Testament

	Page
True Love (I Corinthians 13:1-13)	315
The Christians' Circle of Testimony (I Corinthians 15:1-6)	317
In Vain (I Corinthians 15:1-21)	319
The Firstfruits of the Resurrection (I Corinthians 15:1-23)	320
The Glorified Resurrected Body (I Corinthians 15:51-53)	322
Book of II Corinthians	324
The Face of Jesus (II Corinthians 4:6)	325
The Authority of the Believer (II Corinthians 4:7)	328
Serving Christ (II Corinthians 5:14-21)	331
To Approve Ourselves unto God (II Corinthians 6:1-10)	333
God's Time is at Hand (II Corinthians 6:1-18)	335
Separation from Sin (II Corinthians 6:11-8)	337
God's Unspeakable Gift (II Corinthians 9:15)	339
God's Grace is Sufficient (II Corinthians 12:9)	341
Examine Ourselves (II Corinthians 13:5)	343
Book of Galatians	346
Christ - According to Scripture....(Galatians 4:4-18)	347
The Three Christian Characters (Galatians 5:22-23)	349
Book of Ephesians	351
How to Pray (Ephesians 6:1-24)	352
Spiritual Warfare (Ephesians 6:10-20)	356
Satan's Defeat (Ephesians 6:10-18)	358
Book of Philippians	360
Christ is All (Philippians 1:1-26)	361
Unity in Christ (Philippians 1:1-30)	363
Fellowship in Christ (Philippians 2:1-11)	365
Rejoicing in Christ (Philippians 3:1-14)	367
That I May Know Him (Philippians 3:1-16)	369
The Power of His Resurrection (Philippians 3:7-14)	372
Book of Colossians	375
Christ (Colossians 3:1-17)	376
Book of I Thessalonians	378
The Resurrections (I Thessalonians 4:13-18)	379
Book of II Timothy	382
A Mother's Prayer (II Timothy 1:1-13)	383
God's Divine Rule (II Timothy 1:1-14)	384

Contents – New Testament

	Page
Book of Titus	386
To Be a Pattern (Titus 2:7)	387
Salvation Brought (Titus 2:11-15)	389
Book of Hebrews	390
The Priestly Service of Christ-Office (Hebrew 5:1-10)	391
The Priestly Service of Christ-Offering (Hebrews 9:6-28)	393
The Priestly Service of Christ-Intercession (Hebrews 7:25)	396
Christ our Deliverer (Hebrews 9:24-28)	398
True Faith (Hebrews 11:1-7)	400
The Christian Walk (Hebrews 12:1-2)	401
Looking (Hebrews 12:1-3)	403
Book of James	404
What is Your life? (James 4:12-17)	405
Prevailing Prayer (James 5:16)	406
Book of II Peter	408
The Christian's Crowns (II Peter 1:1-9)	409
Book of I John	412
A Fourfold Attitude Towards Sin (I John 1:1-2:3)	413
How to Promote a Revival (I John 2:15-17)	415
The Sin Question (I John 3:1-24)	416
Propitiation for Our Sins (I John 4:1-2)	418
Book of Revelation	420
What God Sees in the Churches (Revelation 3:1-22)	421
Witnesses Concerning Christ (Revelation 5:1-14)	423
The Final and Last Resurrection (Revelation 20:11-15)	425
The Great White Throne (Revelation 20:11-15)	428
Whom Do You Expect to See in Heaven? (Revelation 21:27)	430
The Final Heaven (Revelation 21:1-8)	433
Pictures of Mark Houseman	435
Quotes of Mark Houseman	438

Old Testament
King James Version

Sermon Outlines from the Book of Genesis

The Creation and the Fall of Man

Genesis 1:1-26

Text: Genesis 1:1-26 - Genesis 2:7 - Genesis 3:15 – Genesis 3:21

I Point: <u>Man was Perfect.</u>
   a. Had fellowship with God.
   b. Was clothed with the garment of righteousness.
   c. Had great intelligence.
   d. Then sin entered.
   e. Consequences - Genesis 3:19-20 "In the sweat of thy face shall thou eat bread, till thou return unto the ground; for out of it wast thou taken: for dust thou art, and unto dust shalt thou return."

II Points: <u>Satan's Attack.</u>
   a. Genesis 3:1-4 – The Temptation of Eve.
      Their admiration was God till that time.
      Satan promised them to be as gods.
      Genesis 3:4 "And the serpent said unto the woman, Ye shall not surely die:"
   b. Eve looked and coveted.
   c. She partook.
   d. Adam and Eve were stripped of all glory.
      Genesis 3:7 "And the eyes of them both were opened, and they knew that they were naked;…"

III Point: <u>God comes down in judgment</u>.
   a. In the cool of the day.
      Genesis 3:8 "And they heard the voice of the LORD God walking in the garden in the cool of the day: and Adam and his wife hid themselves from the presence of the LORD God amongst the trees of the garden." This can be translated storm tempest and judgment.
   b. God gives room for repentance.
   c. Adam will not take the blame.
      Genesis 3:12 "And the man said, The woman whom thou gavest to be with me, she gave me of the tree, and I did eat."

d. Eve will not take the blame.
   Genesis 3:13 "...And the woman said, The serpent beguiled me, and I did eat."
e. God gives the promise of the Saviour.
   Genesis 3:15 "And I will put enmity between thee and the woman, and between thy seed and her seed; it shall bruise thy head, and thou shalt bruise his heel."
f. God shows unto them the Lamb (Christ) slain for their sins. Genesis 3:21 "Unto Adam also and to his wife did the LORD God make coats of skins, and clothed them."
g. The coats of skins are a type of Christ to cover us with the righteousness of God.

Conclusion:
a. Christ, the Lamb of God, takes the blow.
b. The garments of skin are garments of hope until the coming of Christ.
c. The lamb's sacrifice of coats of skins is a type of Christ's sacrifice for us. Revelation 13:8 "...the Lamb slain from the foundation of the world."
d. Are you, my friend, looking forward to that day of perfection when the Lord will come?

The First Sermon Ever Preached
Genesis 2:15-17

The first sermon ever preached on earth was Genesis 2:15-17. "And the LORD God took the man, and put him into the Garden of Eden to dress it and to keep it. And the Lord God commanded the man, saying, Of every tree of the garden thou mayest freely eat. But of the tree of the knowledge of good and evil, thou shalt not eat of it: for in the day that thou eatest thereof thou shalt surely die." (Genesis 2:15-17).
It was a sermon on life and death.
    a. The preacher thereof was God Himself.
    b. This sermon was unto life.

The second sermon ever preached on earth was Genesis 3:1-5. "Now the serpent was more subtil than any beast of the field which the LORD God had made. And he said unto the woman, Yea, hath God said, Ye shall not eat of every tree of the garden? And the woman said unto the serpent, We may eat of the fruit of the trees of the garden: But of the fruit of the tree which is in the midst of the garden, God hath said, Ye shall not eat of it, neither shall ye touch it, lest ye die. And the serpent said unto the woman, Ye shall not surely die: For God doth know that in the day ye eat thereof, then your eyes shall be opened, and ye shall be as gods, knowing good and evil." (Genesis 3:1-5).
    a. The preacher thereof was Satan himself.
    b. This sermon was unto death.

I Point: <u>The nature of these sermons - Obedience and Disobedience.</u>
1. Obedience unto God's command.
    a. The benefits to obedience.
        i. Genesis 2:8-9 - Fellowship with God.
        ii. Dominion over creation. Genesis 1:26 "...and let them have dominion..."
        iii. Painless multiplication of child birth. Genesis 1:28 "...Be fruitful, and multiply..."
2. Disobedience unto God.
    a. The consequences of disobedience.
        i. Death. Genesis 2:17 "...thou shalt surely die."
        ii. Loss of fellowship. Genesis 3:8 "...Adam and his wife hid themselves from the presence of the LORD God..."

  iii. Painful multiplication of child birth. Genesis 3:16 "...in sorrow thou shalt bring forth children;..."
  iv. All labour cursed. Genesis 3:19 "In the sweat of thy face shalt thou eat bread,..."

II Point: <u>Man's choice for life and eternity</u>.
a. Genesis 3:6 - Man chose to disobey.
b. Genesis 3:8 - Man chose to be separated from God.
c. Genesis 3:12-13 – Man accused God for their down fall.

III Point: <u>The condition of man</u>.
a. Genesis 6:5 "And God saw that the wickedness of man was great..."
b. Genesis 6:5 "...and that every imagination of the thoughts of his heart was only evil continually."

IV Point: - <u>The choice of man in these last days</u>.
a. I Timothy 4:1-3 "Now the Spirit speaketh expressly, that in the latter times some shall depart from the faith, giving heed to seducing spirits, and doctrines of devils; Speaking lies in hypocrisy; having their conscience seared with a hot iron;..."

Conclusion: Romans 5:12 "Wherefore, as by one man sin entered into the world, and death by sin; and so death passed upon all men, for that all have sinned:"

Five Steps – How Men Fall

Genesis 3:1-15

Five Steps - How Men Fall.
1. Genesis 3:1 – Listening to slander against God.
2. Genesis 3:4 – Doubting God's word and His love for man.
3. Genesis 3:6 – Looking at what God has forbidden.
4. Genesis 3:6 – Lusting after that which God has prohibited.
5. Genesis 3:6 – Disobedience to God's command.

I Point: The love for the world.
   a. I John 2:15-17 "Love not the world, neither the things that are in the world. If any man love the world, the love of the Father is not in him. For all that is in the world, the lust of the flesh, and the lust of the eyes, and the pride of life, is not of the Father, but is of the world."
   b. Disobedience to God's commands.
   Genesis 3:6 "...she took of the fruit thereof, and did eat, and gave also unto her husband with her; and he did eat."
   Illustration: Where Saul lost out with God. I Samuel 15:23 "...Because thou hast rejected the word of the LORD, he hath also rejected thee from being king."

II Point: The immediate result.
   a. Genesis 3:7 "And the eyes of them both were opened, and they knew that they were naked;..."
   Application: Satan told them that they then will see, and know, and be as God. But the real result was that of Revelation 3:17 "Because thou sayest, I am rich...and knowest not that thou art wretched, and miserable, and poor, and blind, and naked:"
   b. II Corinthians 4:3-4 "But if our gospel be hid, it is hid to them that are lost: In whom the god of this world (Satan) hath blinded the minds of them which believe not, lest the light of the glorious gospel of Christ, who is the image of God, should shine unto them."
   c. Romans 5:12 "Wherefore, as by one man sin entered into the world, and death by sin; and so death passed upon all men, for that all have sinned:"
   d. That is the result of Adam's disobedience.

III Point: <u>To admit their lost condition</u>.
  a. If I could only get the lost to believe that they are lost.
  b. If I could only get it settled in your heart that your loved ones, outside of Christ, are forever lost.
  c. Then salvation is at hand. Luke 19:10 "For the Son of man is come to seek and to save that which was lost."
  This promise is given in Genesis 3:15 "...it shall bruise thy head, and thou shalt bruise his heel."
  And again in Galatians 4:4-5 "But when the fullness of the time was come, God sent forth his Son, made of a woman, made under the law, to redeem them that were under the law..."
  d. Matthew 1:21 "And she shall bring forth a son, and thou shalt call his name JESUS: for he shall save his people from their sins."

IV Point: <u>To see your salvation</u>.
  a. John 12:32 "And I, if I be lifted up from the earth, will draw all men unto me."
  b. Acts 16:31 "...Believe on the Lord Jesus Christ, and thou shalt be saved, and thy house."
  c. John 6:37 "All that the Father giveth me shall come to me; and him that cometh to me I will in no wise cast out."
  d. John 6:47 "Verily, verily, I say unto you, He that believeth on me hath everlasting life."
  e. John 1:12 "But as many as received him, to them gave he power to become the sons of God, even to them that believe on his name:"
  f. Do you see your salvation?

Conclusion: An old Saloon owner tried to disturb a revival meeting. The first night he sent one of his old pals to disturb the meeting, but instead he got saved. The next night he sent another one to disturb the meeting, but he got saved, too. The third night he decided to go himself, and died in the meeting. He then accomplished disturbing the revival meeting.

God's Plan of Salvation through Abel
Genesis 4:1-16

Introduction: I want you to notice that it was God's greatest aim ever since the fall of man to show him the way back to God.

The only way back to God is through Christ.

Here we have Abel - A type of Christ.

1. Genesis 3:15 – The Promise.
2. Genesis 3:21 – The costs of skins.
3. Genesis 4:4 – The sacrifice of Abel.

I Point: God and the fallen race of Adam.

a. The first born - Cain. Genesis 4:1 "And Adam knew Eve his wife; and she conceived, and bare Cain,…"
b. Cain is a type of the mere man of the earth.
Genesis 4:3 "…Cain brought of the fruit of the ground an offering unto the LORD."
c. The first birth is needful. A soul must be born before it becomes a soul.
d. In the natural, a perfect man, a boy who gave his mother great joy. Genesis 4:1 "…I have gotten a man from the LORD."

II Point: God loses no opportunity to show the plan of Salvation.

a. Abel, the second born, must die to show the plan of salvation. Genesis 4:4 "And Abel, he also brought of the firstlings of his flock and of the fat thereof. And the LORD had respect unto Abel and to his offering:"
b. His birth, natural, but to Eve, he was the second born.
c. God's covenant was with the second born.
Genesis 4:2 "…and she again bare his brother Abel. And Abel was a keeper of sheep, but Cain was a tiller of the ground."
d. Abel, the second born, chose a lamb of the firstlings for his offering. Genesis 4:4 "And Abel, he also brought of the firstlings of his flock and of the fat thereof. And the LORD had respect unto Abel and to his offering:"

III Point: God's third man covenant.
1. Adamic – Abel.
2. Abrahamic – Jacob.
3. The Man – Christ Jesus.

IV Point: God's respect toward its offering.
- a. Cain's offering – God had no respect because of what he offered.
- b. Abel's offering – God had great respect because of what he offered.
- c. Because of firmness unto death.

Conclusion: This testimony of Abel condemned Cain.
Genesis 4:10 "And he said, What hast thou done? the voice of thy brother's blood crieth unto me from the ground."

Application: Your testimony condemns the world.
This church stands here for two things; to bless, or to condemn those living around us.

The Righteous Judgment of God

Genesis 6:1-22

I Point: <u>The wickedness of man was great on the earth</u>.
- a. Genesis 6:1-7 - The inter message and the sin from before, such as, Cain, Lamech and others.
  Application: God foresees the millions of little ones coming into this world because of sin. Genesis 3:16 "Unto the woman he said, I will greatly multiply thy sorrow and thy conception;…"
- b. The Holy Spirit was grieved away from them.
- c. Genesis 6:3 - God quit striving with mankind and man became corrupt.

II Points: <u>Judgment predicted</u>.
- a. Genesis 3:5-7 – Judgment.
- b. Genesis 6:14 – Mercy revealed.
- c. Genesis 6:3 - 120 years of chance.
- d. Noah preached by word, deed and life.
- e. Genesis 6:12 – After 120 years.
- f. Genesis 6:15-22 – Object lesson by animals.
  Application: The warning of the day.

III Point: <u>Judgment in action</u>
- a. Genesis 7:1 "…Come thou and all thy house into the ark;…" Noah is taken out of the world.
- b. Genesis 7:16 "And the LORD shut him in."
- c. Genesis 7:17 "…the waters increased, and bare up the ark…"
- d. For 4000 years since the flood we had the chance.
- e. Our ark, Jesus Christ, still calls, still pleads. His servants are still preaching.
  1. John 10:9 "I am the door: by me if any man enter in, he shall be saved,…"
  2. I Corinthians 1:18 "For the preaching of the cross is to them that perish foolishness;…"
  3. Illustration: When Turkey sent all the Christians out of one province – judgment fell.

Compare: <u>The Ark of Noah with the Ark Jesus Christ</u>.
- a. It only had one door.
- b. All had to go through that one door.
  Illustration: The judgment which destroyed the world lifted the ones in the ark near to the heart of God.

After the Flood

Genesis 8:1-22

Introduction: The Ark is a type of Christ. It clearly depicted and explained God's Word.

It is God's aim to present Christ in His types.
1. Tree of Life.
   Genesis 2:9 "...the tree of life also in the midst of the garden..."
2. The Promise.
   Genesis 3:15 "And I will put enmity between thee and the woman, and between thy seed and her seed; it shall bruise thy head, and thou shalt bruise his heel."
3. The Lamb.
   Genesis 3:21 "Unto Adam also and to his wife did the LORD God make coats of skins, and clothed them."
4. As Man in Abel.
   Genesis 4:8 "...Cain rose up against Abel his brother, and slew him."
5. The Ark of Noah.
   Genesis 6:1 "And it came to pass, when men began to multiply on the face of the earth..."

I Point: God's dealings with the Ark.
   a. The Ark went through the judgment.
   b. The Ark took the blows for those inside.
   c. The Ark provides shelter, protection and safety.

II Point: God reveals to Noah that not all who have enjoyed the safety in the Ark will remain faithful.
a. The Raven.
   Genesis 8:7 "And he sent forth a raven, which went forth to and fro..." The raven could feed sweetly on the carcasses floating on the water. This is a picture of the ungodly.
b. The Dove.
   Genesis 8:9 "But the dove found no rest for the sole of her foot..." This is a type of a true Christian.

III Points: God's covenant with Noah
a. Genesis 8: 20 - Noah built an altar and sacrificed.
b. God's token, the rainbow, stands for Christ.
   Genesis 9:13 "I will set my bow in the cloud, and it shall be for a token of a covenant between me and the earth."

c. The colors of the rainbow.
    1. Bluish gray – The calmness of God.
    2. Purple – The royalty of Christ.
    3. Red – The blood of Christ.
    4. Green – The growth of Christ.
    5. Gold – The crown of Christ.

Conclusion:
Illustration: What do the telephone poles on the side of the road teach us?
1. Some are up right.
2. Some are leaning.
3. Some are lying down.
4. Some are hanging as a burden for the rest.
5. Yet, they all support and bare a message.

Which kind of Christian are you? Are you upright and carrying the message of Christ? Are you leaning on others to carry it? Are you lying down and hanging as a burden to those who are carrying the message?

Illustration: Some Christians are like the little girl that received two nickels. Her father said "One is for the offering, and one is for you." But when she lost one she said, "Oh no, I lost God's nickel."

Illustration: A girl came to P. B. I., and there found Christ. Her sister watched her. And after watching her for a while she said, "I don't know what you have, but I want it."

Disobedience
Genesis 11:1-9

Text: Genesis 11:4 "...Go to, let us build us a city and a tower, whose top may reach unto heaven; and let us make us a name, lest we be scattered abroad upon the face of the whole earth."

Introduction: The earth was then about 2000 years old, approximately about 3 or 4 hundred years after the flood.

This Tower of Babel was built in the land of Shinar in the country of Babylon under the leadership of Nimrod.

Genesis 10:8-10 "And Cush begat Nimrod: he began to be a mighty one in the earth. He was a mighty hunter before the LORD: wherefore it is said, Even as Nimrod the mighty hunter before the LORD. And the beginning of his kingdom was Babel,..."

The size of the tower was:
    a. It covered a surface of 4900 square feet.
    b. The base of it was 607 feet square.
    c. The height of it was 607 feet high.

The material was built from:
    a. Brick and mortar.
    b. (Information from exploration about the structure.)

I Point: God's command.
a. Genesis 9:1 "And God blessed Noah and his sons, and said unto them, Be fruitful, and multiply, and replenish the earth."
Application: God still wants us, as Christians, to spread out. Matthew 28:19 "Go ye therefore, and teach all nations,..."

II Points: Men's rebellion.
a. Genesis 11:4 "...let us make us a name,..."
b. Genesis 11:4 "...lest we be scattered abroad..."
This was direct rebellion against God's command.
Illustration: Take city life for example.
    1. How the men would gather together and rebel against God's government.
    2. City life is by far more immoral.
    3. Take the collective farms in Russia, for example:

   i. They hatched laziness.
   ii. They hatched godlessness.
   iii. They hatched rebellion.

III Point: <u>God intervenes</u>.
 a. Genesis 11:5 "And the LORD came down to see…"
  Application: God still comes down to see.
 b. God still has His methods.
 c. He still can confound the works of men.

IV Point: Men's image of God's glory turned to shame.
 a. Genesis 11:9 "Therefore is the name of it called Babel, because the LORD did there confound the language of all the earth: and from thence did the LORD scatter them abroad upon the face of all the earth."

The Abrahamic Covenant

Genesis 12:1-5, Genesis 13:14-18, Genesis 15:2-7,

Genesis 16:1-3, Genesis 17:1-2 & 15-19

Introduction: God is anxious to reveal unto the fallen world, Christ.
1. At the creation – Genesis 2:9 - The tree of Life.
2. At the fall of man – Genesis 3:21 - A Lamb slain.
3. At Cain and Abel's life – Genesis 4:4 – A firstling of the flock.
4. At the flood – Genesis 6:14 – An Ark.
5. At the Abrahamic Covenant – Genesis 17:19 - A son.

In order to reveal these to the world God must have a man whom He can trust.

I Point: Abraham's calling.

a. Genesis 12:1-2 "Now the LORD had said unto Abram, Get thee out of thy country, and from thy kindred, and from thy father's house, unto a land that I will shew thee:"
b. Genesis 17:16 – Abraham's faith.

II Point: God begins to prepare Abraham.

a. Genesis 16:1-3 - Abraham was impatience – (He became a Sara type of Christ.)
b. Genesis 17:18 – Abraham was satisfied with Ishmael.
c. Genesis 21:10 "Cast out this bondwoman and her son:..."
d. It may be grievous to you; as it was to Abraham.

III Points: Cast out this bond woman and her son.

a. That is just the same for as today.
b. Has the Lord something he is doing with your life? Then cast out that bond thing.
c. God could not do much for Abraham until he cast out Ishmael and Hagar.
d. What is it in your life to which the Lord will point his finger and say, "Cast it out?"

e. You may wonder what will become of it.
f. Genesis 21:17-18 "And God heard the voice of the lad; and the angel of God called to Hagar out of heaven, and said unto her, What aileth thee Hagar? fear not; for God hath heard the voice of the lad where he is. Arise, lift up the lad, and hold him in thine hand; for I will make him a great nation."
g. God will take care of your problems, but you must first cast out the bond thing, whatever that may be.

A Message for Fathers
Genesis 18:17-19

Text: Genesis 18:19 "For I know him, that he will command his children and his household after him, and they shall keep the way of the LORD..."

There is no better theme that I can find for Father's Day than to speak on Abraham.

I Points: <u>God's respect to Abraham</u>.
    a. There was no higher compliment that God could pay to Abraham then this, "I know him, that he will command his children and his household after him and they shall keep the way of the LORD,..." (Genesis 18:19).
Application: There is nothing more rejoicing to the heart of a parent than a sober minded, and an honest hearted child.
    b. On the other hand, I do not care how much you have, even if you live in a palace and the floors are spread with Persian rugs, and you lie upon silken cushions, or roll down the streets in the best and finest vehicles ever put out; if you have a godless drunken loafer of a boy, or a frivolous flirty-headed girl who gads about the streets with every Tom, Dick and Harry, let me tell you that such parents, in spite of all they have, or all that they are, they are of all parents most miserable.
    c. And who is to be blamed? According to our text, it can be traced down to some defect in the home.
Every gambler, every drunkard, and every fallen woman, once upon a time was as pure as the morning dew.
No drunkard ever intended to be a drunkard; but, he followed someone before him.
Illustration: Look at what smoking does to a fellow. How childish it appears to the rest of us; yet, if a boy sees his father smoking he thinks it is smart.
What you do in moderation your children will do in excess. You need to teach your children by a good and godly example. God could not say of this father, "I know him; he will command his children after him."
Remember, you leave marks behind you every day of your life.

II Point: <u>Abraham the intercessor.</u>
Genesis 18:23 - He interceded for Lot, and so saved his life from destruction.
   a. Intercede to the Father in heaven for your children and save them from destruction.
      Sometimes you feel you should pray, but you put it off and put it off. Yes, you say, I'll wait until I finish my job and then I'll pray. But it is too late, the spirit has left you and you have no more desire to pray. Genesis 6:3 "And the LORD said, My spirit shall not always strive with man,..." Fathers, pray for your children when the spirit bids.

      Churches are praying for revival, but are not willing to pay the price. Members do not pray. They do not give up their bad habits. They do not tithe.

      Fathers, you teach your children by your example. Teach them to follow good and godly habits.

      Illustration: A farmer taught his pigs to follow him when he sprinkled peas on the ground. They followed him everywhere. But later he led them to the slaughter house, for they were used to following his peas. Fathers, your children will follow your lead. Lead them to Christ.

Isaac – A Type of Christ
Genesis 22:1-14

Introduction: God is still in the effort to prepare Abraham for the great revelation he had in store for the world at that age.

I Point: <u>The preparation of Abraham</u>.
1. Loss of country.
2. Loss of home.
3. Loss of loved ones.
4. Loss of Isaac his only child.
a. Genesis 22:2 "…Take now thy son, thine only son Isaac, whom thou lovest, and offer him there for a burnt-offering upon one of the mountains which I will tell thee of."
b. Did Abraham have reasons to refuse?
Did he have reason to doubt if this truly was from God? Yes! But he walked so close to God that he knew perfectly well it was God who spoke.

II Point: <u>Isaac a type of Christ</u>.
a. Genesis 22:6 – Isaac bared the wood.
Genesis 22:9 - Abraham bound Isaac, his own son, and laid him on the altar upon the wood.
b. Genesis 22:13 - God shows to Abraham the substitute.
A ram caught in the thicket.
1. Revelation 13:8 "…the Lamb slain from the foundation of the world."
2. John 1:29 "…Behold the Lamb of God, which taketh away the sin of the world."
3. John 8:56 "…Abraham rejoiced to see my day:…"

III Point: <u>The Son question settled</u>.
a. The Son question at hand. Matthew 27:22 "…What shall I do then with Jesus which is called Christ?"

Matthew 27:1 "When the morning was come,…"
1. They bound Him.
2. They condemned Him.
3. They killed Him. (Matthew 27:1-2 & 22).

IV Point: <u>The greatest salvation day the world has ever seen</u>.
a. Matthew 27:22 - Two candidates.
1. God's Son - God's representative.
2. Barabbas – Satan's representative.
3. Your choice.

Conclusion: What will you do with Jesus, which is called Christ?

A Bride for Isaac
Genesis 24: 1-27

Introduction: Today we shall see a well-disciplined family in whom God was first in all things, and of whom God had said: "For I know him, (Abraham) that he will command his children and his household after him, and they shall keep the way of the LORD…" (Genesis 18:19).

I Point: Family discipline.

    a. Genesis 24:1-8 – Abraham was old; but yet, he had the say so and the care of his household.
    b. Isaac, though he was the only son, was not spoiled.
    c. Abraham had one aim in mind, and that was to serve the Lord, either by life or by death.
    d. Abraham knew why he had come out from Ur.
        1. Did you come out from "Ur" - the world?
        2. Do your children see that in your life God is first?
    e. Abraham was able to talk with Isaac in regards to whom he should marry.
    Application: Many of our parents, today, have lost complete control of their children as to whom they should marry.

This is the natural side of the blessing this message brings forth. But now let us see the spiritual side it reveals.

II Point: The Bride of Isaac.

    a. Genesis 24:2-10 – Eleazar was the servant of Abraham. He was a type of the Holy Spirit going out to win a bride for Isaac.
    b. Rebekah – A type of the "blood bought" ones - The bride of Christ.
    c. She was active, willing and loving. Genesis 24:58 "…she said, I will go…"
    d. She meets Isaac, her bridegroom, in humility.
    e. Her joy is complete when the arms of her bridegroom are around her.
    Application: Isaiah 62:5 "…as the bridegroom rejoiceth over the bride, so shall thy God rejoice over thee."

III Point: <u>The bridegroom is soon to come</u>.

Illustration: Why was Queen Elizabeth crowned as queen?
She was crowned because she loved the King.

Revelation 22:17 "And the Spirit and the bride say, Come. And let him that heareth say, Come. And let him that is athirst come. And whosoever will, let him take the water of life freely."

John 15:16 "Ye have not chosen me, but I have chosen you, and ordained you, that ye should go and bring forth fruit, and that your fruit should remain…"

Conclusion: Are you ready to meet Christ as His bride?

The Deceitfulness of the Human Heart
Genesis 27:1-33

Introduction: So far we have had the Lord's concern to show to the world Calvary. In different types we have had it presented. The type of the Holy Spirit in the form of Eleazar, Abraham's servant, is going out to win a bride for Isaac. Today we have the nature of the human heart with which God has to deal with present.

I Point: <u>Esau</u> - <u>The carefree stomach filling kind</u>.
    a. Esau's life. (Genesis 25:27-34).
        1. Out for sport and fun in life.
        2. Genesis 25:30 "...Feed me, I pray thee..."
        3. Esau had no aim in life. Genesis 25:32 "...what profit shall this birthright do to me?"
        4. Genesis 25:34 "...thus Esau despised his birthright." What did God think of him?
    b. God calls these profane people.
    c. Hebrew 12:16-17 "Lest there be any fornicator, or profane person, as Esau, who for one morsel of meat sold his birthright. For ye know how that afterward, when he would have inherited the blessing, he was rejected: for he found no place of repentance, though he sought it carefully with tears."

II Point: <u>Jacob</u> <u>was so ambitious to get places that he forgets</u>
      <u>God</u>.
    a. First, I want you to notice that Jacob was, at that time, an unsaved man.
    b. Jacob was one of those fellows that can put on a good front and pass for a Christian. He was one who could lie his way in, and lie his way out.
    c. He lied to his father. Genesis 27:19 "And Jacob said unto his father, I am Esau thy firstborn;..."
    d. He stole Esau's birthright, and stole his brother's blessing.

    Application: These kind of folks are very hard to reach for Christ. They are a great stumbling block to Christianity.

III Point: <u>God cornered Jacob</u>. (Genesis 28:10-15).
    a. We see Jacob was caught in his sin. Genesis 27:41 "And Esau hated Jacob because of the blessing wherewith his father blessed him:..."

    b. We see he had to flee. Genesis 27:43 "Now therefore, my son, obey my voice; and arise, flee thou to Laban my brother to Haran;"
    c. Genesis 28:10-15 - Now we find him lying, caught, and found out of the LORD.
    d. He felt uncomfortable. Genesis 28:17 "And he was afraid, and said, How dreadful is this place!..."
    Illustration: An infidel got into the wrong row boat and did not like his company. When you are unsaved, you feel uncomfortable around Christians.

IV Point: Jacob's ladder (Genesis 28:10-17).
    a. Great fear came upon Jacob. He was out of fellowship with God.
    b. He makes a covenant with God. Not for salvation, but for a good life and protection in this life only.
    c. Genesis 18:20-21 "And Jacob vowed a vow, saying, If God will be with me, and will keep me in this way that I go, and will give me bread to eat, and raiment to put on, So that I come again to my father's house in peace; then shall the LORD by my God."
    d. But God is not through with Jacob yet.

Conclusion: How many are here who try to use the look of Christianity for going into the world? Take Jacob as an example.

Realizing the Presence of God
Genesis 28:10-22

I Point: <u>Jacob's obedience unto sins</u>.
    a. Genesis 27:1-4 – Isaac's act against God's will.
    b. Genesis 27:8 – Rebekah's eagerness to have the Lord's will performed without even counseling God or the Holy Spirit.
    Application: This is a perfect picture of us. People look up to us and take our words as from the LORD.
    c. Jacob's obedience unto sin. Genesis 27:14 "And he went, and fetched, and brought them to his mother: and his mother made savoury meat, such as his father loved."
    d. Because of his consent to his mother's plan, it was necessary for him to add one lie to another. He truly received God's blessing, but not in God's way. Who was to be blamed? The one looked up to as a servant of God. Oh, what a lesson!

II Point: <u>Jacob thinks himself forsaken and rejected of God</u>.
    a. He had to leave his loved ones. Genesis 28:10 "And Jacob went out from Beer-sheba, and went toward Haran."
    b. Alone and friendless, the darkness covers him. Moreover, he goes to sleep. Genesis 28:11 "And he lighted upon a certain place, and tarried there all night, because the sun was set; and he took of the stones of that place, and put them for his pillows, and lay down in the place to sleep."
    Application: What a picture! His own loved ones helped him to get to this place.

III Point: <u>He realized God's presence</u>.
    a. Genesis 28:12 "And he dreamed, and behold a ladder set up on the earth, and the top of it reached to heaven: and behold the angels of God ascending and descending on it." Jacob discovers that heaven and earth are not as far apart as he had thought.
    b. He realizes that God can see him in the midst of darkness.
    c. Genesis 28:12 - He realizes there is access to heaven and sees angels ascending and descending to help him in time of trouble should he call to God for help.
    d. He sees the Lord standing above it. Genesis 28:15 "And, behold, the LORD stood above it, and said, I am the LORD God of Abraham thy father, and the God of Isaac:…"

e. Does Jacob rejoice? No!
   Instead he says, "...How dreadful is this place!" (Genesis 28:16-17).
   Application: If God visits us, when we are out of His will, we don't feel happy about it, but it appears to be a dreadful time or place.

IV Point: <u>Jacob bargains with God</u>.
   a. Genesis 28:18-22 - He bargained for material blessings.
   b. This is a perfect picture of a man under conviction.
   If you do this, I'll do that. That was the reason why Jacob had another wrestle with the Lord at "Penuel." (Genesis 32:24-32).

Conclusion: For 20 long years, we notice that God could bless Jacob only materially when he lived with Laban. For that was his bargain with God. Oh, what a picture for us. Oh, that we may not ask so much for material things, but to know Him! I am convinced if Jacob would have asked to know Him he would have received as Solomon did.

May this be our prayer: Philippians 3:10 "That I may know him, and the power of his resurrection, and the fellowship of his sufferings, being made conformable unto his death;"

His Chosen Man
Genesis 31:3

Introduction: In this message we shall see God's long suffering and loving patience with a stubborn and stiff-necked person.

I Point: God calls Him.
    a. Return! Genesis 31:3 "And the LORD said unto Jacob, Return unto the land of thy fathers..."
Tell briefly how it came that Jacob was where he was.
    b. Jacob obeyed. Genesis 32:1 "And Jacob went on his way, and the angels of God met him."
    c. God's delight. The invisible band of angels around Jacob to protect him. Genesis 32:2 "And when Jacob saw them, he said, This is God's host:..."

II Point: Jacob's mistrust.
    a. Genesis 32:3-5 – Jacob communed with flesh and blood, instead of trusting in the Lord.
    b. Genesis 32:6-8 – Great fear fell upon Jacob. Jacob was yet trying to plan his way out alone.

III Point: Jacob calls on God.
    a. Jacob prayed. Genesis 32:9 "And Jacob said, O God of my father Abraham, and God of my father Isaac,..."
    b. He confessed his unworthiness. Genesis 32:10 "I am not worthy of the least of all the mercies, and of all the truth, which thou hast shewed unto thy servant;..."
    c. He prays for mercy. Genesis 32:11 "Deliver my, I pray thee, from the hand of my brother,..."
    d. He takes God at His word of promises. Genesis 32:12 "And thou saidst, I will surely do thee good..."
    e. Genesis 32:13-21 – He makes restitution.
    f. But all this could not give Jacob peace with God.

IV Point: In prayer alone with God.
    a. He wrestled all night. Genesis 32:24 "And Jacob was left alone; and there wrestled a man with him until the breaking of the day."
    b. God takes Jacob at his word and touches his thigh. Genesis 32:25 "And when he saw that he prevailed not against him, he touched the hollow of his thigh; and the hollow of Jacob's thigh was out to joint, as he wrestled with him."

c. In order to bless him, God had to take actions against him. God had to break his stubborn will.
   Application: How many are here upon whom the Lord must take action just like this. I am one of them upon whom the Lord showed this mercy. (God put me in bed with tuberculosis.)

V Point: <u>Jacob clings to God</u>.
   a. Genesis 32:26 "…I will not let thee go, except thou bless me."
   b. Genesis 32:27-28 – His name was changed.

VI Point: <u>Jacob's conversion</u>.
   a. His name was changed from Jacob to Israel.
   Genesis 32:27-28 "And he said unto him, What is thy name? And he said, Jacob. And he said, Thy name shall be called no more Jacob, but Israel:…" (From sinner to saint.)
   b. Jacob's interest in God. Genesis 32:29 "…Tell me, I pray thee, thy name…"
   Application: A man who accepts Christ is interested in His Word.
   c. God honours his interest in Him.
   Genesis 32:29 "And he blessed him there."
   d. Genesis 32:30 "And Jacob called the name of the place Peniel: for I have seen God face to face…"

VII Point: <u>Jacob's life after accepting God</u>.
   a. Genesis 32:31 "And as he passed over Peniel the sun rose upon him, and he halted upon his thigh."
   b. He saw it all now.
   c. He halted upon his thigh.
   d. He became a living testimony.
   e. Genesis 33:3 – Jacob's perfection in Christ. No longer stiff-necked, he bowed himself.

Conclusion: Oh, that you may wrestle with God, as Jacob wrestled. And cling to God as Jacob clung. And that you may inquire as Jacob inquired.

Sermon Outlines from the Book of Exodus

Moses Hid in the Bulrushes
Exodus 2:1-10

I Point: <u>The children of Israel in prosperity</u>.
  a. Exodus 1:7 "And the children of Israel were fruitful, and increased abundantly, and multiplied, and waxed exceeding mighty; and the land was filled with them."
  b. By this time they had lived 350 years in Egypt.
  But they forgot God.
     i. Prosperity was too great.
     ii. The young people began to intermarry with the Egyptians.
     iii. Sins of modern days were present.
  Illustration: The people liked to feed on the old carcasses of the world.

II Point: <u>Judgment from the Lord</u>.
  a. Exodus 1:11 "...set over them taskmasters..."
  b. Exodus 1:14 "And they made their lives bitter with hard bondage,..."
  c. They killed the male children of the Israelites.
  Illustration: All the riches of this world according to Proverbs 23:5 will fly away on wings. "Wilt thou set thine eyes upon that which is not? for riches certainly make themselves wings; they fly away as an eagle toward heaven." (Proverbs 23:5).

III Point: <u>They cried unto God</u>.
  a. God sent a deliverer; but, in the form of a little babe.
  b. For 40 years they kept on program, and the boy who was to be their Saviour grew day by day as their prayers grew for 40 long years in slavery.
  c. After 40 years he presents himself as their deliverer, but he was rejected, because he was not according to what they had expected. And they had to wait for another 40 years in the wilderness.
  d. Moses is a type of Christ.
  He came as a deliverer in the form of a babe, and was rejected; but yet, he was the only deliverer the children of Israel could have.
  e. Christ came as a babe, and was rejected; but, He is the only deliverer the world can have.

Conclusion: Your answer to your prayer might be here, but in its infancy. Keep praying.

Moses and the Burning Bush
Exodus 3:1-12

Introduction: Moses had fled from Egypt, and had joined himself to Jethro the Midian Priest. Moses married one of his seven daughters, Zipporah, and lived there for 40 long years.

I Point: <u>God heard the prayers and cries of the children of Israel</u>.
   a. Exodus 3:7 "And the LORD said, I have surely seen the affliction of my people which are in Egypt, and have heard their cry by reason of their taskmasters; for I know their sorrows."
        i. He hath seen.
        ii. He hath heard.
        iii. He hath known.
   b. Application: God's ear is not hardened that He cannot hear. His arm is not shortened that He cannot reach.
God knows your sorrows. He feels your pain.

II Point: <u>Moses's call.</u>
   a. Exodus 3:2 "And the angel of the LORD appeared unto him in a flame of fire out to the midst of a bush:..."
Application: When God calls He appears.
   b. He appears in a great way and wonderful way.

III Point: <u>Moses's response</u>.
   a. Exodus 3:3 "And Moses said, I will now turn aside and see this great sight, why the bush is not burnt."
   b. God has respect.
Application: When Moses turned to see, God called him. No one will ever be called except he turns to see God.
   c. God called him out of the midst of the fire.
   d. He introduces Himself as the God of old.
Exodus 3:6 "...I am the God of thy father, the God of Abraham, the God of Isaac, and the God of Jacob..."
   e. He reveals to Moses His name. Exodus 3:14 "And God said unto Moses, I AM THAT I AM: and he said, Thus shalt thou say unto the children of Israel, I AM hath sent me unto you."
   f. God tells Moses His plan.

IV Point: <u>Moses's appointment</u>.
  a. Exodus 3:10 "Come now therefore, and I will send thee unto Pharaoh, that thou mayest bring forth my people the children of Israel out of Egypt."
  b. The one who was rejected became the deliverer.
  c. Humbleness of heart. Exodus 3:11 "And Moses said unto God, Who am I, that I should bring forth the children of Israel out of Egypt?"
  d. Exodus 3:12 "And he said, Certainly I will be with thee; and this shall be a token unto thee, that I have sent thee: When thou hast brought forth the people out of Egypt, ye shall serve God upon this mountain."

  Illustration: God there set a bush on fire, in Moses's heart.
  God had set a bush on fire in Paul's heart on the road to Damascus.
  God had set a bush on fire in the hearts of the early Christians when they burned like torches inwardly and also outwardly.

Conclusion: The burning bush is a type of Christ.
Did the Lord set a bush on fire in your heart?

The Passover in Egypt
Exodus 12:1-13

Introduction: <u>The 10 different plagues of Egypt</u>
1. Judgment: <u>Water</u> was turned into blood.
2. Judgment: <u>Frogs</u> covered all of Egypt.
3. Judgment: <u>Lice</u> covered all of Egypt.
4. Judgment: <u>Flies</u> covered the country of Egypt.
5. Judgment: <u>Pestilence</u> on the cattle of Egypt.
6. Judgment: <u>Boils</u> covered all the people and animals.
7. Judgment: <u>Hail</u> covering all of Egypt.
8. Judgment: <u>Locust</u> covering all of Egypt.
9. Judgment: <u>Darkness</u> covered the earth.
10. Judgment: <u>Death</u> - Judgment upon the first born in Egypt.

I Points: <u>God's command to the Passover</u>.
   a. Exodus 12:5 "Your lamb shall be a male without blemish…"
   b. Exodus 12:13 "And the blood shall be to you for a token upon the houses where ye are: and when I see the blood, I will pass over you…"
   c. Some may have said, "I don't believe in this." But if they did not put the blood on their doorpost, the first born in their household died.

II Point: <u>They were to put the blood on with hyssop</u>.
   a. Hyssop is for:
      1. Cleaning – Leviticus 14:4-6.
      2. Scarlet wool - Leviticus 14:4.
      3. Blood - Leviticus 14:51-52.
   b. Numbers 19:6 - For sacrifice for sin offerings.
   c. I Kings 4:33 - In the wisdom of Solomon where he speaks to the reign of Israel it speaks of hyssop.
   d. David says, Psalm 51:7 "Purge me with hyssop, and I shall be clean…"
   e. When Christ died they used hyssop to give Him the vinegar. John 19:29 "…and they filled a spunge with vinegar, and put it upon hyssop, and put it to his mouth."
   f. Moses sealed the covenant with these three items: scarlet wool, hyssop, and blood. Hebrews 9:19 "…he took the blood of calves and of goats, with water, and scarlet wool, and hyssop, and sprinkled both the book, and all the people."

III Point: <u>The eating of the Passover lamb, and the unleaven bread, and the bitter herbs.</u>
   a. Exodus 12:8 – The Lamb was typical of Christ.
   b. Exodus 12:8 – The unleaven bread that goes with it is the sinless life.
   c. Exodus 12:8 – The bitter herbs is an illustration of the bitter persecution that goes with it to all those who believe and live for Christ.

IV Point: <u>The readiness to go.</u>
   a. Exodus 12:11 "And thus shall ye eat it; with your loins girded, your shoes on your feet, and your staff in your hand..."
   b. Exodus 12:11 "...and ye shall eat it in haste: it is the LORD'S Passover."

   Illustration: As long as we are in this world, we should live as if always ready to meet the Lord. When the Lord will pass over us, and all His redeemed shall come out of the world, then all the unsaved people, in and of the world, will face death - The great tribulation.

   c. Exodus 12:13 "...when I see the blood, I will pass over you, and the plague shall not be upon you to destroy you, when I smite the land of Egypt."

Christ's Deity

Exodus 6:1-3

Text: Exodus 6:3 "And I appeared unto Abraham, unto Isaac, and unto Jacob, by the name of God almighty, but by my name JEHOVAH was I not known to them."

Introduction: Many people say of Jesus Christ that He was divine, but not Deity; that he was a perfect revelation of God, but not God. But let us search the scriptures, for they testify of Him.

I Point: <u>He declares his Deity</u>.
  a. To Moses - Exodus 3:14 "And God said unto Moses, I AM THAT I AM: and he said, Thus shalt thou say unto the children of Israel, I AM hath sent me unto you."
  b. "JEHOVAH".
    Exodus 6:3 "...by my name JEHOVAH was I not known unto them."
    Jehovah means: "Lord," "Saviour," "Joshua," "Jesus."
    As the "Lord Jesus" was I not known unto them.
    John 18:6 "...I am he..." or "...I AM THAT I AM:..." (Exodus 3:14).
    John 18:6 "As soon then as he had said unto them, I am he, they went backward, and fell to the ground."
    Christ surrendered His Deity to God the Father, and went through as a man in His humanity.
  c. He claimed to be the LORD of the Old Testament.
    Psalm 110:1 "The LORD said unto my Lord, Sit thou at my right hand, until I make thine enemies thy footstool."
  d. He also taught His absolute identity with God.
    John 10:30 "I and my Father are one."
    John 14:9 "...he that hath seen me hath seen the Father;..."
  e. Jesus was not just divine; He is "Deity."

II Point: <u>Jesus proves His Deity</u>.
  a. He accepts worship.
    Matthew 14:33 "Then they that were in the ship came and worshipped him, saying, Of a truth thou art the Son of God."

Matthew 28:9 "...And they came and held him by the feet, and worshipped him."

John 20:28 "And Thomas answered and said unto him, My Lord and my God."

    b.   Jesus proves His Deity because He forgives sins.

Mark 2:5 "When Jesus saw their faith, he said unto the sick of the palsy, Son, thy sins be forgiven thee."

Luke 7:48 "And he said unto her, Thy sins are forgiven."

III Point: Jesus proves His Deity.

    a.   Jesus displayed <u>Omnipotent power.</u>

Luke 8:24 "...Then he arose, and rebuked the wind and the raging of the water: and they ceased, and there was a calm."

John 6:19 – "...they see Jesus walking on the sea..."

John 6:1-14 - Jesus fed five thousand with five loaves and two fishes.

John 2:1-11 – Jesus made the water into wine.

    b.   Jesus displayed <u>Omniscience.</u>

John 11:11-14 – Jesus was 60 miles away when Lazarus died, and He knew it.

    c.   Jesus displayed <u>Omnipresence</u>.

John 3:13 "And no man hath ascended up to heaven, but he that came down from heaven, even the Son of man which is in heaven."

Passing Through the Red Sea
Exodus 12:37-38

Introduction
1. We saw the blood on the door posts.
2. We saw the Passover Lamb.
3. We find the Israelites pushed out of Egypt because they partook of the Paschal Lamb.

I Point: Pushed out of Egypt.
    a. Exodus 12:33 "And the Egyptians were urgent upon the people, that they might send them out of the land in haste..."
Application: A person that has partaken of Christ is out of place among the rest of the world.
    b. According to the Egyptians, God led them the wrong way. Exodus 13:18 "But God led the people about, through the way of the wilderness of the Red Sea..."
Your way and my way seems wrong in the eyes of the world.

II Point: Through the Red Sea.
    a. Exodus 14:21 "And Moses stretched out his hand over the sea; and the LORD caused the sea to go back by a strong east wind all that night, and made the sea dry land, and the waters were divided."
    b. Moses lifting up his hands over them. Exodus 14:21 "And Moses stretched out his hand over the sea:"
    c. The Red Sea opened up. Exodus 14:22 "And the children of Israel went into the midst of the sea upon the dry ground..."
Illustration: If you and I follow the Lord, even the sea will turn into a paved highway.

III Point: The distancing of Egypt.
    a. Exodus 14:24 "And it came to pass, that in the morning watch the LORD looked unto the host of the Egyptians through the pillar of fire and of the clouds, and troubled the host of the Egyptians."
Illustration: There is a way that seems right unto men, but then they often are the ways of death.
You cannot pretend to walk Jesus' way and be His enemy.

    b. Some went along not as enemies, but of course, not as Israelites either, but only as a mixed multitude. But we read where they all died in the wilderness.
    c. You may cross the dividing line and appear to be a Christian, but you cannot feed on Christ, the manna. (Exodus 16:14-17). Numbers 11:4 "And the mixt multitude that was among them fell..."

Conclusion:
1. Did you partake of Christ, the Passover Lamb?
2. Did the world push you out from their society?
3. Did you pass through the Red Sea? (A division).
4. Did you see the hand of the Lord upon you?

Manna – A Type of Christ
Exodus 3:7

Introduction: Today we shall look into:
1. The life of the children of Israel in Egypt.
2. Their deliverance out of Egypt.
3. God's dealing with them in the wilderness.
4. The sifting out of the mixed multitude from amongst them.

I Point: Life in Egypt.
- a. Exodus 3:7 "And the LORD said, I have surely seen the affliction of my people which are in Egypt, and have heard their cry by reason of their taskmasters; for I know their sorrows;"
  Application: For 430 years in Egypt they were:
  1. Slaves to the Egyptians.
  2. Most cruelly treated.
  3. They cried unto God.

II Point: Their deliverance.
- a. Exodus 12:37-38
  1. God's dealings with the Egyptians.
  2. The Passover Lamb. A type of Christ revealed.
- b. Remedy: Exodus 12:13 "And the blood shall be to you for a token upon the houses where ye are: and when I see the blood, I will pass over you,..."
  Application for present days.
  This is death without remedy if not under the blood; but, salvation for all and everyone if under the blood.

III Point: God's dealing with them in the wilderness.
- a. Exodus 16:15 "And when the children of Israel saw it, they said one to another, It is manna: for they wist not what it was, And Moses said unto them, This is the bread which the LORD hath given you to eat."
  Manna - A type of Christ.
  1. Exodus 16:31 "And the house of Israel called the name thereof Manna: and it was like coriander seed, white; and the taste of it was like wafers made with honey."
  2. It is the bread sent from heaven.
  3. Psalm 78:25 "Man did eat angels' food."
  4. Sweet in Christ.

5. John 6:48 "I am the bread of life."
  6. John 6:51 "I am the living bread which came down from heaven: if any man eat of this bread, he shall live for ever: and the bread that I will give is my flesh, which I will give for the life of the world."
  7. All are to partake of it, or die without it.
     Application for today: Christ is the Living Bread.

IV Point: <u>The sifting out of the mixed multitude from amongst the true children of Israel.</u>
  a. Numbers 11:4 "And the mixt multitude that was among them fell a lusting:…."
  1. Who is this mixed multitude?
  2. How did they get in with the children of Israel?
  b. Illustration:
     1. They are not of Israel. (They are Egyptians.)
     2. They have not been moved by the power of God and were trying to hide themselves amongst the children of Israel.

  c. Application for our day.
     1. There are many unconverted members in Christian churches today.
     2. They cannot feed on Christ, the Manna – The Bread of heaven.
     3. They are lusting after the things of the world.
     4. No other food is granted – only Christ – The Manna.
     5. Acts 4:12 "Neither is there salvation in any other: for there is none other name under heaven given among men, whereby we must be saved."

The Golden Calf
Exodus 32:1-35

Introduction: The Lord has bought the people through the Red Sea. Then He gave them manna to eat, and water out of the rock to drink. He made it so that their clothing did not wear, out and their strength did not lack.

I Point: Idleness.
- a. Exodus 32:6 "...and the people sat down to eat and to drink, and rose up to play."
- b. Exodus 32:22 "...they are set on mischief."

II Point: Moses interceding for them before God.
- a. Exodus 31:18 "...upon mount Sinai, [God gave Moses] two tables of testimony, tables of stone, written with the finger of God."
- b. God can speak to your leader and to your Pastor, but if the people in the camp do not get busy, all is in vain.
  Illustration: Exodus 32:7 - While some are praying, others will corrupt themselves.
- c. Exodus 32:8 "They have turned aside quickly out of the way which I commanded them:...."
  Application: The human heart.
- d. Exodus 32:11-14 – Moses is an advocate.
  1. I John 2:1 "...And if any man sin, we have an advocate with the Father, Jesus Christ the righteous:"
- e. Moses - A type of Christ.
- f. The children of Israel are a type of the "so called" Christians.

III Point: The commandments of the Lord were broken.
- a. Exodus 32:19 - Moses "...cast the tables out of his hands, and brake them beneath the mount."
- b. The people sinned, because the commandments were already broken in their hearts.
- c. The judgment of God had fallen. Exodus 32:28 "...and there fell of the people that day about three thousand men."
- d. Moses yet pleads for the people.
  Exodus 32:32 "...blot me, I pray thee, out of the book which thou hast written." Moses - a type of Christ.
  Illustration: No one can know real love for a child like the mother that suffered in travail.

The Tabernacle in the Wilderness
Exodus 25:1-9

Text: Exodus 25:8 "And let them make me a sanctuary; that I may dwell among them."

Introduction: <u>The Tabernacle</u>.
- a. To whom was it given?
- b. When was it given?
- c. For what reason was it given?

I Point: <u>To whom was it given?</u>
- a. To the children of Israel.
- b. His chosen ones.
- c. He had delivered them.
  1. They had crossed the Red Sea.
  2. They were living on manna – A type of Christ.
  3. But they still were in the wilderness.

Application: To us He gives the order to build Him a Tabernacle.

II Point: <u>Still in the wilderness, means we are still</u>:
- a. In the world.
- b. Living on manna – Christ.
- c. We are being distinguished by the place we worship.

Application: You will reveal the expression and looks of the table you are feasting at. That is why it is so important that you go to a place of worship where they feast on Christ.

III Point: <u>For what main reason was it given?</u>
- a. For Christ to dwell with us. Exodus 25:8 "And let them make me a sanctuary; that I may dwell among them."
- b. To reveal Christ Jesus:
  1. Fine linen – Symbol of righteousness.
  2. Brass – Symbol of judgment.
  3. Silver – Symbol of redemption.
  4. Gold – Symbol of heaven.
- c. To reveal unto us our complete unworthiness.
  1. Trespass offering – When convicted of sin.
  2. Sin offering – You see your own sinfulness.
  3. Peace offering – When you are at rest, you give thanks and appreciation unto God.

      4. Meat offering – When Christ lives in us and He is our meat.
      5. Burnt offering – Willing to do His will. (Romans 12:1).
- d. To reveal unto us our guide – The Holy Spirit.
  1. Exodus 27:20 "And thou shalt command the children of Israel, that they bring thee pure oil olive beaten for the light, to cause the lamp to burn always."
  The Pure Oil. The pure oil is a type of the Holy Spirit used to throw light upon the shewbread - a type of Christ.
  2. If you want to show forth Christ you must be filled with the oil – The Holy Spirit.
  You are the candlestick.
- e. The Golden Alter upon which incense was burned.
  Sweet perfumes of three different kinds.
  1. Stac-te – This comes from a tree.
  2. On-y-cha – This comes from a crab that lives in the depths of the Red Sea.
  3. Gal-bon-um – This comes from a desert shrub.

IV Point: <u>The Mercy Seat</u>
- a. Only the High Priest can enter in.
  Our High Priest, Jesus Christ, entered in once for all, and set down at the right hand of God to intercede for us.

Conclusion: Where do we stand?

Sermon Outlines from the Book of Numbers

Man's Rebellion and God's Judgment

Numbers 21:5-9

Introduction: Previous to this we fine the children of Israel receiving Manna to eat. Now we fine them rebelling against their food, telling Moses that this manna is loathsome. Thus we find them working themselves up to a rebellion against God and Moses.

I Point: <u>A Great Rebellion</u>.
- a. Numbers 21:5 "And the people spake against God, and against Moses,..."
- b. Application: Is not this a perfect picture of our days?
  1. In what was it that you rebelled against God last?
  2. Is it trouble in the home, or perhaps with your neighbor? Or perhaps you are somewhat troubled by the way the preacher behaves. Or your wife or husband causes you some headache. And, of course, there is the general condition of the world.
  3. God offers you manna – Christ. He is the remedy for all your troubles, but you still reject and rebel.

II Point: <u>A Great Ruin</u>.
- a. Numbers 21:6 "...and much people of Israel died."
  Application: Is not this the reason why we have all this trouble in the world?
- b. Galatians 6:7 "Be not deceived; God is not mocked: for whatsoever a man soweth, that shall he also reap."
- c. Numbers 21:6 "And the LORD sent fiery serpents among the people,..."
- d. Because of great rebellion, there is great suffering.

III Point: <u>A Great Repentance</u>.
- a. Pray for us was their request. Numbers 21:7 "...We have sinned, for we have spoken against the LORD and against thee;..."
  Application: This holds true even today.
- b. II Chronicles 7:14 "If my people, which are called by my name, shall humble themselves, and pray, and seek my face, and turn from their wicked ways; then will I hear from heaven, and will forgive their sin, and will heal their land."
  Application: This also means that you and I need to repent.

IV Point: <u>A Great Remedy</u>.

    a.   Numbers 21:8 "And the LORD said unto Moses, Make thee a fiery serpent, and set it upon a pole: and it shall come to pass, that every one that is bitten, when he looketh upon it, shall live."

    b.   Application: Are we not all bitten?
1. Romans 5:12 "Wherefore, as by one man sin entered into the world, and death by sin; and so death passed upon all men, for that all have sinned:"
2. Romans 3:10 "...There is none righteous, no, not one:"
3. Romans 3:23 "For all have sinned, and come short of the glory of God;"

    c.   This same sin passed onto all men, and therefore it is the same remedy for all men.
1. John 3:14 "And as Moses lifted up the serpent in the wilderness, even so must the Son of man be lifted up:"
2. John 12:32 "And I, if I be lifted up from the earth, will draw all men unto me."

V Point: <u>A Great Respect</u>.

    a.   Numbers 21:8 "...that every one that is bitten, when he looketh upon it, shall live."

    b.   Application: Look and live!
1. But He respects action upon His promises.
Acts 10:34 "Then Peter opened his mouth, and said, Of a truth I perceive that God is no respecter of persons:"
2. Exodus 12:13 "And the blood shall be to you for a token upon the houses where ye are: and when I see the blood, I will pass over you..."

VI Point: <u>The Great Recovery</u>.

    a.   Numbers 21:9 "And Moses made a serpent of brass, (the serpent is a type of Christ made sin for us) and put it upon a pole, and it came to pass, that if a serpent had bitten any man, when he beheld the serpent of brass, he lived."

    b.   Application: This is the only recovery for you and me.
John 3:14 "And as Moses lifted up the serpent in the wilderness, even so must the Son of man be lifted up:"

VII Point: <u>A Great Rejoicing</u>.

    a.   Numbers 21:17-18 "Then Israel sang this song, Spring up, O well; sing ye unto it: The princes digged the well, the nobles of the people digged it, by the direction of the lawgiver, with their staves…"

Conclusion: You too will sing and rejoice when you know Christ as your personal Saviour.

Sermon Outlines from the Book of Deuteronomy

City of Refuge

Deuteronomy 19:4-5

Text: Deuteronomy 19:5 "...he shall flee unto one of those cities, and live:"

Introduction:
1. Explain what a refuge city is for.
2. What a refuge city stands for is symbolic of Christ.
3. What you may expect of a refuge city.

I Point: Deuteronomy 14:5 - City of Refuge.
- a. What is a city of refuge?
    1. A place of refuge.
    2. A place of justice.
    3. A place where life may be saved.
- b. Is a refuge city of necessity?
    1. It is a commandment of God.
    2. It is the dwelling place of God.
    3. It is loved by the just.
    4. It is hated by the unjust.

II Point: The refuge city – symbolic of Christ.
- a. Christ - the refuge from our avenger.
    1. Any person outside of Christ is not safe.
- b. Who is the avenger?
    1. <u>Satan!</u> I Peter 5:8 "Be sober, be vigilant; because your adversary the devil, as a roaring lion, walketh about, seeking whom he may devour:"
    2. <u>Our flesh</u>. Philippians 3:3 "...have no confidence in the flesh." Galatians 5:17 "For the flesh lusteth against the Spirit, and the Spirit against the flesh:..."

III Point: Deuteronomy 19:5 "...he shall flee unto one of those cities, and live."
- a. John 10:9 "I am the door: by me if any man enter in, he shall be saved..."
- b. John 3:36 "He that believeth on the Son hath everlasting life: and he that believeth not the Son shall not see life;..."
- c. John 6:37 "All that the Father giveth me shall come to me; and him that cometh unto me I will in no wise cast out."

Illustration: Luke 7:36-48 – The woman which was a sinner fled to the refuge place at the feet of Jesus.
- 1. When Mary lost her brother, Lazarus, she fled to the feet of Jesus for comfort. John 11:32 "And when Mary was come where Jesus was, and saw him, she fell down at his feet;…"
- 2. Christ Jesus is a refuge place, for everyone who will come unto Him.

IV Point: <u>What you may expect in the refuge city.</u>
- a. Protection for everyone, Jew and Gentile alike.
  - 1. You may expect absolute justice.
  - 2. If you are not guilty, you live; but, if you are guilty, you die.
- b. In God's sight all are guilty.
- c. Romans 3:9 "…both Jews and Gentiles, that they are all under sin;"
  - 1. Romans 3:23 "For all have sinned, and come short of the glory of God;"
  - 2. Ezekiel 18:20 "The soul that sinneth, it shall die…"
- d. Your death penalty is paid in the death of Christ your refuge city.
  - 1. All are guilty, all must come. Isaiah 1:18 "Come now, and let us reason together, saith the LORD: though your sins be as scarlet, they shall be as white as snow; though they be red like crimson, they shall be as wool."

Conclusion: You can no more say, "Well, I never do anything bad, and if I do, I really don't want to do it." You are guilty.

Romans 3:9. "…they all are under sin;"

Romans 10:13 "For whosoever shall call upon the name of the Lord shall be saved."

John 6:37 "All that the Father giveth me shall come to me; and him that cometh to me I will in no wise cast out."

Sermon Outlines from the Book of Joshua

Be Strong and of Good Courage
Joshua 1:1-9

Text: Joshua 1:2 "…now therefore arise, go over this Jordan,…"

I Point: <u>God sees the need</u>.
- a. Joshua 1:2 "Moses my servant is dead;…"
- b. The people are still on this side of the Jordan.
  Application: The great men of God in our days have died.
- c. The people are still groping around in the wilderness and darkness of sin.

II Point: <u>God looks for a leader</u>.
- a. Joshua 1:2 "…now therefore arise, go over this Jordan,…"
  Application: God looks today in just the same manner.
  Illustration: We are the torch bearers: our father's flung the torch to us when they died: You and I must bear it in our generation.

III Point: <u>God promises to stand with His man.</u>
- a. Joshua 1:5 "…as I was with Moses, so I will be with thee:…"
- b. Joshua 1:5 "…I will not fail thee, nor forsake thee."
  Application: Has the Lord been with your forefathers?
  Illustration: The God that lived in Moses' day is just the same today.

IV Point: <u>God's expectancy of His man</u>.
- a. Joshua 1:7 "Only be thou strong and very courageous, that thou mayest observe to do according to all the law…"
- b. Joshua 1:9 "…be not afraid, neither be thou dismayed: for the LORD thy God is with thee whithersoever thou goest."
  Application: Proverbs 29:25 "The fear of man bringeth a snare: but whoso putteth his trust in the LORD shall be safe."
- c. Psalm 118:6 "The LORD is on my side; I will not fear:…"

V Point: <u>God's formation from whence comes all strength</u>.
- a. Joshua 1:8 "This book of the law shall not depart out of thy mouth; but thou shalt meditate therein day and night, that thou mayest observe to do according to all that is written therein: for then thou shalt make thy way prosperous, and then thou shalt have good success."
- b. Then you will be a leader.
- c. Then you will be a messenger.
- d. Then you will be a deliverer.

Seven Kings

Joshua 8:25-29

Theme: There were seven kings hanged on a tree: The king of Ai, the five kings of the Amorites, and the King of the Jews.

Introduction: Here we have seven kings. All of them were hanged on trees, crucified, and buried behind large stones. But only one arose – The King of the Jews.

I Point: <u>The king of an earthy kingdom</u>.
- a. The king of Ai was hanged and buried with great stones marking the place until this day.
- b. Joshua 8:29 "And the king of Ai he hanged on a tree until eventide: and as soon as the sun was down, Joshua commanded that they should take his carcase down from the tree, and cast it at the entering of the gate of the city, and raise thereon a great heap of stones, that remaineth unto this day."
  Application: The king of Ai trusted in his armies, he trusted in his strength, and in earthly weapons. But where is he now?

II Point: <u>The five kings of the Amorites</u>.
- a. Joshua 10:15-17 "And Joshua returned, and all Israel with him, unto the camp of Gilgal. But these five kings fled, and hid themselves in a cave at Makkedah. And it was told Joshua, saying, The five kings are found hid in a cave at Makkedah."
- b. Joshua 10:26-27 "And afterward Joshua smote them, and slew them, and hanged them on five trees: and they were hanging upon the trees until the evening. And it came to pass at the time of the going down of the sun, that Joshua commanded, and they took them down off the trees, and cast them into the cave wherein they had been hid, and laid great stones in the cave's mouth, which remain until this very day."
  Application: In the natural way of thinking it was impossible for Joshua even to think of fighting against these five confederate allied kings. But the Lord shall fight for you. Just look and see Joshua 10:11-14 "...And the sun stood still, and the moon stayed,..." (Joshua 10:13).

III Point: <u>The King of the Jews</u>.

    a. Matthew 27:31 "they...led him away to crucify him."
Application: I want you to notice that He too, as all the other kings, was buried behind a great stone.
The Roman soldiers "rolled a great stone to the door of the sepulchre..." (Matthew 27:60).
But note carefully: Three days later the stone was rolled away, while the stones sealing the burial place of the other kings are still there unto this day.

    b. Matthew 28:6 "...He is risen." That is what the angel said whose countenance was like lightning and his raiment white as snow.
How blessed that we have a risen, and ascended Saviour, and King who is "alive forevermore." And because He lives we shall live also.

IV Point:

    a. The graves and tombs of His loved ones shall also have the stones rolled away on that Great Day when we are called to meet Him in the air.

    b. I Corinthians 15:51-58 "Behold, I shew you a mystery; We shall not all sleep, but we shall all be changed, In a moment, in the twinkling of the eye, at the last trump: for the trumpet shall sound, and the dead shall be raised incorruptible, and we shall be changed."

    c. I Thessalonians 4:13-18 "But I would not have you to be ignorant, brethren, concerning them which are asleep, that ye sorrow not, even as others which have no hope. For if we believe that Jesus died and rose again, even so them also which sleep in Jesus, will God bring with him. For this we say unto you by the word of the Lord, that we which are alive and remain unto the coming of the Lord shall not prevent them which are asleep. For the Lord himself shall descend from heaven with a shout, with the voice of the archangel, and with the trump of God: and the dead in Christ shall rise first: Then we which are alive, and remain shall be caught up together with them in the clouds, to meet the Lord in the air: and so shall we ever be with the Lord. Wherefore comfort one another with these words."

Joshua's Last Charge
Joshua 24:14-31

Text: Joshua 24:15 "...choose you this day whom ye will serve;..."

Introduction: This was Joshua's last charge to Israel before he died. God gives them a summary of His watchful care over them through the wilderness.

I Point: <u>The Summary</u>.
  a. Fifteen times God pointed out to them where He personally intervened to help them.
  b. The challenge - Joshua 24:14 "Now therefore fear the LORD, and serve him in sincerity and in truth:... "
  Application: How many times has the Lord helped you?

II Point: <u>Joshua 24:15 "...choose you this day whom ye will serve;"</u>
  a. Joshua 24:15 - The people served strange gods. Such as their forefathers had served.
  b. Joshua setting the example. Joshua 24:15 "...as for me and my house, we will serve the LORD."
  c. Joshua 24:16-19 – The people would like to serve God and also idols. (Other gods).
  d. Joshua wants them to put away their strange gods.

III Point: <u>Their Hypocrisy</u>.
  a. Joshua 24:19 "...Ye cannot serve the LORD:..." and other gods.
  b. Joshua 24:22 "...Ye are witnesses against yourselves..."
  c. Joshua 24:23 "put away...the strange gods which are among you, and incline your heart unto the LORD God..."
  d. Joshua brings them under other orders. Joshua 24:27 "...Behold, this stone shall be a witness unto us;..."

IV Point: <u>The people went home to serve their strange gods</u>.
  a. Joshua 24:28 - Joshua had done all he could.
  b. Joshua 24:29 - They were alright as long as Joshua lived.
  c. Joshua 24:31 "And Israel served the LORD all the days of Joshua,..."
  d. Joshua 24:30 - Joshua died. They buried him, and then they continued to serve strange gods.
  Application: This is a human heart:

Conclusion: How many will go home from here with more condemnation heaped on their hearts, then when they come in? There are many people who will give up everything for Christ sake, except their sin.

Sermon Outlines from the Book of Judges

Compromising

Judges 2:1-15

Text: Judges 2:10 "...and there arose another generation after them, which knew not the LORD, nor yet the works which he had done for Israel."

I Point: <u>Their freedom</u>.

    a. Judges 2:1 – God heard their cry.
    b. Judges 2:1 – He brought them out.
    c. Judges 2:1 – He sware unto them.
    d. Judges 2:1 – He makes a covenant.

II Point: <u>Their duties to God</u>.

    a. Judges 2:2 "And ye shall make no league with the inhabitants of this land;..."
    b. Judges 2:2 "...ye shall throw down their altars:..."

III Point: <u>Their compromise</u>.

    a. Judges 2:2 "...but ye have not obeyed my voice:..."
    Application: God cannot forgive sin. Sin must be paid for; either by Christ or by you.

IV Point: <u>God's withdrawal</u>.

    a. Judges 2:3 "Wherefore I also said, I will not drive them out from before you; but they shall be as thorns in your sides, and their gods shall be a snare unto you."
    b. Their hypocrisy.
        1. Judges 2:4 - They wept.
        2. Judges 2:5 - They sacrificed.
        3. Judges 2:6 - They possessed the land.
        4. Judges 2:7 - They even served the Lord, to please Joshua, as long as he lived.

V Point: <u>Their consequences of sin</u>.

    a. Judges 2:10 "...and there arose another generation after them, which knew not the LORD,..."
    b. Exodus 20:5 "...I the LORD thy God am a jealous God, visiting the iniquity of the fathers upon the children unto the third and fourth generation of them that hate me;"

VI Point:
  a. Has your father and mother been freed from sin?
  b. Were you brought out from the world? (Egypt).
  c. Did the Lord make a covenant with you?
  d. Did you teach it to your sons and daughters?
  e. Did you help them to make a covenant with God?
  f. Did your sons and daughters see Christ in you?
  g. Or did they see you make a league with the world?
  h. Do you look on without control when your child is drinking, smoking, cursing, and disobeying?
  i. Is it not because you have neglected to tell them about Christ?
  j. If so, you are just reaping the consequences for your league with the inhabitants of this land. (The world).

Conclusion: Parents, do not obstruct the way of your children, and keep them from this free and full salvation, that was purchased for us by Jesus Christ on the cruel Cross of Calvary, which fits and prepares us for heaven and the glorious world to come.

Galatians 6:7 "Be not deceived, God is not mocked: for whatsoever a man soweth, that shall he also reap."

Proverbs 29:1 "He, that being often reproved, hardeneth his neck, shall suddenly be destroyed, and that without remedy."

Blessed and Tragic Unconsciousness

Judges 16:20

Text: Judges 16:20 "...The Philistines be upon thee, Samson. And he awoke out of his sleep, and said, I will go out as at other times before, and shake myself. And he wist not that the LORD was departed from him."

Introduction: There are two kinds of unconsciousness. One is a blessed unconsciousness, and the other is a tragic unconsciousness.

I Point: <u>The blessed unconsciousness</u>.
- a. Exodus 34:29 "...Moses wist not that the skin of his face shone while he talked to him."
- b. He was in touch with God.
- c. He was in harmony with God.
- d. He was in intersession before God.

    Application: When you are doing these things before God your face will shine.
    Stephen's face was like the face of an angel when they stoned him. Acts 6:15 "And all that sat in the council, looking stedfastly on him, saw his face as it had been the face of an angel."

    Illustration: If you are in touch with God you will not need to tell others. Others will see it.

II Point: <u>The tragic unconsciousness</u>.
- a. Judges 16:20 "...The Philistines be upon thee, Samson. And he awoke out of his sleep, and said, I will go out as at other times before, and shake myself. And he wist not that the LORD was departed from him."
- b. Samson, the Nazarite, kept company with the Philistines.
- c. He played with them. Tell the story of the lion.
  Judges 14:18 "...What is sweeter than honey? and what is stronger than a lion?..."
- d. He fell in love with them. Judges 16:4 "And it came to pass afterward, that he loved a woman in the valley of Sorek, whose name was Delilah."
- e. He partook of their sin and fell asleep.
  Judges 16:19 "And she made him sleep upon her knees;..."

  f. Judges 16:20 "...And he wist not that the LORD was departed from him."
  Application: Oh, my friend, you who play with sin and think you are today just as good a Christian as you were before, this is a tragic unconsciousness that has come over you.
  g. Judges 2:10 "...and there arose another generation after them, which knew not the LORD, nor yet the works which he had done for Israel." They knew not!
  Our world knows not that they have backslidden. The world is unconscious and will wake up in tragedy.

Conclusion: Which is true in your life, a blessed unconsciousness or a tragic unconsciousness?

Sermon Outlines from the Book of I Samuel

Another Year – Another Milestone

I Samuel 7:1-7

Text: I Samuel 7:12 "...Hitherto hath the LORD helped us."

Introduction: Today we stand at the end of another year. Another milestone in our life will be set.

I Point: Your enemy
- a. I Samuel 7:7 – The Philistines.
- b. I Samuel 7:8 – Israel's prayer.
- c. I Samuel 7:9 – Samuel's offering.
  Illustration: Ira D. Sankey sang the song called "Shepherd Song" on a boat in 1860. There was a man in the audience with a gun who planned on shooting him. But after he heard the song, he couldn't shoot him. God protected Sankey.
  Application: How many times in this past year did Satan aim at you?

II Point: God's protection.
- a. I Samuel 7:10 – The LORD thundered upon their enemy's.
- b. I Samuel 7:11 – Israel pursued.
  Illustration: David Brainerd was a missionary to the Delaware Indians. God protected him in the hour of death.

III Point: Your responsibility.
- a. I Samuel 7:12 – Ebenezer – means "Hitherto hath the LORD helped us." (I Samuel 7:12).
- b. Your responsibility is to be a witness for the Lord.
  Ira Sankey led the man, who was about to shoot him, to the Lord.
  How long since you testified for Jesus?
  How long since you tried to win a friend to Christ?
  How long has Jesus waited for you to speak a word for Him?
  How long will it take you to obey the Master?

IV Point: God's blessing.
- a. I Samuel 7:13 – The Philistines were subdued.
- b. I Samuel 7:14 - There was peace.
  Peace in their hearts because they put away the strange gods; and peace in their country because their enemy was subdued.

Conclusion: Will you make peace with God today?

Disobedience and Obedience
I Samuel 15:1-23

Theme: The result of disobedience and obedience.

Text: I Samuel 15:22 "...Behold, to obey is better than sacrifice, and to hearken than the fat of rams."

Introduction: Two Points - disobedience and obedience will be presented. I would like to ask you on which side are you?

I Point: Disobedience.
   a. This is the very first sin.
   b. This is the very greatest sin.
   c. This is the most common sin.
   d. This is the sin of today.

1st – The disobedience of Adam and Eve.
1. Because of disobedience we are all plunged into sin. We are all, by nature, born sinners.
   a. Genesis 3:6 "And when the woman saw that the tree was good for food, and that it was pleasant to the eyes, and a tree to be desired to make one wise, she took of the fruit thereof, and did eat, and gave also unto her husband with her; and he did eat."
2. What was the result of this act of disobedience?
   a. Genesis 3:16 "Unto the woman he said, I will greatly multiply thy sorrow and thy conception; in sorrow thou shalt bring forth children,..."
   b. Genesis 3:17 - "And unto Adam he said:...cursed is the ground for thy sake; in sorrow shalt thou eat of it all the days of thy life:"

2nd - The disobedience of King Saul.
1. Saul's first disobedience.
   a. I Samuel 13:9 "And Saul said, Bring hither a burnt-offering to me, and peace offerings. And he offered the burnt-offering."
2. Saul's second disobedience.
   a. The command of the Lord was, "Now go and smite Amalek, and utterly destroy all..." (I Samuel 15:3).
   b. Saul disobeyed. I Samuel 15:9 "But Saul and the people spared Agag, and the best of the sheep,..."
   c. Saul refused to acknowledge his sin.
      I Samuel 15:20 "And Saul said unto Samuel, Yea, I have obeyed the voice of the LORD,..."

      d.   Saul blames others for his own fault.
           I Samuel 15:21 "But the people took of the spoil,…"
3. What was the result of this act of disobedience? Saul was rejected to be king of Israel.
      a.   I Samuel 15:23 "…Because thou hast rejected the word of the LORD, he hath also rejected thee from being king."
      b.   I Samuel 15:15 - Sacrifice. What was God's advice?
           I Samuel 15:22 "…Behold, to obey is better than sacrifice, and to hearken than the fat of rams."

II Point: <u>Obedience.</u>

<u>Six illustrations of Obedience.</u>
You must remember that in obedience you will meet up with things that will seem and look foolish to you and others. I Corinthians 1:25 "…The foolishness of God is wiser than men; and the weakness of God is stronger than men."

<u>Illustration (No. 1): - Ezekiel's Life - Ezekiel 37:3</u>.
The Lord asked Ezekiel to do something that seems foolish.
      a.   Ezekiel 37:3 "And he said unto me, Son of man, can these bones live? And I answered, O Lord GOD, thou knowest."
      b.   Ezekiel 37:4 "Again he said unto me, Prophesy upon these bones, and say unto them, O ye dry bones, hear the word of the LORD."
           Ezekiel 37:5 "Thus saith the Lord GOD unto these bones; Behold, I will cause breath to enter into you, and ye shall live."
      c.   Ezekiel 37:10 - Ezekiel's answer, "So I prophesied as he commanded me, and the breath came into them, and they lived, and stood up upon their feet, an exceeding great army."

<u>Illustration (No. 2): - Gideon's Life - Judges 7:1-25</u>.
      a.   His enemies, the Midianites, were as many as the sand on the sea shore.
      b.   He had his own army of 32,000 men. God says, Judges 7:2 "…The people that are with thee are too many…" So, 22,000 went home, leaving 10,000. Even then God said, Judges 7:4 "…The people are yet too many;…"
      c.   God chose only 300 men to fight the Midianites. This looks foolish, but God said, Judges 7:7 "…By the three hundred men that lapped will I save you,…"

Illustration (No. 3): - Moses's Life - Exodus 14:16.
   a. Exodus 14:16 "..But lift thou up thy rod, and stretch out thine hand over the sea, and divide it: and the children of Israel shall go on dry ground through the midst of the sea."
   b. It looked foolish. But clouds of dust must have risen in the midst of the sea. Exodus 14:22 "And the children of Israel went into the midst of the sea upon the dry ground:..."

Illustration (No. 4): – Joshua's Life - Joshua 3:13.
   a. Joshua 3:13 "And it shall come to pass, as soon as the soles of the feet of the priests that bear the ark of the LORD, the Lord of all the earth, shall rest in the waters of Jordan, that the waters of Jordan shall be cut off from the waters that come down from above; and they shall stand upon a heap."
   b. Joshua 3:17 "...and all the Israelites passed over on dry ground,..."

Illustration (No. 5): - The Blind Man – John 9:7.
   a. John 9:7 "...Go, wash in the pool of Siloam, (which is by interpretation, Sent)."
   b. Joshua 9:7 "He went his way therefore, and washed, and came seeing."

Illustration (No. 6): – The Lame Man – Acts 3:6.
   a. Acts 3:6 "Then Peter said, Silver and gold have I none; but such as I have give I thee; In the name of Jesus Christ of Nazareth rise up and walk."
   b. Acts 3:8 "And he leaping up stood, and walked,..."

Conclusion: All this was accomplished because of obedience.

Sermon Outlines from the Book of II Samuel

Humbleness
II Samuel 6:1-24

Text: II Samuel 6:22 - David said, "And I will yet be more vile than thus, and will be base in mine own sight:..." Or as John the Baptist puts it: John 3:30 "He must increase, but I must decrease."

Introduction: To be base or humble in my eyes.
1. You are not always humble when you look humble.
2. You are not always humble when you feel humble.
3. You are not always humble when you think you are humble.
4. What God calls humble: Psalm 51:17 "The sacrifices of God are a broken spirit: a broken and a contrite heart, O God, thou wilt not despise."

I Point: How David tried to serve the Lord.
   a. II Samuel 6:1-3 – He did great preparation to bring the ark to Jerusalem.
   b. Serving in the flesh. II Samuel 6:5 "...played before the LORD on all manner of instruments..."
   c. God takes action. II Samuel 6:7 "And the anger of the LORD was kindled against Uzzah, and God smote him..."
   d. II Samuel 6:8 "And David was displeased because the LORD had made a breach upon Uzzah:..." David sympathized with sin, and is therefore equally guilty.
   e. Great fear came upon David. II Samuel 6:9-10 "And David was afraid of the LORD that day..."
   f. David turned in fear away from God, and lost the blessing God had for him. II Samuel 6:11 "And the ark of the LORD continued in the house of Obed-edom the Gittite three months: and the LORD blessed Obed-edom..."

III Point: David's repentance.
   a. II Samuel 6:13 – He sees his own wicked heart.
   b. II Samuel 6:13 – He repents.
   c. He goes after the blessing. II Samuel 6:13 "And it was so, that when they that bare the ark of the LORD had gone six paces, he sacrificed oxen and fatlings."

III Point: <u>David serves the Lord in humility.</u>

a. He was in contriteness and in brokenness of heart.
b. II Samuel 6:13 – He bears the Ark of the Lord on the shoulders of the priests.
c. II Samuel 6:14 – He became humble.
d. II Samuel 6:15 – He became like one of the servants.

IV Point: <u>He was despised</u>.

a. II Samuel 6:16 "...Michal, Saul's daughter looked through a window, and saw King David leaping and dancing before the LORD; and she despised him in her heart."
b. God now takes the center place in David's heart.
II Samuel 6:17 "...David offered burnt-offerings and peace-offerings before the LORD."

V Point: <u>David now becomes a mighty blessing.</u>

a. II Samuel 6:18 - David "...blessed the people in the name of the LORD of host."
b. David fed the people. II Samuel 6:19 "...to every one a cake of bread, and a good piece of flesh, and a flagon of wine..."
c. II Samuel 6:20 – He is yet more despised by Michal.
d. II Samuel 6:20 – He humbles himself yet more and more.
e. He became a broken and contrite person whom the Lord could use mightily in His great plan. II Samuel 6:22 "And I will yet be more vile than thus, and will be base in mine own sight:..."

Conclusion: Has the Lord delt with you in this way? Are you broken and contrite at heart? Psalm 51:17 "The sacrifices of God are a broken spirit: a broken and a contrite heart, O God, thou wilt not despise."

Sermon Outlines from the Book of I Kings

A Man's Knees in the Sand
I Kings 18:42-46

Text: I Kings 18:42 "...And Elijah went up to the top of Carmel; and he cast himself down upon the earth, and put his face between his knees,..."

Introduction: Before us here, we have the story of the children of Israel going through three and a half years of famine, because of their sin. Elijah had prayed that the Lord should not permit it to rain for three and a half years; as per James 5:17 "Elias was a man subject to like passions as we are, and he prayed earnestly that it might not rain: and it rained not on the earth by the space of three years and six months." Next, we have seven different companies doing everything they can think of in order to somehow improve the situation of the world; such as: politics, good works, and working out their troubles. But God was looking for one thing by which He would improve the world, and that was a simple sign – a man's knees in the sand, or to see someone praying. II Chronicles 7:14 "If my people, which are called by my name, shall humble themselves, and pray, and seek my face, and turn from their wicked ways; then will I hear from heaven, and will forgive their sin, and will heal their land."

There Are Seven Companies:

First Company: We will call them "The Ahabites."
I Kings 18:42 "So Ahab went up to eat and to drink...."
Illustration: This is the jolly-go-lucky group: eat, drink and be merry.
Application: This company is very great in our days - feeding their stomachs and gratifying their cravings for amusement and pleasure.

Second Company: Known as The Hiders. These are known as the seven thousand who had not bowed their knees to Baal. I Kings 19:18 "Yet, I have left me seven thousand in Israel, all the knees which have not bowed unto Baal..."
Application: But they kept hid, having not the boldness to come out with their testimony. And if they did bow their knees to God, is questionable, for God was still looking for that sign.

Third Company: Known as The Mourners over the drought. I Kings 18:21 "And Elijah came unto all the people, and said, How long halt ye between two opinions? if the LORD be God, follow him: but if Baal, then follow him. And the people answered him not a word."
Application: We surely can find a large company of this kind. They are gazing mournfully at the deep cracks in the earth, but they will not close a single one of them by their mourning.

Fourth Company: Known as <u>The Straddles</u>. The sample shown was Obadiah. He was a believer in Jehovah, but for his job's sake he was a follower of Ahab. I Kings 18:3 "And Ahab called Obadiah, which was the governor of his house..."
Application: I believe we have plenty of these kinds nowadays. They don't want to lose their job, so they are afraid to stand up for what's right.

Fifth Company: Known as <u>The Bread and Water Prophets</u>. They are a hundred prophets of the Lord in a cave divided into two companies, looking for their daily bread and water to be brought to them by Obadiah, when he himself was out of fellowship with the Lord. I Kings 18:4 "Obadiah took an hundred prophets, and hid them by fifty in a cave, and fed them with bread and water."
Application: This is the saddest spectacle on the whole earth. Here were men called of God to preach, but instead they were satisfied with just bread and water. Such preachers we have many of in our day. They are not willing to speak out and preach the truth.

Sixth Company: Known as <u>The Sky Gazers</u>. He looked toward the sea. I Kings 18:43-44 "...Go up now, look toward the sea..."
Application: Of this kind we have many. They are looking and gazing into the sky to see a sign. They are looking for God to move; whereas, God is looking for them to get on their knees and pray, producing the sign He is looking for.

Seventh Company: <u>One Man</u> – Elijah.
I Kings 18:42 "...And Elijah went up to the top of Carmel; and he cast himself down upon the earth, and put his face between his knees."
Application: Elijah was the only one who showed the sign God was looking for; the sign of a man's knees in the sand. Others could have produced this sign, but didn't.

Conclusion: When God saw this sign, we read that the sky was over cast with clouds and a sound of abundance of rain was heard. Yes, it is only then, when God sees the sign of a man's knees on the floor, He will answer.

II Chronicles 7:14 "If my people, which are called by my name, shall humble themselves, and pray, and seek my face, and turn from their wicked ways; then will I hear from heaven, and will forgive their sin, and will heal their land."

<u>Close with this illustration</u>: A mother knelt at her chair every morning and prayed. Her little son watched her and noticed that her knees left an imprint in the rug. Years passed and his mother passed away, and her son intended to tear down the old house. Walking through it for the last time he noticed the knee-prints in the rug where his mother used to pray. There and then he knelt in those knee-prints on the rug and accepted Jesus Christ as his Saviour and Lord.

Sermon Outlines from the Book of II Kings

Digging Ditches in Faith
II Kings 3:5-24

Text: II Kings 3:16 "And he said, Thus saith the LORD, Make this valley full of ditches."

Introduction: There are a number of dry valleys which the Lord must lead us into, in order to show us the fountain of life in the midst of the dry valley.

I Point: <u>The Valley of Death</u>.
- a. II Kings 3:9 "So the king of Israel went, and the king of Judah, and the king of Edom: and they fetched a compass of seven days' journey: and there was no water for the host..."
  Illustration: God had to bring these kings first into this dry valley before He could let them see the victory. If not, they would have lasted and thus sinned against God.

The different valleys the Lord may lead you into:
1. The valley of death.
2. The valley of sickness.
3. The valley of want.
4. The valley of doubt.
5. The valley of disappointment.
6. The valley of discouragement.
7. The valley of despair.

- b. What purpose has God in taking you into these different valleys?
  1. You then will call upon the Lord when you are at the end of yourself.
  2. II Kings 3:11 "Jehoshaphat said, Is there not here a prophet of the LORD, that we may enquire of the LORD by him?"

II Point: <u>God's answer</u>:
- a. II Kings 3:16 "...Thus saith the LORD, Make this valley full of ditches."
- b. There was no rain.
- c. There was no river anywhere in sight.
- d. It was a dry valley. A valley of death.
- e. But God said at such time to them, "Make this valley full of ditches." (II Kings 3:16).

Application: It looked ridiculous to them, and more so to their enemies. But it was the wisdom of God.
- f. People may wonder if you are alright, but your job is to make the dry valley full of ditches, so that God may fill them with the abundance of His grace.
- g. Don't ask God for the possible things you can do yourself. Ask Him for the impossible things, for He is the God of the impossible.

III Point: <u>God did the impossible</u>.
- a. This is what God did with the ditches. II Kings 3:20 "And it came to pass in the morning...Behold, there came water by the way of Edom, and the country was filled with water."
- b. It was victory to the faithful ones.
- c. The ditches confused the enemy and allowed the defeat of the Moabites.

    II Kings 3:21-24 "And when all the Moabites heard that the kings were come up to fight against them, they gathered all that were able to put on armour and upward, and stood in the border. And they rose up early in the morning, and the sun shone upon the water, and the Moabites saw the water on the other side as red as blood: And they said, This is blood: the kings are surely slain, and they have smitten one another...And when they came to the camp of Israel, the Israelites rose up and smote the Moabites, so that they fled before them: but they went forward smiting the Moabites, even in their country."

Conclusion: The ditches allowed Israel to conquer the enemy.
Do you have enough faith to obey the Lord even when what He asks you to do seems foolish?

Seven Dunks in the Muddy Jordan
II Kings 5:1-12

Introduction: Leprosy in the Old Testament always applied to sin. In other words, Naaman was a good man, but he is a sinner.

I Point:
- a. II Kings 5:1 – Naaman was captain of the host of the king of Syria.
- b. II Kings 5:1 – He was an honorable man.
- c. He was a man who was loved by his captives, such as the little Israelite maiden.
- d. II Kings 5:5 – He was respected by the king of Syria, and also the country.
- e. II Kings 5:5 – He was rich of gold and silver.
- f. II Kings 5:9 – He went to the prophet's house.
- g. He was all these things, "...but he was a leper." (II Kings 5:1).

    Application: These words "But he was a leper" tells me something about the rest of us.
    1. You might be a great man, a learned man, but still a sinner.
    2. You might be honorable in your country, in your town, and in your neighborhood, honest in all your dealings, but in God's sight you are a sinner.
    3. You might have done great things for your country, your town, your church, and your home. But if you don't know the Lord Jesus Christ as your own personal Saviour, you are still a leper, a sinner condemned to die.

II Point: What must I do?
- a. Do exactly what Naaman did. OBEY!
    II Kings 5:10 "...Go and wash in Jordan...seven times..."
- b. Was that hard? No, it was simple. "But Naaman was wroth..." (II Kings 5:11).
- c. Naaman says, "Are not...rivers of Damascus better..." "...may I not wash in them and be clean?" (II Kings 5:12).
- d. But Naaman was still a leper.
- e. "...So he turned and went away in a rage." (II Kings 5:12).
- f. But his little servant maiden urged him. So what did he do?
- g. II Kings 5:14 "Then he went down, and dipped himself seven times in the Jordan, according to the saying of the man of God: and his flesh came again like unto the flesh of a little child, and he was clean."

Conclusion: There is only one way, one door, one formula where to wash our sins away, and that is Christ Jesus our Lord.

It is not what you may do, or what your church may do, but what Christ has done.

Salvation in Time of Great Need
II Kings 6:24-& 7:1-10

Text: II Kings 7:9 "...this day is a day of good tidings, and we hold our peace:..."

Introduction: There was famine, siege and starvation in Samaria.

I Point: <u>The condition of Samaria</u>.
- a. Read II Kings 6:24-31.
  Illustration: The conditions are as they were during the Russia Revolution of 1917.
- b. The people's attitude towards God, men and government.
  1. II Kings 6:27 – Against God.
  2. II Kings 6:31 – Against Elisha.
  3. II Kings 6:6:1-2 – Considered it as impossible for God.

<u>There were four lepers.</u>

II Point: <u>This is the desperation of these four lepers</u>.
1. Poverty.
2. Pain.
3. Banishment.
4. Friendless.

III Point: <u>Their decision</u>.
Before you can make any decision you must be convinced in your heart and mind that it is the only and best thing for you to do.

- a. II Kings 7:4 – The four lepers were convinced of death. "If we say, We will enter into the city, then the famine is in the city, and we shall die there; and if we sit still here, we die also…"
- b. They made the decision. They decided to go into the Syrian camp.
- c. They acted upon their decision.
  Illustration: The prodigal son.
  Luke 15:17-18 "And when he came to himself, he said, How many hired servants of my father's have bread enough and to spare, and I perish with hunger? I will arise and go to my father…"

IV Point: <u>The four lepers discovery.</u>
- a. After the decision and action has been made, then you may look for discovery.
- b. The Lord had well taken care of the Syrians. The Syrians fled the camp. II Kings 7:7 "For the Lord had made the host of the Syrians to hear a noise of chariots, and a noise of horses, even the noise of a great host…"
- c. The lepers' discovery.
  II King 7:8 "And when these lepers came to the uttermost part of the camp, they went into one tent, and did eat and drink, and carried thence silver, and gold, and raiment, and went and hid it;…"
  1. The Syrians were gone.
  2. There was bread enough and to spare.
  3. It was their duty to minister now unto others.

V Point: <u>Their labour of love.</u>
- a. II Kings 7:9 "…this day is a day of good tidings…"
- b. They went and told the good news of their discovery.
- c. II Kings 7:10 "So they came and called unto the porter of the city; and they told them saying, We came to the camp of the Syrians, and, behold, there was no man there, neither voice of man…" They saved the nation.
- d. Bread in abundance. II Kings 7:16 "And the people went out, and spoiled the tents of the Syrians. So a measure of fine four was sold for a shekel, and two measures of barley for a shekel, according to the word of the LORD."

Conclusion: If you are a Christian, do your labour of love.

The High Cost of Doubting
II Kings 19:14-19 & 35

Introduction: The high cost of living is hard on every hand. Few, however, stop to consider the high cost of doubting. A study of the word of God reveals doubt is costly.

One pays for doubt without being sure that the payment was necessary. We do not know or see what God would have done had we only trusted Him.

<u>Six Examples of Doubt</u>.

I Point: <u>First example: The life of King Hezekiah</u>.
- a. The king of Assyria threatened Hezekiah. (II Kings 19:10-12).
  Application: This is a familiar trick of Satan. He makes us fear to trust God.
- b. King Hezekiah here stands for an example.
  Because of his doubt in the Lord he had to pay to Sennacherib gold and silver. In order to pay this heavy tribute he stripped the Lord's house.
  Application: Doubt cost Hezekiah and his kingdom heavily.
- c. Hezekiah prayed, and 185,000 Assyrians were slain.
  II Kings 19:35 "And it came to pass that night, that the angel of the LORD went out, and smote in the camp of the Assyrians an hundred four score and five thousand: and when they arose early in the morning, behold, they were all dead corpses."
  Application: Have you prayed? Have your problems and enemy numbered to 185,000? God can take care of them in one night.

II Point: <u>Second example: Jacob fleeing from home</u>.
- a. Rebecca, his mother, doubted that God would keep His promise that the elder should serve the younger.
- b. This doubt cost Jacob his home.
- c. God appeared to Jacob. He, for a while, believed, then he doubted.
- d. This doubt cost Jacob 200 goats, 220 sheep, 30 camels, 50 head of cattle, and 580 head of stock.
  Application: Doubting is costly.

III Point: Third example: Moses is called of God to a great task.
   a. He was to be a leader, and priest, and prophet to Israel.
      Moses doubted because he was slow of speech.
   b. Because of this doubt Moses lost the priesthood. It was given to Aaron.
   c. Aaron became a regular annoyance and great trouble to Moses a number of times.
      Application: Has God appointed you to be a leader? Don't excuse yourself not to be one. By doubting in God your cost will be very heavy.

IV Point: Fourth example: God had promised.
   a. The children of Israel to possess the land.
   b. But at the border they doubted. Twelve spies were sent, and they came back with doubt in their hearts.
   c. The result of it was that they all died in the wilderness, except for the two that did not doubt – Caleb and Joshua. And the Israelite children had to wonder for another forty years in the wilderness.
      Application: Doubt will cost you.

V. Point: Fifth example: The Life of Abraham.
   a. Sarah doubted when God told them that they will have a son. She gave Hagar to Abraham for a wife, and Ishmael was born.
   b. Sarah had trouble at once, and all these many years Israel has been at war with the Ishmaelite's. Sarah's doubt cost heavy.

VI Point: Sixth example: Peter's lack of faith.
   a. Peter, in faith, stepped out on the rough sea, but a moment of doubt nearly cost him his life.
      Matthew 14:31 "...O thou of little faith, wherefore didst thou doubt?"

Conclusion: The books where your record is being made is not yet open. I wonder what doubt is costing you today. Doubt may cost you your business, or your heavenly responsibilities. Many, because of doubt, have moved out of God's will. Doubt keeps many Christians from full surrender.

Sermon Outlines from the Book of I Chronicles

Jabez - The Man of Prayer

I Chronicles 4:9-10

Theme: Jabez, the man of prayer, in the midst of spiritual declension.

Text: I Chronicles 4:10 "And Jabez called on the God of Israel, saying, Oh that thou wouldest bless me indeed, and enlarge my coast, and that thine hand might be with me, and that thou wouldest keep me from evil, that it may not grieve me!

Introduction:
1. First, we want to notice the time of Jabez's life. (It was after the captivity of Babylon).
2. How he came into the world. (In great sorrow.) He was sorrow to his mother at his birth.
3. He became the greatest blessing to Israel in his days. Also to his sorrowing mother.

I Point: His Birth.
   a. Born in great sorrow. I Chronicles 4:9 "...and his mother called his name Jabez, saying, Because I bare him with sorrow."
   b. I Chronicles 4:9 – He realized that the name Jabez meant, "man that causes grief."
   c. He had a reputation to outlive, and a name to overcome, and a debt of pity to pay to his mother.

II Point: His Character.
   a. I Chronicles 4:9 "And Jabez was more honourable than his brethren:..."
   b. He became the pride of his mother.
   c. He became a mighty doctor of the Law and savior of Israel.

III Point: His Rewards.
   a. Cities were named after him.
   b. Disciples followed him.
   c. Nations respected him.

IV Point: The secret of it all.
   a. He was a man who believed the God of Israel.
   b. He was a man of prayer.

V Point: <u>Nature of prayer</u>.
1. I Chronicles 4:10 "And Jabez called on the God of Israel, saying, Oh that thou wouldest bless me indeed,..."
   He called upon the blessing of Abraham to come upon him.
   The greatest prayer a man can say is to ask for God's blessing.
   At that time Israel had experienced the crises.
2. I Chronicles 4:10 "...and enlarge my coast,..."
   Israel at that time was cramped together by their enemies.
   And he was a man who prayed for enlargement.
3. I Chronicles 4:10 "...that thine hand might be with me..."
   He realized that his own hand and might was weakened by his enemies.
   He cast himself upon the Lord.
4. I Chronicles 4:10 "...that thou wouldest keep me from evil, that it may not grieve me!"
   His name means grief and sorrow. His prayer is that he may live above his name, above sin, and above his sorrow. What a prayer!

VI Point: I Chronicles 4:10 "...And God granted him that which he requested."

Conclusion: Here is a man who lived in a most critical age. He came into the world in the most critical way. His very name spelled grief and sorrow. Yet he proved himself to be a man of God, a man of prayer. He became a doctor of the Law, and a savior of the nation. You and I have the same chance, for we have the same God!

Sermon Outlines from the Book of II Chronicles

Power through Prayer
II Chronicles 16:9

Text: II Chronicles 16:9 "For the eyes of the LORD run to and fro throughout the whole earth, to shew himself strong in the behalf of them whose heart is perfect toward him..."

I Point: The divine channel of power.

    a. We are constantly in a stretch, if not in a strain, to devise new methods, new plans, and new organization to advance the church, and to build our work with God.

    b. But God's plan is to make much of us to build His work through us, and not through methods, nor through organizations.

Illustration: Robert Murray M'Cheyne (1813-1843) said, "Study universal holiness of life. Give yourself to prayer, and get your texts, your thoughts, and your words from God."

Application: God declares that the eyes of the Lord run to and fro throughout the whole earth to shew Himself strong in the behalf of them whose heart is perfect toward Him. He then proves to us that the divine channel of power is through us.

The Holy Ghost does not flow through methods, but through men. He does not anoint plans, but men. He is looking for men of prayer.

II Point: What God would have us do?

    a. Edward M. Bounds (1835-1913) the great man of prayer said: "Prayer to the preacher is not simply the duty of his profession, but a privilege, and a necessity."

Air is no more necessary to the lungs than prayer is to the preacher. It is absolutely necessary for the preacher to pray, and it is also absolutely necessary that the preacher be prayed for. These two propositions are welded into a union which ought never to know any separation: The preacher must pray and the preacher must be prayed for.

    b. The praying members are to the preacher as Aaron and Hur were to Moses. They held up his hands during the battle, and decided the issues that were raging around them.

Illustration: Units of prayer combined, like drops of water, make an ocean which defies resistance.

The Apostle Paul said:

1. <u>To the Ephesians:</u> "Praying always with all prayer and supplication in the spirit, and watching thereunto with all perseverance and supplication for all saints; And for me, that utterance may be given unto me, that I may open my mouth boldly, to make known the mystery of the gospel." (Ephesians 6:18-19).

2. <u>To the Colossians:</u> Paul emphasizes "Withal praying also for us, that God would open unto us a door of utterance, to speak the mystery of Christ, for which I am also in bonds: That I may make it manifest, as I ought to speak." (Colossians 4:3-4).

3. <u>To the Thessalonians</u>: Paul says it sharply, "Brethren, pray for us." (I Thessalonians 5:25).

4. <u>To the Corinthians:</u> Paul calls for help in prayer.
II Corinthians 1:11 "Ye also helping together by prayer for us, that for the gift bestowed upon us by the means of many persons thanks may be given by many on our behalf."

5. Then he says to them all, "Finally, brethren, pray for us, that the word of the Lord may have free course, and be glorified, even as it is with you:" (II Thessalonians 3:1).

Conclusion: The plea and the purpose of the Apostle Paul was to put the churches to praying. Christian, are you praying?

Sermon Outlines from the Book of Nehemiah

The Fight of a Christian
Nehemiah 4:1-23

Text: Nehemiah 4:4 "Hear, O our God; for we are despised; and turn their reproach upon their own head…"

Introduction: As you all know, the children of Israel are always representing the Christians. This chapter particularly reveals the fight between the power of light and the power of darkness. Ephesians 6:12 "For we wrestle not against flesh and blood, but against principalities, against powers, against the rulers of the darkness of this world, against spiritual wickedness in high places."

I Point: <u>The people, the children of Israel, in captivity</u>.
   a. Satan was quite content to keep God's people in captivity. Therefore, they were left alone by him.
   Application: You are left alone by Satan as long as you are in his captivity.
   b. But there came a time when the people called upon the name of the Lord; and God heard their cry.
   c. The enemy heard of these things. Nehemiah 2:10 "…it grieved them exceedingly that there was come a man to seek the welfare of the children of Israel."
   Satan loves to see you in misery.
   In other words, misery loves company.
   d. Misery and belittlement is used in order to defer them from their idea. Nehemiah 2:19 "…they laughed us to scorn, and despised us,…"

II Point: <u>The people came back from the captivity</u>.
   a. The fight is won.
   The enemy "…was wroth, and took great indignation, and mocked the Jews." (Nehemiah 4:1).
   b. How to overcome such mockery.
   Pray to God. Nehemiah 4:4 "Hear, O our God; for we are despised;…"
   c. Nehemiah 4:7-8 - The enemy comes in like a flood.
   d. Nehemiah 4:9 - But the Lord shall raise up a defense against the enemy.
   > "No man can be wholly the Lord's unless he is wholly consecrated to the Lord; and no man can know whether he is thus wholly consecrated except by tribulation. That is the test. To rejoice in God's will, when that will imparts

nothing but happiness, is easy even for the natural man. But no one but the new man can rejoice in the Divine will when it crosses his path, disappoints his expectations, and overwhelms him with sorrow. Trial therefore, instead of being shunned, should be welcomed as the test – the only true test – of a true state. Beloved souls, there are consolations which pass away, but true and abiding consolations ye will not fine except in entire abandonment, and in that love which loves the Cross. He who does not welcome the Cross does not welcome God" (Madame Guyon - 1648-1717).

III Point: <u>Co-operation in the fight</u>.
    a.   Nehemiah 4:13 & 16-The people were at work with families, all for one cause.

IV Point: <u>Enemies</u>.
    a.   Nehemiah 6:1-2 - If the enemy cannot get you in wrath, he then will come as an angel of light.
    b.   He also will use your own friends to destroy you.
        Nehemiah 6:8 & 11 - Nehemiah was a man filled with the Lord to do His will.

Sermon Outlines from the Book of Job

Satan's Desire
Job 1:1-12

Introduction: What we have learned thus far in this study relates to Satan as the "prince" or "god" of this world, the spirit that now worketh in the children of disbelief or disobedience which is the mass of unregenerated mankind. But he also exercises certain privileges and powers against the saints of God. To him is given the privilege of harassing, sifting, and testing the saints. This history of Job is a case in point.

I Point: Satan's desire
- a. Job 1:11 "But put forth thine hand now, and touch all that he hath, and he will curse thee to thy face."
  Application: It is Satan's desire that God would touch us or test us.
- b. This many times God does. And then He gives us the victory to stand up under the testing.
- c. Sometimes saints fall and turn against the Lord. (John 6:63-69).
- d. Again, sometime they stand true as Job did. (Job 1:20-22).
  Application: Troubles never come singularly. If you stand against one, look for the next, for Satan has given a blow and you fell not, but got weak; or he saw you rise against him. He will be furious. Satan's desire is to get you to lose out with God, in any way possible, either through sickness or health as he said "Skin for skin." Job 2:4 "And Satan answered the LORD, and said, Skin for skin, yea, all that a man hath will he give for his life."
  1. In Luke 13:10-16, we read about a daughter of Abraham, whom Satan had bound with physical affliction for 18 years.
  2. In II Corinthians 12:7, Paul's infirmities are called by him, "a thorn in the flesh, the messenger of Satan to buffet me,..."
  3. Look at Peter's experience. Luke 22:31-32 "And the Lord said, Simon, Simon, behold, Satan hath desired to have you, that he may sift you as wheat: But I have prayed for thee, that thy faith fail not: and when thou are converted, [hast turned back again] strengthen thy brethren."
  Satan was granted the privilege of sifting the chief apostle.

4. We find in I Corinthians 5:5 that Satan also destroys the flesh of carnal Christians in the church.
   I Corinthians 5:5 "To deliver such an one unto Satan for the destruction of the flesh, that the spirit may be saved in the day of the Lord Jesus."
   Application: Just as this world with its glory is delivered to Satan, so are saints sometimes delivered unto Satan. But Satan exercises these powers under restriction. God limits him, or else we would all be consumed in one day. Remember the swine in Luke 8:33-33.

II Point: God's protection.
   a. Psalm 37:28 "For the LORD loveth judgment, and forsaketh not his saints; they are preserved for ever:…"
   b. Psalm 37:23-24 "The steps of a good man are ordered by the LORD: and he delighteth in his way. Though he fall, he shall not be utterly cast down: for the LORD upholdeth him with his hand."
   c. Romans 8:35-39 "Who shall separate us from the love of Christ?…"

III Point: Satan's devices.
   a. In view of the fact that God has these wonderful protections, Satan is at no loss for a method of attack upon a saint. He employs various artful devices.
   b. Some of his choice snares are:
      1. Pride.
      2. Covetousness.
      3. Affliction.
      4. Animosity.
   The devil is never happier than when he can get people mad at each other.
      i. That was the point that gave rise to Lot saying, "Let's choice Sodom."
      ii. That was the thing that caused Paul and Barnabas to separate.
      iii. That was what broke the church asunder in Corinth.
      iv. And that is what causes our churches today to split.

Conclusion: The only and foremost thing in Christian life is to defeat Satan in the name of Jesus Christ our Lord.

The Manifestation of His Own

Job 1:1-22

Theme: God takes delight in the manifestation of His own.

Introduction: Job is a man of whom the Lord could say, "...was perfect and upright, and one that feared God, and eschewed evil." (Job 1:1)

In such a man God will take delight to manifest him before the world, Satan, and also heaven.

John 3:21 "But he that doth truth cometh to the light, that his deeds may be made manifest, that they are wrought in God."

I Point: What kind of a man was Job?
1. A perfect man.
2. An upright man.
3. One the feared God.
4. One that eschewed evil.
5. Job was a man in whom God could take delight.

II Point: Job's manifestation:
  a. How, and before whom, will God manifest His own?
1. Before heavenly host.
2. Before Satan.
3. Before men in the world.

Application (No. 1): Luke 12:8 "Also I say unto you, Whosoever shall confess me before men, him shall the Son of man also confess before the angels of God:"

Application (No. 2): Job 1:8 "And the LORD said unto Satan, Hast thou considered my servant Job, that there is none like him in the earth..."

Application (No. 3): Psalm 23:5 "Thou preparest a table before me in the presence of my enemies:..."

III Point: Job's suffering because of his manifestation:
  a. Satan hates you when you are manifested by God.
    Application: Christ, after the proclamation that He was the Son of God.
    Job 1:9 "Then Satan answered the LORD, and said, Doth Job fear God for nought?"

VI Point: <u>Job's earthly promotion</u>.
    a. God will never permit temptation to come upon you, unless He can trust you to be faithful.
    b. Men who have done much for the LORD have also suffered much, because Satan hates such, and strikes to the utmost of his knowledge.

V Point: <u>Heavenly promotion</u>.
Five things not found in heaven.
1. Heaven is a place without tears.
   Revelation 21:4 "And God shall wipe away all tears from their eyes;…"
2. Heaven is a place without death.
   Revelation 21:4 "…and there shall be no more death…"
3. Heaven is a place without sorrow.
   Revelation 21:4 "…neither [is there found] sorrow,…"
4. Heaven is a place without crying.
   Revelation 21:4 "…nor [is there found] crying,…"
5. Heaven is a place without pain.
   Revelation 21:4 "…neither shall there be any more pain: for the former things are passed away."

Conclusion: Are you in the place today that God can manifest you, through sorrow and suffering on earth in the land of the dying? Then you shall be promoted in the land of the living where there is no more death.

Sermon Outlines from the Book of Psalm

Temperance
Psalm 1:1-6

Introduction: Looking for a text to speak on temperance, there are many texts, such as Proverbs 16:25 "There is a way that seemeth right unto a man, but the end thereof are the ways of death."

And Proverbs 14:34 "Righteousness exalteth a nation: but sin is a reproach to any people."

Also Proverbs 31:4-10; or Amos 2:6-8.

There are many and very hard portions of the scripture against hard drink, but which shall I speak from?"

Just for a few minutes let me speak from Psalm 1:1-6. Psalm 1:1 "BLESSED is the man that walketh not:..."
This is the introductory to the entire Psalter.

I Point: Psalm 1:1
1. Walking in the counsel of the ungodly.
2. Standing in the way of sinners.
3. Sitting in the seat of the scornful.
   Application: That is the picture of the ungodly.

II Point: Psalm 1:2
a. "But his delight is in the law of the LORD;"
b. "...and in his law doth he meditate day and night."
   Application: This is the picture of the godly that fear the Lord.

III Point: Psalm 1:3
a. The godly "...shall be like a tree planted by the rivers of water..."

IV Point: Psalm 1:4
a. "The ungodly are not so:...."
b. "...but are like the chaff..."
c. "...which the wind driveth away."

V Point: Psalm 1:6
a. "For the LORD knoweth the way of the righteous:...."
b. "...but the way of the ungodly shall perish."
   Illustration: Proverbs 9:10 "The fear of the LORD is the beginning of wisdom: and the knowledge of the holy is understanding."

God's Hand Upon a Nation

Psalm 2:1

Introduction: God is looking down from the heavens.

I Point: Proverbs 14:34 "Righteousness exalteth a nation: but sin is a reproach to any people."
    a. Looking into history of old, we see that God used one nation to destroy another nation.
    b. That does not mean that the one nation is absolutely righteous, and the other found unrighteous; but the one is probably found somewhat more righteous.
    c. Remember, God used Babylon to destroy Israel.

II Point: Psalm 111:10 "The fear of the LORD is the beginning of wisdom: a good understanding have all they that do his commandments: his praise endureth for ever."
    a. Again, looking a little into the past, we can see that those nations that forgot God are the losers in the end.
    b. That was my experience in Russia, a nation that forgot God.

III Point: The victory of a nation begins at home.
    a. The hand that rocks the cradle rules the world.
    b. The boy who knelt at his mother's knees, found a place of refuge and comfort in the battle field.
    c. The privileged child is the one who has a Christian home, and a Christian country.

IV Point: God's plan in the victory.
    1. First, to have fear of the LORD.
    2. Second, to rule in righteousness.
    3. Third, to bring the gospel to every nation.
    4. Fourth, to give God the glory.

V point: Five tragedies.
    1. A face without eyes.
    2. A desert without water.
    3. A sky without stars.
    4. A heart without Christ.
    5. A nation without God.

The Fragility of Human Life

Psalm 39:4

Text: Psalm 39:4 "LORD, make me to know mine end, and the measure of my days, what it is; that I may know how frail I am."

Psalm 39:5 "Behold, thou hast made my days as an handbreadth; and mine age is as nothing before thee: verily every man at his best state is altogether vanity. Selah."

I Point: The fragility of human life.
- a. When a baby is born:
  1. The most helpless.
  2. Altogether dependent.
  3. Growing up as tender plant.

   Illustration: A mother wrote in an album to her son. "When you were born, you cried, and the rest of us laughed rejoicing over you. Live your life so that when you die, all the rest of us will cry, but you will be able to laugh and rejoice in the presence of the Lord forever."

II Point: <u>The brevity of human life.</u>
- a. From infancy to childhood sorrow begins.
- b. Problems, difficulty, and pain are at hand every day.
- c. All this is given so that man will keep the end of life in view.
- d. This life is but a preparation for the life to come.

   Psalm 39:5 "Behold, thou hast made my days as an handbreadth; and mine age is as nothing before thee: verily every man at his best state is altogether vanity. Selah."

Conclusion: What are you doing with your life? You say you are doing all you can. But the question really is, "What are you doing with Jesus?"

Hebrews 2:3 "How shall we escape, if we neglect so great salvation; which at the first began to be spoken by the Lord, and was confirmed unto us by them that heard him."

He Brought Me Out of a Horrible Pit
Psalm 40:1-17

Text: Psalm 40:1-3 "I waited patiently for the LORD; and he inclined unto me, and heard my cry. He brought me up also out of an horrible pit, out of the miry clay, and set my feet upon a rock, and established my goings. And he hath put a new song in my mouth, even praise unto our God: many shall see it, and fear, and shall trust in the LORD."

Introduction: This morning we want to look into this wonderful Psalm and see if there are not any instructions for us.

I Point: <u>I waited patiently</u>.
- a. Psalm 40:1 "I waited patiently for the LORD; and he inclined unto me, and heard my cry."
   Illustration: There was a little girl whose father promised her that he would get her out of the school should it ever catch on fire. One day the school house did catch on fire and the little girl waited patiently in the corner for her father. And he did come and get her. She trusted him and waited patiently.
- b. To wait upon the Lord you must have:
   1. Faith in Him.
   2. Faith in His strength.
   3. Faith in His ability.
   4. Psalm 40:1 "...and he inclined unto me, and heard my cry."

II Point: <u>A horrible pit.</u>
- a. Psalm 40:2 "He brought me up also out of an horrible pit..."
   Application: That proves that we are down helpless in a pit. A pit of sin.
   Illustration: Like the pit where Jeremiah was cast into. Jeremiah 38:6 "Then took they Jeremiah, and cast him into the dungeon...And in the dungeon there was no water, but mire: so Jeremiah sunk in the mire."
- b. The miry clay of sin. Psalm 40:2 "...out of the miry clay..."

III Point: <u>Set my feet.</u>
- a. <u>Psalm 40:2 "...and set my feet upon a rock..."</u>
- b. The Rock is Jesus Christ.
- c. Psalm 40:2 "...and established my goings."

Application: A Christian, who is on the Rock - Christ Jesus, has a different path to go. You don't go the same way as you went before. God will establish a new direction and a new purpose for you.

IV Point: <u>A new song.</u>
- a. Psalm 40:3 "And he put a new song in my mouth..."
    1. Your longings are different.
    2. Your songs are different.
    3. Your praise is different.
    4. Psalm 40:3 "...even praise unto our God:..."

In heaven, we read, that there will be much singing.

But there is no singing heard in the pit. The Bible tells us that in hell "...there shall be wailing and gnashing of teeth." (Matthew 13:50).

Conclusion: Are you lifted out of the horrible pit?
If not, why not take His hand now.

Revival - Part III
Psalm 42:1-11

Theme: How to promote a revival?

I Point: <u>Why we have not a revival.</u>
    a. When Israel was down cast and over run by their enemies, David, the great intercessor, stands before God in prayer.
    b. Psalm 42:1 "As a hart panteth after the water brooks, so panteth my soul after thee, O God."
    c. John 7:37-38 "In the last day, that great day of the feast, Jesus stood and cried, saying, If any man thirst, let him come unto me, and drink. He that believeth on me, as the scripture hath said, out of his belly shall flow rivers of living water."
    d. Ephesians 4:30 "And grieve not the Holy Spirit of God, whereby ye are sealed unto the day of redemption."
    e. Why we have not a revival:
        1. Because we have lost the panting after God.
        2. Because we have lost the thirsting after God.
        3. Because we have grieved the Holy Spirit.

II Point: <u>How to promote a revival.</u>
    a. By reading God's Word.
    Why we have not revival?
        1. Because we neglect the Word of God.
    b. Proverbs 6:22 "When thou goest, it (the Word of God) shall lead thee; when thou sleepest, it shall keep thee; and when thou awakest, it shall talk with thee."
    c. John 6:48 "I am that bread of life."
    d. John 6:53 "...Verily, verily, I say unto you, Except ye eat the flesh of the Son of man, and drink his blood, ye have no life in you."
    e. Why we have not revival?
        1. Because we have neglected to feed upon the Word of God.

III Point: <u>Unbelief.</u>
    a. Jeremiah 25:4 "...ye have not hearkened, nor inclined your ear to hear."
    b. The children of Israel were on the way to destruction, but they did not believe it.
    Read - I John 1:10 and I John 5:10.
    c. If we try to justify ourselves before God, and say we are not guilty and that we have not sinned; in these points of omission, we make Him a liar and His word is not in us; or we have not been feeding on His word as we should have.

IV Point: Neglect of prayer.
  a. Psalm 55:17 "Evening, and morning, and at noon, will I pray, and cry aloud: and he shall hear my voice."
  b. Do we make it a matter of prayer? And do we weep over our sins of neglect?
  c. I Thessalonians 5:17 "Pray without ceasing."

V Point: Lack of love for lost souls.
  a. Philippians 2:21 "For all seek their own, not the things which are Jesus Christ's."
  b. Paul found it so in his days. People were too busy seeking their own, instead of Christ.
  Illustration: It is as much the duty of the church to awake as it is for the fireman to awake when a fire breaks out at night. Sleep? Should the fireman sleep and let the whole city burn down? What would you think of such a fireman? Yet, their guilt would not compare to the guilt of Christians who sleep.

VI Point: Your own life.
  a. Why we have not a revival is because of neglect to watch our own lives and conduct.
  b. Ephesians 5:15-16 "See then that ye walk circumspectly, not as fools, but as wise, Redeeming the time, because the days are evil."
  c. Colossians 4:5 "Walk in wisdom toward them that are without, redeeming the time."
  Application: I know of a man who redeemed the time. He was anxious to lead souls to Christ, so he asked the Lord to bring them to the field where he had to work on the farm. And as they came there to ask for directions, he led them to Christ.

VII Point: Neglect of self-denial.
  a. Are you willing to suffer reproach for the name of Christ; to give up luxuries, comforts, anything to save a soul from hell?
  b. Romans 8:13 "...but if ye through the Spirit do mortify the deeds of the body, ye shall live."
  c. James 5:7 "Be patient therefore, brethren, unto the coming of the Lord..."

*This is Part III of the Revival Series:
Part I - Isaiah 44:22, page 133.
Part II - Acts 5:1-16, page 271.
Part III – Psalm 42:1-11, page 112.

Where is Thy God?

Psalm 42:7-11

Text: David wrote: Psalm 42:3 "My tears have been my meat day and night, while they continually say unto me, Where is thy God?" Psalm 42:10 "As with a sword in my bones, mine enemies reproach me; while they say daily unto me, Where is thy God?"

Introduction: Where is Thy God? This is the word of reproach of an enemy to a saint in deep distress, when all the waves and billows are gone over him.

Many a time the devil says to the believer who is struggling with temptation, "Where is thy God?"

Many times:
1. The world says it.
2. Sorrow says it.
3. Fear says it.
4. Sickness says it.
5. Perplexity says it.

It is well to answer this question by the Word of God that endureth forever. Tell them:

I Point: <u>He is above us.</u>
   a. Deuteronomy 4:39 "Know therefore this day, and consider it in thine heart, that the LORD he is God in heaven above, and upon the earth beneath: there is none else."
   b. Ephesians 1:21-23 "Far above all principality, and power, and might, and dominion, and every name that is named, not only on this world, but also in that which is to come: And hath put all things under his feet, and gave him to be the head over all things to the church, Which is his body, the fullness of him that filleth all in all."

II Point: <u>He is around us.</u>
   a. Psalm 34:7 "The angel of the LORD encampeth round about them that fear him, and delivereth them."
   b. Psalm 125:2 "As the mountains are round about Jerusalem, so the LORD is round about his people from henceforth even for ever."
   c. John 10:28-30 "And I give unto them eternal life; and they shall never perish, neither shall any man pluck them out of my hand."

    d. II Kings 6:17 "...the mountain was full of horses and chariots of fire round about Elisha."
    Illustration: Tell the story of Elisha with horses and chariots and angels all around.

III Point: <u>His is before us</u>.
    a. Exodus 13:21 "And the LORD went before them by day in a pillar of a cloud, to lead them the way; and by night in a pillar of fire, to give them light; to go by day and by night:"
    b. Deuteronomy 1:30 "The LORD your God which goeth before you, he shall fight for you..."
    c. Deuteronomy 31:3 "The LORD thy God, he will go over before thee, and he will destroy these nations from before thee, and thou shalt possess them:..."
    d. Romans 8:31 "What shall we then say to these things? If God be for us, who can be against us?"

IV Point: <u>He is behind us</u>.
    a. Exodus 14:19 "And the angel of God, which went before the camp of Israel, removed and went behind them; and the pillar of the cloud went from before their faces, and stood behind them:"
    b. Isaiah 30:21 "And thine ears shall hear a word behind thee, saying, This is the way, walk ye in it, when you turn to the right hand, and when ye turn to the left."
    Illustration: This being behind means also He will be behind you in your business, your undertakings, and your successes in life. He will bless you if you are walking with Christ hand in hand.

V Point: <u>He is beneath us</u>.
    a. Deuteronomy 33:27 "The eternal God is thy refuge, and underneath are the everlasting arms:"
    b. Song of Solomon 2:6 "His left hand is under my head, and his right hand doth embrace me."
    Illustration: God says, I will uphold thee with the right hand of my righteousness as he did to Jacob of old, but if you don't learn, he may use that left hand to make you obey.

VI Point: <u>He is with us</u>.
    a. Matthew 28:20 "…lo, I am with you alway, even unto the end of the world. Amen."
    b. God said to Jacob, Genesis 28:15 "And behold, I am with thee, and will keep thee in all places whither thou goest…"
    c. Isaiah 43:2-3 "When thou passest through the waters, I will be with thee; and through the rivers, they shall not overflow thee: when thou walkest through the fire, thou shalt not be burned; neither shall the flame kindle upon thee. For I am the LORD thy God…"
    d. II Timothy 4:17 "Notwithstanding the Lord stood with me, and strengthened me…and I was delivered out of the mouth of the lion."
    e. Hebrews 13:5 "…for he hath said, I will never leave thee, nor forsake thee. So that we may boldly say, The Lord is my helper, and I will not fear what man shall do unto me."

VII Point: <u>He is within me.</u>
    a. John 14:16-17 "And I will pray the Father, and he shall give you another Comforter, that he may abide with you for ever; Even the Spirit of truth; whom the world cannot receive, because it seeth him not, neither knoweth him: but ye know him; for he dwelleth with you, and shall be in you."
    b. I Corinthians 6:19 "What? know ye not that your body is the temple of the Holy Ghost which is in you, which ye have of God, and ye are not your own?"
    c. Colossians 1:27 "…Christ in you, the hope of glory:"
    d. Ezekiel 36:27 "And I will put my spirit within you, and cause you to walk in my statutes, and ye shall keep my judgments, and do them."

Conclusion: So, when people say, "Where is thy God?" you can say with confidence:
1.. He is above me.
2. He is around me.
3. He is before me.
4. He is behind me.
5. He is beneath me.
6. He is with me.
7. He is within me.
8. Indeed, He and I are one.

What is Man?
Psalm 90:1-17

Theme: Psalm 8:4 "What is man, that thou art mindful of him…"

Introduction: God has once again granted us to see what human life really is.

I Point: What is man?
- a. Psalm 90:5-6 "…they are like grass…In the morning it flourisheth, and groweth up; in the evening it is cut down and withereth."
- b. Job 7:7 "O remember that my life is wind:…"
- c. James 4:14 "…For what is your life? It is even a vapour, that appeareth for a little time, and then vanisheth away."

II Point: Is that the end of life?
- a. This is only a preparation for the life to come.
  Psalm 90:4 "For a thousand years in thy sight are but as yesterday when it is past, and as a watch in the night."
- b. In the natural.
  Psalm 90:10 "The days of our years are threescore years and ten; and if by reason of strength they be fourscore years, yet is their strength labour and sorrow; for it is soon cut off, and we fly away."
- c. What have you accomplished?
  Hebrews 9:27 "And as it is appointed unto men once to die, but after this the judgment:"

III Point: Man's responsibility
- a. Psalm 90:12 "So teach us to number our days, that we may apply our hearts unto wisdom."
- b. What is expected of man?
  John 3:3 "…Except a man be born again, he cannot see the kingdom of God."
- c. John 3:7 "Marvel not that I say unto thee, Ye must be born again."
- d. How much time have you to think about it?
  II Corinthians 6:2 "…I have heard thee in a time accepted, and in the day of salvation have I succoured thee: behold, now is the accepted time; behold, now is the day of salvation."

A true story: The Eagle at Niagara

A gentleman standing by Niagara saw an eagle swoop down on a frozen lamb incased in a floating piece of ice. The eagle stood upon it as it was "drifting" on toward the rapids. Every now and again the eagle would proudly lift his head into the air to look around him, as much as to say: "I am 'drifting' on toward danger, but I know what I am doing; I will fly away and make good my escape before it is too late." When he neared the falls he stopped and spread his powerful wings and leaped for his flight; but, alas! While he was feasting on that dead carcass his feet had frozen to the fleece. He leaped and shrieked and beat upon the ice with his wings until the ice-frozen lamb and eagle went over the falls and down into the chasm and darkness below.

I know there are some here who will, or are right now, doing as this eagle did at the Niagara. You may say, "I know what I'll do. I'll stop before it's too late. But alas! It may be too late now.

The Priestly Service of Christ – The Coming Again

Psalm 110 (Part Four)

Introduction: Christ was appointed as Priest, Hebrews 7:17 "...after the order of Melchisedec." So, therefore, He is a King as well as a Priest. At His second coming He will enter into His Kingly position and begin to execute His Kingly office.

I Point: Christ is a King.
- a. Psalm 110:4 and Hebrews 7:12-17 – Here Christ is represented to us as Priest and King after the order of Melchisedec.
- b. Matthew 2:1-2 and 11 – Jesus was born King of the Jews.
- c. Jesus claimed to be a King. Matthews 27:11 "And Jesus stood before the governor: and the governor asked him, saying, Art thou the King of the Jews? And Jesus said unto him, Thou sayest."
- d. Matthew 27:27-37 – Read it – Jesus died as King of the Jews. Matthew 27:37 "And set up over his head his accusation written, THIS IS JESUS THE KING OF THE JEWS."
- e. Revelation 4:2-3 - Jesus is enthroned as King in heaven.
Application: First we had Christ as the offering.
Life must come through death. Christ died that you and I might live.
Example: A mother must go to the very gates of death to give life to a child.

II Point: Christ was promised a kingdom.
- a. The kingdom of heaven. (Daniel 2:44-45).
He is coming again! And the dead in Christ shall rise first. Then, we which are alive and remain shall be caught up together in the air, where, we shall receive the rewards and appointments to rule and reign with him on earth. Then Jesus shall reign as King and High Priest for one thousand years. Oh, beloved, just picture the glorious resurrection at the rapture.

    b. Zechariah 14:9 "And the LORD shall be king over all the earth: in that day shall there be one LORD, and his name one."
    c. Luke 1:31-33 - Jesus, shall sit on the throne of His father David and reign forever.
Luke 1:32 "He shall be great, and shall be called the Son of the highest: and the Lord God shall give unto him the throne of his father David:"

III Point: <u>Christ will enter into his inheritance at His second coming.</u>
    a. Luke 19:12 He went "…to receive for himself a kingdom, and to return."
        1. He comes.
        2. He fights the battle.
        3. He sets up His kingdom and appointed you and me as His representatives. He gave you the pounds to work which He expects you to present to Him at His coming, together with the pounds you gained for Him. You then will be appointed accordingly to what you raised for Him.
    b. He comes as KING OF KINGS.
Revelation 19:11 "And I saw heaven opened, and behold a white horse; and he that sat upon him was called Faithful and True…"
    c. Revelation 19:16 "And he hath on his venture and on his thigh a name written, KING OF KINGS, AND LORD OF LORDS."
    d. Revelation 20:1-4 - He will rule for a thousand years.
    e. Revelation 20:6 "Blessed and holy is he that hath part in the first resurrection: on such the second death hath no power, but they shall be priests of God and of Christ, and shall reign with him a thousand years."

  *This is Part IV of the Priestly Service of Christ:
    Part I – Office - Hebrews 5:1-10, page 391.
    Part II – Offering - Hebrews 9: 6-28, page 393.
    Part III – Intercession - Hebrews 7:25, page 396.
    Part IV – The Second Coming - Psalm 110, page 119.

No Hiding Place
Psalm 139:1-24

Text: Psalm 139:7 "Whither shall I go from thy spirit? or whither shall I flee from thy presence?"

I Point: Psalm 139:1-6
   a. Psalm 139:1 "O Lord, thou hast searched me, and known me."
   b. Psalm 139:1 – He knows me.
   c. Psalm 139:2 – He understands me.
   d. Psalm 139:3 – He compassest me.
   e. Psalm 139:4 – He knows my words while they were yet in my tongue.
   f. Psalm 139:5 – He laid his hand upon me.
   g. Psalm 139:7 "Whither shall I go from thy Spirit? or whither shall I flee from thy presence?"

II Point: Confession of unworthiness.
   a. Psalm 139:7-13 – No hiding place left for me.
   b. Psalm 139:7 - I cannot flee.
   c. Psalm 139:8 – I cannot ascend.
   d. Psalm 139:8 – I cannot descend.
   e. Psalm 139:9 – The sea cannot hide me.
   f. Psalm 139:11 – Darkness cannot hide me.
   g. Psalm 139:13 – "For thou hast possessed my reins: thou hast covered me in my mother's womb."

III Point: Praising God.
   a. Psalm 139:14 "I will praise thee; for I am fearfully and wonderfully made: marvellous are thy works; and that my soul knoweth right well."
   b. Psalm 139:15 – I am praising God for the substance used to make me, and the curious ways he took to lead me.
   c. Psalm 139:19 – I am praising God for his mighty power. He is the power which upholds the world. It is a miracle.

IV Point: - My stand with God against sin.
   a. Psalm 139:20 – The enemies of God.
   b. Psalm 139:21 – Hating sin.
   c. Psalm 139:23-24 – Appealing to God to be searched.
   "Search me, O God, and know my heart: try me, and know my thoughts: And see if there be any wicked way in me, and lead me in the way everlasting." (Psalm 139:23-24).

Sermon Outlines from the Book of Proverbs

A Father's Day Sermon
Proverbs 14:34

Text: Proverbs 14:34 "Righteousness exalteth a nation: but sin is a reproach to my people."

Introduction: God is looking from heaven into this world, into each home, and into each heart.

I Point: <u>God has a divine rule</u>.
   a. First, we shall look into the divine rule God has for parents.
      1. God's rule for parents is the last rule on His parental love.
      2. His love is fulfilled in sacrifice. (Calvary).
   b. Second, we shall notice God's respect unto those that obey His rule.

   Illustration: II Timothy 1:5 "When I call to remembrance the unfeigned faith that is in thee, which dwelt first in thy grandmother Lois, and thy mother Eunice; and I am persuaded that in thee also."
   This can be also spoken of fathers and grandfathers.

   c. <u>God's outline to parental success</u>:
      1. Deuteronomy 6:5-7 "And thou shalt love the LORD thy God with all thine heart, and with all thy soul, and with all thy might. And these words, which I command thee this day, shall be in thine heart: And thou shalt teach them diligently unto thy children, and shalt talk to them when thou sittest in thine house, and when thou walkest by the way, and when thou liest down, and when thou risest up."

II Point: <u>Should you neglect this command, this is what happens:</u>
   a. Judges 2:10-11 "And also all that generation were gathered unto their fathers: and there arose another generation after them, which knew not the LORD, nor yet the works which he had done for Israel. And the children of Israel did evil in the sight of the LORD, and served Baalim:"

Conclusion: Fathers, obey God's parental rules and teach your children about God.

The Gospel in a Proverb
Proverbs 16:1-9

Text: Proverbs 16:6 "By mercy and truth iniquity is purged: and by the fear of the LORD men depart from evil."

Introduction: A proverb is a truth in a nutshell. They are burrs that stick to clothing not readily shaken off or forgotten.

I Point: Two names for sin.
1. Iniquity - This is the "God-ward" aspect of sin.
    i. It is the sin of insult, indignity, and dishonor done to God.
    ii. Of course, all manner of sin outrages the whole order of God.
2. Evil – This is the "man-ward" aspect of sin.
    i. Sin brings men into evil condition.
    ii. The way of transgression is hard.
    iii. Sin ruins lives.

II Point: Two requirements.
1. Iniquity must be purged.
2. Evil must be departed.
    Application: How shall this evil and iniquity be purged? Or how shall we escape the just judgment due to us?
    God's claims come first.
    Application – There is a common mistake that conversion, all at once, corrects moral evil. Oh no! It no more does so then it would mend a broken leg.
    But true conversion, supplies a new motive and love for God and righteousness.
    After conversion, evil must be retraced.
    The farther you went in evil the farther you must retrace.

III Point: How is iniquity purged?
  a. By mercy and truth.
  b. Truth and honesty - you and I must supply.
  c. Mercy and righteousness - God will supply.
    Do not expect mercy from God unless you produce a proof to God that you are honest.
    All this was made possible at Calvary when, "Mercy and truth are met together; righteousness and peace have kissed each other." (Psalm 85:10).

Conclusion: Depart from evil. Step by step – new ways of life are learned, and evil departed.

Sermon Outlines from the Book of Isaiah

The Devil
Isaiah 14:12-17

Introduction: The devil, as sinful and wicked as he is, has still a majesty office and power.

The Devil:
1. He was created in beauty, wisdom, might and perfection.
2. He was made ruler and representative over the world before the creation of man.
3. He snatched at equality with God and fell.
4. He resented the creation of man to take his place as the vicegerent of God.
5. He planned to destroy man by putting into man's heart the suggestion to reach for equality with God.
6. Because of his partnership with man he regained, in a measure, his title as prince and god. (Is. 14:12-14)(Gen. 3:5-7).

I Point: The Devil's character:
   a. Paul says to the church at Corinth, II Corinthians 11:3 "But I fear, lest by any means, as the serpent beguiled Eve through his subtilty, so your minds should be corrupted from the simplicity that is in Christ."
   b. Matthew 13:19 "When any one heareth the word of the kingdom, and understandeth it not, then cometh the wicked one, and catcheth away that which was sown in his heart..."
   c. When any one hath permitted by the subtilty of the devil to snatch away the seed of the Word of God, he or she then is this in the eyes of Christ: John 8:44 "Ye are of your father the devil, and the lusts of your father ye will do. He was a murderer from the beginning, and abode not in the truth, because there is no truth in him..."

II Point: Satan's ten distinct titles.
1. II Corinthians 11:14 "...an angel of light."
2. I Peter 5:8 "...a roaring lion..."
3. Ephesians 2:2 "...prince of the power of the air..."
4. Colossians 1:13 "...power of darkness..."
5. John 14:30 "...prince of this world..."
6. Revelation 12:9 "...the great dragon..."
7. Serpent.
8. Devil, Satan.
9. II Corinthians 4:4 "...god of this world..."
10. Revelation 9:11 "...angel of the bottomless pit,..."

III Point: <u>Satan's work</u>.

   a. I Peter 5:8 "...seeking whom he may devour:"
   b. Matthew 13:25 - Sowed tares, evil doctrine, and leaven.
   c. II Corinthians 4:4 "...blinded the minds of them which believed not..."
   d. Revelation: 12:10 "...the accuser of our brethren...which accused them before our God day and night."
   e. Luke 22:31 "...sift you as wheat:"
   f. I Corinthians 5:5 - The Apostle Paul said to the church of Corinth in regards to that wicked person in I Corinthians 5:5 "To deliver such an one unto Satan for the destruction of flesh..."
   Application: His complete aim is to destroy, kill, and torture.

IV Point: <u>Satan has subordinates</u>.

   a. Ephesians 6:12 - Principalities, powers, world rulers, spiritual hosts.
   b. Matthew 25:41 tells us there is "...everlasting fire, prepared for the devil and his angels:"

V Point: <u>Satan's destiny</u>.

   a. Revelation 12:7-9 - He was "cast out" of heaven.
   b. Revelation 20:1-3 – He shall be cast into the bottomless pit during Christ's reign of 1000 years.
   c. He will be cast into the lake of fire forever and ever. Revelation 20:10 "And the devil that deceived them was cast into the lake of fire and brimstone...and shall be tormented day and night for ever and ever."

Satan's Downfall
Isaiah 14:12-17

Introduction: Satan's downfall is the subject we shalt now discuss.

Ezekiel 28:13-14 - Satan once stood as the great ruler over God's creation and as the anointed cherub, from the midst of the stones of fire. Then he reached the peak of his light, because of his uplifted heart, and God cast him out of heaven. Now today, as per Israel's writing, we see him as a down fallen cast off and doomed enemy of God.

I Point: Pride

  a. Pride before the fall.
Isaiah 14:14 "I will ascend above the heights of the clouds; I will be like the most High."

Application: We notice that Satan was created perfect by God, but he sinned, and the chief sin was pride.

Illustration: It is this pride that ruined the world, and sent Adam and Eve out of the garden. It is this pride that causes all the trouble in the world and pride always goes before a fall.

That was the charge God made against Satan and that is the charge that God makes against you and me.

Illustration: That was the type of sin that Satan tried to bring Christ to fall by in the forty days of temptation.

Illustration: Satan is not so much interested in the gross sins of the flesh. He is much more interested in thwarting the will of God in men's lives.

When Satan comes between, that means pride comes between you and God.

  b. His downfall out of heaven.
But he still has access to the throne of God along with other angelic beings.
We see that in Job 1:6 "Now there was a day when the sons of God came to present themselves before the LORD, and Satan came also among them."
I Peter 5:8 "Be sober, be vigilant: because your adversary the devil, as a roaring lion, walketh about, seeking whom he may devour:"
Even in his downfall, he still has power and dominions.

II Point: <u>Satan's dominion</u>.
  a. Satan uses the kings and princes of the world to defy God's people. Daniel 10:13 "But the prince of the kingdom of Persia withstood me one and twenty days: but, lo, Michael, one of the chief princes, came to help me; and I remained there with the kings of Persia."
  b. When we turn to the New Testament we find that Christ designates Satan as the "prince of this world."
  John 16:11 "...the prince of this world is judged."
  c. Paul goes a step farther. He calls Satan the god of this world or the god of this age. II Corinthians 4:4 "In whom the god of this world hath blinded the minds of them which believe not..."
  d. In Ephesians 2:2, Paul designates him as "...the prince of the power of the air..."
  e. Then in Ephesians 6:11-18 - Paul admonishes us to arm ourselves against Satan.

I want you to notice that Paul informs us that Satan is not alone in this operation. He has others associated with him. Both Peter and Jude inform us of fallen "...angels which kept not their first estate,... (Jude 1:6).

Illustration: I want to call your attention to the fact that this world is rubbed over by Satan.

Matthew 4:1 and Luke 4:1 - This is where Satan tempted Christ to fall down and worship him. Matthew 4:9 "...All these things will l give thee, if thou wilt fall down and worship me."

Luke 4:6 "And the devil said unto him, All this power will I give thee, and the glory of them: for that is delivered unto me; and to whomsoever I will I give it."

I want you to notice that Christ did not contradict or dispute this claim of Satan. And if it had been a lie, then Christ would have known it, and it would not have been a temptation.

Conclusion: I call your attention also just as Satan once offered the kingdom and glory of this world to Christ, so he will one day bestow them upon the antichrist. (II Thessalonians.2:3-4).

But just a few verses farther we are told that He, "Christ" will destroy that wicked one. (II Thessalonians 2:5-10).

Final conclusion: So when we gather up all the threads of the scripture teaching, we find that Satan has "charge" of this world, he does not own it. He is merely its prince, its god, its ruler because it is given to him until that glorious day when "...The kingdoms of this world are become the kingdoms of our Lord, and of his Christ; and he shall reign for ever and ever."(Rev. 11:15). Hallelujah! Amen!

A Bed Too Short
Isaiah 28:14-21

Theme: A bed that is too short.
Text: Isaiah 28:20 "For the bed is shorter than that a man can stretch himself on it: and the covering narrower than that he can wrap himself in it."

I Point: <u>What does this bed mean?</u>
  a. Isaiah 28:15 "Because ye have said, We have make a covenant with death, and with hell are we at agreement; when the overflowing scourge shall pass through, it shall not come unto us: for we have made lies our refuge, and under falsehood have we hid ourselves:" The bed spoken of here means, a plan, a goal, and a self-satisfied assurance that they will escape judgment.
  b. They say, Isaiah 28:15 "...We have made a covenant..."
       1. With death.
       2. With hell.
  c. We have reached an agreement; they are self-satisfied, that judgment shall not come unto them.
  d. The reason for their self-satisfied hope is:
       1. They have made lies their refuge.
       2. Under falsehood have they hid themselves.
     Application: We think we can lie our way out of anything. We say, "I can pretend to be good. I can put up a Christian front. I can fool God. I can prove myself in my falsehood."

II Point: <u>What does it prove to them</u>?
  a. They are selling themselves short.
  b. What kind of a bed are you trying to sleep in?
  c. Have you made an agreement with death and with hell?
  d. Are you trying to rest on a self-righteous made bed? You may rest on it, but you will not be able to sleep.
  e. Are you trying to cover yourself with your own home-made cover-ups? You soon will find out that they are too short, and too narrow.

Conclusion: God says, Isaiah 28:17-18 "Judgment also will I lay to the line, and righteousness to the plummet: and the hail shall sweep away the refuge of lies, and the waters shall overflow the hiding place. And your covenant with death shall be disannulled, and your agreement with hell shall not stand; when the overflowing scourge shall pass through, then ye shall be trodden down by it."
It is God's foundation, God's cornerstone, God's rest.

Radiant Gems
Isaiah 43:1-11

Theme: Radiant gems from the wonderful Word of God.

Introduction: In Isaiah 43:1-5 there are five beautiful gems of scripture, which like diamonds of rare brilliance, become increasingly so as we group them together with their radiance blending with each other.

These five radiant gems are:
1. I have redeemed thee.
2. I have called thee.
3. I have loved thee.
4. I am with thee,
5. I will gather thee.

I Point: Isaiah 43:1 "…for I have redeemed thee…"
- a. The cost of it:
  - i. I Peter 1:18-19 "Forasmuch as ye know that ye were not redeemed with corruptible things, as silver and gold, from your vain conversation received by tradition from your fathers; But with the precious blood of Christ, as of a lamb without blemish and without spot:"
- b. The extent of it:
  - ii. John 10:28 "And I give unto them eternal life; and they shall never perish, neither shall any man pluck them out of my hand."
- c. The result of it:
  - iii. John 5:24 " Verily, verily, I say unto you, He that heareth my word, and believeth on him that sent me, hath everlasting life, and shall not come into condemnation; but is passed from death unto life."

II Point: Isaiah 43:1 "…I have called thee by thy name;…."
Called to what?
- a. To sonship:
  John 1:12 "But as many as received him, to them gave he power to become the sons of God, even to them that believe on his name:"
- b. To fellowship:
  I Corinthians 1:9 "God is faithful, by whom ye were called unto the fellowship of his Son Jesus Christ our Lord."

   c. <u>To service</u>:
      John 15:16 "Ye have not chosen me, but I have chosen you, and ordained you, that ye should go and bring forth fruit, and that your fruit shall remain: that whatsoever ye shall ask of the Father in my name, he may give it you."

III Point: <u>Isaiah 43:4 "...I have loved thee:..."</u>
   a. With divine love, unchangeable love.
      Romans 8:35 "Who shall separate us from the love of Christ?..."
      When we have trouble seeing we go get spectacles. I want you to see Him. I want you to get the spectacles of love to see the altogether lovely one, who says "I have loved thee."

IV Point: <u>Isaiah 43:5 "Fear not: for I am with thee</u>..." In what?
   a. <u>In prayer</u>.
      Matthew 18:20 "For where two or three are gathered together in my name, there am I in the midst of them."
   b. <u>In suffering</u>.
      Matthew 11:28 "Come unto me, all ye that labour and are heavy laden, and I will give you rest."
   c. <u>In service</u>.
      John 15:16 "Ye have not chosen me, but I have chosen you, and ordained you... "
      Application: Do you, my friend, realize that He is with thee.
      The greatest verse I ever found in time of great need is Isaiah 41:10 "Fear thou not; for I am with thee: be not dismayed; for I am thy God: I will strengthen thee; yea, I will help thee; yea, I will uphold thee with the right hand of my righteousness."

V Point: <u>Isaiah 43:5 "...I will...gather thee</u>..." Where?
   a. <u>To be with me</u>.
      John 14:1 "Let not your heart be troubled: ye believe in God, believe also in me."
   b. <u>For your reward</u>.
      Revelation: 22:12 "And, behold, I come quickly; and my reward is with me, to give every man according as his work shall be."
   c. <u>For your place</u>.
      John 14:2 "...I go to prepare a place for you."

Conclusion: Did you notice how these prophetical words of Isaiah, given to Israel, fit in so perfect in the outline of Jesus Christ to His redeemed. Are you, my friend, one that looks forward to the gathering, when Christ will come to receive His bride?

Revival – Part I
Isaiah 44:22

Text: Isaiah 44:22 "I have blotted out, as a thick cloud, thy transgressions, and, as a cloud, thy sins: return unto me; for I have redeemed thee."

Introduction: What for, and when is a revival needed?

I Point: <u>What is a revival</u>?
  a. A revival consists of the return of the church from her backslidings.
    Hosea 11:7 "And my people are bent to backsliding from me: though they called them to the most High, none at all would exalt him."
    Isaiah 44:22 "...return unto me; for I have redeemed thee."
    Illustration: The idea that it takes something very peculiar to promote a revival is unscriptural. The churches have been trying now everything: picture shows, music, programs, and feasting. But there is one thing they have not done. They have not returned from their backsliding. The church has not returned to their knees.
  b. A revival always includes conviction of sin on the part of the Christians.
    Romans 3:10 "As it is written, There is none righteous, no, not one:"

    Romans 3:11 "There is none that understandeth, there is none that seeketh after God."

    Romans 3:12 "They are all gone out of the way, they are together become unprofitable; there is none that doth good, no, not one."
    Romans 3:23 "For all have sinned, and come short of the glory of God;"
    I Peter 4:17 "For the time is come that judgment must begin at the house of God: and if it first begin at us, what shall the end be of them that obey not the gospel of God?"
    Application: It is the church that must come back to God first.
  c. Revival is nothing else than a new beginning of obedience to God.
    I John 2:15 "Love not the world, neither the things that are in the world. If any man love the world, the love of the Father is not in him."

Application: Faith renewed brings a tender burning love for souls, and breaks the power of the world and sin in a Christian.
Illustration: If you say you love Jesus, I shall ask you one question: "Have you lead a soul to Him?"
d. In a revival Christians have deep feelings about Christ. And their feeling for Christ is noticed wherever they go.
Matthew 12:36 "But I say unto you, That every idle word that men shall speak, they shall give account thereof in the day of judgment. For by thy words thou shalt be justified, and by thy words thou shalt be condemned."

Application: Idle words have no place when a revival is on. Strong language has no place, and words of accusation of others have no place. Each is too busy seeing and judging his own sins.
John 8:9 "And they which heard it, being convicted by their own conscience, went out one by one, beginning at the eldest, even unto the last:..."

Application: A revival breaks out in the hearts of the accusers:

II Point: <u>When is revival needed?</u>
a. Revival is needed when there is a lack of brotherly love.
I John 4:7-8 "Beloved, let us love one another: for love is of God; and every one that loveth is born of God, and knoweth God. He that loveth not knoweth not God; for God is love."
When there are dissensions, jealousies, and evil speaking, it shows that Christians are out of communion with God, and a revival will put an end to such things.
Colossians 3:8-9 "But now ye also put off all these: anger, wrath, malice, blasphemy, filthy communication out your mouth. Lie not one to another, seeing that ye have put off the old man with his deeds;"
I Peter 4:8 "And above all things have fervent charity among yourselves: for charity shall cover the multitude to sins."
I Peter 4:15 "But let none of you suffer as a...busybody in other men's matters."
b. Revival is needed when there is a worldly spirit in the church.
Mark 8:36 "For what shall it profit a man, if he shall gain the whole world, and lose his own soul?"

I Timothy 6:9 "But they that will be rich fall into temptation and a snare, and into many foolish and hurtful lusts, which drown men in destruction and perdition."
- c. Revival is needed when the church finds its members in gross sins.
  Ephesians 4:25 "Wherefore putting away lying, speak every man truth with his neighbour: for we are members one of another."
- d. Revival is needed when the wicked things triumph over the church.
  Psalm 94:3 "LORD how long shall the wicked, how long shall the wicked triumph?"
  Exodus 11:7 "...the LORD, doth put a difference between the Egyptians and Israel."
  And God hath put a difference between the wicked and the righteous.

III Points: How to bring revival.
- a. Rodney Gipsy Smith was once asked how to start a revival. He answered: "Go home, lock yourself in your room and kneel down in the middle of your floor. Draw a chalk mark all around yourself and ask God to start the revival inside that chalk mark. When He has answered your prayer, the revival will begin."
- b. Dr. R. A. Torrey wrote, "I can give you a prescription that will bring revival to any church."
  1. Let a few Christians get thoroughly right with God themselves. This is the prime essential. If not done, the plan will fail.
  2. Let them give themselves to prayer for revival until God opens the heavens and comes down.
  3. Let them put themselves at God's disposal to use as He sees fit in winning others to Christ. THAT IS ALL. This is sure to bring revival.

*This is Part I of the Revival Series:
Part I - Isaiah 44:22, page 133.
Part II - Acts 5:1-16, page 271.
Part III – Psalm 42:1-11, page 112.

Sermon Outlines from the Book of Ezekiel

As God Sees You

Ezekiel 8:8-9

Theme: You cannot hide from God.

Introduction: God looks down right upon this town, upon this place, and upon you and me. At this very day, at this very moment, He sees the hidden things in your life. He grieves with compassion over you. He gives His Holy Spirit charge over you, to convict you, to love you. He sends messengers to plead with you. He sends sickness to draw you in love, unto Himself.

I Point: <u>Now shall we see how our text reveals this unto us.</u>
    a. God sees the works of man in a gross manner.
        1. As you and I would see a mess of corruption.
Genesis 6:12 "And God looked upon the earth, and, behold, it was corrupt; for all flesh had corrupted his way upon the earth."
    b. Take the life of a city.
        1. Take the life of a little town.
        2. Take the life of a sinful home.
        3. Take the life of a filthy person.
        4. Take the life of a corrupted church.
    c. He sees a heap of mess just climbing one on top of the other
    d. As you and I would see a piece of flesh under corruption.
        1. He divides it into classes upon the individual once as we shall see in our text.
        2. He reveals these things unto His people, by the mouth of Ezekiel.

II Point: <u>What men do</u>.
    a. Ezekiel 8:1 – God sees a jewel (Ezekiel) mingled with the mess of corruption. (church bodies)
Ezekiel 8:3 – God lifted Ezekiel up that he may see as God sees.
    b. If you and I could see the corruption of mankind as God sees it, we would not think it is cruel of God to destroy man: by floods, earthquakes, Sodom and Gomorra, etc.

III Point: <u>How God reveals it unto Ezekiel</u>.
  a. Ezekiel 8:5-6 - Idolatry, to provoke God that He should turn from them. These are sins done <u>in the open</u>.
  b. Ezekiel 8:7-12 – God also reveals unto Ezekiel <u>the hidden sins </u>of man.
     1. Idol worship.
     2. Devil worship.
     3. Self-worship.
     4. Church worship.
  c. What have you, my friend, hid in your heart? Whatever it is, it is not hid from God.
  d. Ezekiel 8:13-16 – We see God's people with their backs toward the temple.
  e. Willingly rejecting God and worshipping the devil.

Here are a few of today's false worship and idolatry.

Christian Science	Mohamedism	Christian Delphiniums
British Israelism	Agnosticism	Humanism
Modernism	Mormonism	Russellism
Kenosis Theory	Evolution	Soul Sleeping Religion
Jehovah Witness	Spiritism	Seventh Day Adventism
Sweden Borginism	Unitarianism	Atheism

IV Point: <u>God takes action</u>.
  a. Ezekiel 8:17-18 "...mine eye shall not spare, neither will I have pity: and though they cry in mine ears with a loud voice, yet will I not hear them."
  b. Ezekiel 9:1 "...Cause them that have charge oven the city to draw near, even every man with his destroying weapon in his hand."
     Do we see such orders given by God today?

V Point: The Christian is to be recognized.
  a. Ezekiel 9:4 "...set a mark upon the foreheads..."
  b. Ezekiel 9:7 - Defile the house of God where there are corrupt people.
  c. Can we see the mark on true Christians today in time of trouble?
     Illustration: Some Christians are like leaven bread. (Dough) They look good until they receive a punch. Then down they go.

Satan – Part One
Ezekiel 28:11-19

Introduction:
1. Satan is a personality of power and great importance. He is superior to man, but inferior to God, the Lord Jesus Christ, and the Holy Spirit.
2. Satan uses his power. II Corinthians 11:14 "...for Satan himself is transformed into an angel of light." And he has false ministers of righteousness for the deception of human beings.
3. II Corinthians 11:15 "Therefore it is no great thing if his ministers also be transformed as the ministers of righteousness; whose end shall be according to their works."
4. He leaves a trail, by his power that cannot be erased.

I Point: A birds-eye view of what Satan has done.
   a. He beguiled Eve and caused the down fall of the human race. Genesis 3:13 "...The serpent beguiled me, and I did eat."
   b. He afflicted Job. Job 1:12 "And the LORD said unto Satan, Behold, all that he hath is in thy power;..."
   c. I Chronicles 21:1 "And Satan stood up against Israel, and provoked David to number Israel."
   d. Zechariah 3:1 "And he shewed me Joshua the high priest standing before the angel of the LORD, and Satan standing at his right hand to resist him."
   e. Satan tempted the Lord Jesus Christ in the wilderness saying, Matthew 4:9 "...All these things will I give thee, if thou wilt fall down and worship me."
   f. He entered into Judas and caused him to betray the Lord for 30 pieces of silver. Luke 22:3 "Then entered Satan into Judas surnamed Iscariot..."
   g. He caused Peter to swear and deny His Christ. Luke 22:31-32 "And the Lord said, Simon, Simon, behold, Satan hath desired to have you, that he may sift you as wheat:"
   h. He filled the heart of Ananias and Sapphira and caused them to lie to the Holy Ghost. Acts 5:3 "But Peter said, Ananias, why hath Satan filled thine heart to lie to the Holy Ghost,..."

- i. He hindered Paul in his missionary journey.
  I Thessalonians 2:18 "Wherefore we would have come unto you, even I Paul, once and again; but Satan hindered us."
- j. He snatches the word out of unbeliever's hearts. Matthew 13:19 "When any one heareth the word of the kingdom, and understandeth it not, then cometh the wicked one, and catcheth away that which was sown in his heart..."
- k. He blinds the minds of them that believe not.
  II Corinthians 4:4 "In whom the god of this world hath blinded the minds of them which believe not..."
- l. He sows tares among the wheat. Matthew 13:39 "The enemy that sowed them is the devil..."
- m. He destroys the flesh of carnal Christians. I Corinthians 5:5 "To deliver such an one unto Satan for the destruction of the flesh, that the spirit may be saved in the day of the Lord Jesus,"

Application: No wonder he is called the god of this world as per Luke 4:5-6 and II Corinthians 4:4.

II Point: <u>He will establish his rule against the world</u>.
- a. Revelation: 13:1-6 – (read).
- b. Revelation 13:11-17 -He will inaugurate the World Religious System.
- c. Revelation 12:13-17 - He will instigate unparalleled persecution to the Jewish people.
- d. He will march the armies of the world into the Battle of Armageddon. Revelation 16:16 "And he gathered them together into a place called in the Hebrew tongue Armageddon."

III Point: <u>His final place</u>.
- a. Revelation 20:1-3 – Satan will be conquered. Praise be to God. And he will be put into the bottomless pit during the Millennium.
- b. He will be ultimately tormented in the lake of fire for ever and for ever. Revelation 20:10 "And the devil that deceived them was cast into the lake of fire and brimstone...and shall be tormented day and night for ever and ever."

Conclusion: This is but a very brief introduction of the person of the devil. Next time, I want you to see all his titles. They are a large number of them, but, of course, not all were flattering to him, but just as the Bible calls him.

Satan – Part Two
Ezekiel 28:11-19

Introduction: The Bible teaches that there is abroad in the universe a superhuman being, a personality that opposes God and His will. He has some 30 title names of which are not flattering to him.

I Point: <u>Satan's Titles.</u>
1. Revelation 9:11 - He is called "Abaddon" in the Hebrew tongue, and "Apollyon in the Greek tongue which means "destroyer."
2. II Thessalonians 2:8-10 - He is called "Belial" which means the "lawless one."
3. Matthew 12:27-29 - He is called "Beelzebub" which means "the prince of demons."
4. I John 3:12, Revelation 12:3 - He is called "a great red dragon" which means a liar and a father of lies, a thief, a murder, or "the wicked one."
5. Isaiah 14:12-14 - He is called "Lucifer."
6. Revelation 9:11 - He is called the" angel of the abyss."
7. Revelation 12:9 - He is called "that old serpent."
8. Ephesians 2:2 - He is called "the prince of darkness."
9. Ephesians 2:2 - He is called "the prince of the air."
10. John 12:31 - He is called "the prince this world."
11. Satan is the god of this age (world) which means, Ephesians 2:2 "...the Spirit that now worketh in the children of disobedience:"
12. Thirty-five times he is called "The Devil" which means "accuser or slanderer."
13. Fifty-two times he is called "Satan" which means "enemy or adversary."

II Point: <u>Where did this being come from</u>?
   a. Ezekiel 28:11-13 "Moreover the word of the LORD come unto me, saying, Son of man, take up a lamentation upon the king of Tyrus, and say unto him, Thus saith the Lord GOD; Thou sealest up the sum, full of wisdom, and perfect in beauty. Thou hast been in Eden the garden of God; every precious stone was thy covering, the sardius, topaz, and the diamond, the beryl, the onyx, and the jasper, the sapphire, the emerald, and the carbuncle, and gold: the workmanship

of thy tabrets and of thy pipes was prepared in thee in the day that thou wast created."
   a. Answer: He came from Eden from the mount of God, meaning from the upper light of God.

III Point: What is his origin?
   God create him.
   a. Ezekiel 28:14-17 "Thou art the anointed cherub that covereth; and I have set thee so; thou wast upon the holy mountain of God; thou hast walked up and down in the midst of the stones of fire. Thou wast perfect in thy ways from the day that thou wast created, till iniquity was found in thee. By the multitude of thy merchandise they have filled the midst of thee with violence, and thou hast sinned: therefore I will cast thee as profane out of the mountain of God: and I will destroy thee, O covering cherub, from the midst of the stones of fire. Thine heart was lifted up because of thy beauty; thou hast corrupted thy wisdom by reason of thy brightness: I will cast thee to the ground, I will lay thee before kings, that they may behold thee."
   b. Satan was created by God. This fact is brought out in Ezekiel 28:13 and 15 "From the day that thou was created."

IV Point: How was he created?
   a. He was not created as a hideous, repulsive being with forked hoofs, spear-pointed tail, horns upon his head and carrying a pitchfork; but, Ezekiel 28:12 "...Thou sealest up the sum, full of wisdom, and perfect in beauty."
   b. Application: Satan is no fool. He is wiser than the wisest of man. That is why he can outsmart the wisest man.
   c. Genesis 3:1 - He is subtle.
   d. Ezekiel 28:14 - He is an angelic being.

There was three of highest authority: Michael, Gabriel, and Lucifer, the anointed cherub. This last one is the devil.

Conclusion: Ezekiel 28:15 - He was created a sinless and perfect being. But Satan became a sinful creature as scripture tells us because of pride.

Sermon Outlines from the Book of Daniel

The Prophet Daniel – Part One

The Man

Daniel 1:1-21

Introduction: The book of Daniel with its great prophecies, both fulfilled and unfulfilled, is one of the most interesting portions of God's Holy Word.

Before we follow this blessed book in a series of studies, a few general remarks on prophecy and its importance may be in order. Prophecy is history prewritten. The center of all prophecy is the Lord Jesus Christ.

- a. His suffering.
- b. His glory.
- c. His two comings.
    1. As man of sorrow to suffer and to die.
    2. As King of Glory to reign.

I Point: <u>The larger part of scripture is prophecy</u>.
- a. It is sad to say that many churches today ignore and neglect the story of prophecy such as Daniel and Revelation.
- b. The greater majority of professing Christians have little desire to know what God has said concerning the future.
    1. Unfortunately, thousands of fortunetellers, astrologers, and demon possessed medians make a fine living because of the ignorance of Christians.

II Point: <u>The division and analysis of the Book of Daniel</u>.
- a. The Book of Daniel is composed of two parts and it was written in two languages.
    1. The first six chapters do not contain prophecies; but, Daniel here stands as the divinely chosen interpreter of what has been revealed to Nebuchadnezzar in dreams.
- b. The invasion of Jerusalem.
    This is called "the times of the Gentiles" counting from the time God withdrew from Jerusalem where His glory dwelt. These times of the Gentiles will continue till Jesus Christ again establishes His throne on earth. Then the times of the Gentiles is ended.

2. The second part of the Book of Daniel is chapter's seven to twelve. We find here the communication Daniel had with God, and these are no longer dreams, but visions. These visions also concern the times of the Gentiles.
  c. Also note that these two parts are written in two different languages. Chapters eight and twelve are written in Hebrew. The other chapters are written in Aramaic. The reason for this is that it was written in the language of the empires it concerns.

III Point: The personality of Daniel.
  a. He was a man of faith, and a man of prayer. He was one with whom God talked.
  b. I want you to notice that Daniel outlived the 70 year captivity, and saw again when Jehovah led his children back to the Promised Land to get ready for the birth of Christ.

IV Point: The first chapter of Daniel.
  a. The year 606 B.C. was the first besiege of Jerusalem. Nebuchadnezzar took part of the people and their king, Jehoiakim. Daniel 1:1 "In the third year of the reign of Jehoiakim king of Judah came Nebuchadnezzar king of Babylon unto Jerusalem, and besieged it."
  b. In 598 B.C. Nebuchadnezzar came again and took away a larger number of people including Ezekiel.
  c. In 587 B.C. Nebuchadnezzar completed his besiege and burned Jerusalem. This is when the "times of the Gentiles" begins.
  d. This third time is when Daniel, Hananiah, Mishael and Azariah were taken and placed under the custody of the king's eunuch, Melzar.

V Point: You will recall that the king renamed them.
  a. Daniel, which means "God of my judge" was renamed Belteshazzar, which means "Bels Prince."
  b. Hananiah, which means "Beloved of the Lord" was renamed Shadrach, which means "Sungod."
  c. Mishael, which means "Who is as God" was renamed Meshach, which means "god of Venus" which is the Babylonian god.

d. Azariah, which means "The Lord is my help" was renamed Abednego, which means "Servant of Nebo" which is another one of their false gods.

> Application: The object of this name change was to wipe out the memory of Jerusalem. Daniel 1:8 "But Daniel purposed in his heart that he would not defile himself..." He made this step known unto the king, and God met him and his fellows.

> Our constant danger is that we give up our separation and being set apart for God and go along with the world. "And be not conformed to this world: but be ye transformed by the renewing of your mind, that ye may prove what is that good, and acceptable, and perfect, will of God." (Romans 12:2).

Conclusion: We find our churches today are sympathizing with the backslidden young folks, and compromise to have them join somewhat with the world. All because we have not purposed in our heart to serve the Lord by life or death, as did Daniel and his companions. We must purpose in our heart to remain set apart and separated from the world. "Wherefore come out from among them, and be ye separate, saith the Lord..." (II Corinthians 6:17).

The Prophet Daniel – Part Two
Nebuchadnezzar's Dream
Daniel 2:19-49

Introduction: The second chapter is the foundation of all the visions following in this great Book of Daniel.

I Point: Dreams and Visions.
  a. Two nations are involved – The Gentile nation and the Jewish Nation.
     1. The Gentile nation received the matters of God by dreams.
     2. The Jewish Nation received matters by visions.
  b. The revelations here shown to both of them are the "times of the Gentiles."
     1. This particular word we find not in the Book of Daniel, but it refers to Daniel in the New Testament in Luke 21:24 "And they shall fall by the edge of the sword, and shall be led away captive into all nations: and Jerusalem shall be trodden down of the Gentiles, until the times of the Gentiles be fulfilled."
     2. The times of the Gentiles did not begin when the Jews rejected Christ on the cross, but in the days of Daniel in the year 587 B.C.
  c. Jerusalem had been supreme because the throne of the glory of Jehovah was there. But when the Lord drew out of Jerusalem, the place was then in the hands of the Gentiles.
  d. This will be under the Gentiles till the "fulness of the Gentiles" is come. Romans 11:25 "For I would not, brethren, that ye should be ignorant of this mystery, lest ye should be wise in your own conceits; that blindness in part is happened to Israel, until the fulness of the Gentiles be come in."
  e. The "fulness of the Gentiles" is to be distinguished from the "times of the Gentiles." This expression "the fulness of the Gentiles" is only found once in the New Testament, and it refers to the number of that people taken out from among the Gentiles – The Church. Then the removal of the Church will take place. That then, is the end of the Gentile rule and the number is full.
  f. Then once again the Jewish history will be resumed.

II Point: <u>The Division of Chapter 2.</u>

a. There are six divisions in Chapter 2.
   1. The forgotten dreams of the king. (Daniel 2:1-13).
   2. The prayer meeting. (Daniel 2:14-18).
   3. The praise meeting. (Daniel 2:19-25).
   4. Daniel before the king. (Daniel 2:26-36).
   5. The revelation & interpretation of the dream. (Dan. 2:37-45).
   6. The effect upon Nebuchadnezzar and the promotion of Daniel and his companions. (Daniel 2:46-49).
b. The prayer meeting and the praise meeting. Daniel gives God all the glory. He, as well as his companions, hide behind the Lord so deeply that only God Jehovah is seen.
   1. Wisdom and might are His.
   2. He changes the times and seasons.
   3. He removeth kings and setteth up kings.
   4. He giveth wisdom unto the wise and knowledge to them that know understanding.
   5. He revealeth the deep and secret things.
   6. He knoweth what is in the darkness and the light dwelleth with Him.
   7. He gives praise for the revelation of what has been asked.
   Application: If that is the way we come, then God will talk through us; and as King Nebuchadnezzar, they to whom you speak will see the power of God, as Nebuchadnezzar saw it and fell on his face before his captives.

III Point: <u>The revelation and interpretation (Daniel 2:31-35).</u>

a. The image!
   1. The image, in the form of a man, reveals to us the race of man "the times of the Gentiles." This "Man's Day" will continue until the "Lord's Day" begins.
b. Note the composition of the image of the man.
   1. Gold - head.
   2. Silver – arms.
   3. Brass and iron – chest and legs.
   4. Iron and clay - the feet and the ten toes.

Application: These four parts of the image present to us four world empires which have and still are to appear on the earth.

That is history written in advance.
  1. Gold - Empire in the Gentile rule was Babylon.
  2. Silver – The Medes and Persians made of King Darius.
  3. Brass – Greco-Macedonia, the King of Greece – Alexander the Great.
  4. The monarchy during the time of the Gentiles is represented by the long legs and ten toes – the Roman Empire. It has the longest part of the body and of time, and it is of iron which subdues all other metals.
- c. The ten toes. They stand for 10 kings. Daniel 2:44 "And in the days of these kings shall the God of heaven set up a kingdom, which shall never be destroyed: and the kingdom shall not be left to other people, but it shall break in pieces and consume all these kingdoms, and it shall stand for ever."
- d. The stone cut out of the mountain without hands.
Daniel 2:45 "Forasmuch as thou sawest that the stone was cut out of the mountain without hands, and that it brake in pieces the iron, the brass, the clay, the silver, and the gold; the great God hath made known to the king what shall come to pass hereafter: and the dream is certain, and the interpretation thereof sure."
- e. Mathew 21:44 "And whosoever shall fall on this stone shall be broken; but on whomsoever it shall fall, it will grind him to powder."
- f. The Stone is Christ.
  1. The Jews stumbled and fell over the stone and was broken.
  2. The Church is built upon the Stone.
  3. But the Gentiles who reject Christ, this stone will fall on them and grind them to pieces.
  4. This will take place at the Second Coming of Christ.

IV Point: <u>The effect of the interpretation upon Nebuchadnezzar</u>.
  1. He was silent.
  2. He was astonished.
  3. He fell to the earth and worshipped Daniel.
  4. He acknowledged Daniel's Lord as the God of gods.
  5. Daniel's exaltation, and at his request, his three friends are exalted with him. This is a perfect type of Christ who said, "And the glory which thou gavest me I have given them;..." (John 17:22).

The Prophet Daniel – Part Three
The Moral and Religious Conditions of the Times of the Gentiles.

Daniel 3:1-28

Introduction:
1. Last time we had the dream of Nebuchadnezzar. Here the king begins to see that there is a God above gods. And he is trying to worship this God in his own strength in the flesh, and to exalt himself.
2. The next four chapters, which follow the great dream, are of historical character. They do not contain direct prophesies, but record current events which transpired during the reign of Nebuchadnezzar, Belshazzar, and Darius the Mede.
3. It covers the age of Daniel from 14 years old, when he was taken to Babylon, til 80 years old, when he was cast into the lion's den under the reign of Darius the Mede in 538 B.C. or 68 years after Daniel had been brought to Babylon.

I Point: The Image of Gold.

   a. Nebuchadnezzar had heard from Daniel's own lips "...Thou art this head of gold." (Daniel 2:38).
   Application: The king became puffed up, and in the pride of his heart attempted to unify the religious worship of his vast empire.
   b. It was an image of a man – "self." The dream humbled him for a moment, but then Satan, taking a hand in it, lifted him up. He was not yet converted, but believed only in his head that there was a God above gods.
   c. Daniel 3:1 "Nebuchadnezzar the king made an image of gold, whose height was threescore cubits, (that is 60 cubits or 90 feet high), and the breadth thereof six cubits:..." (that is 9 feet wide). This is the number of man. Seven is God's number. This reminds me of 666. It was the beginning of the times of the Gentiles. This type of worship, which is idolatry, is reproduced in Rome, which is called in Revelation – Babylon. This new religion promised to the people sweet music with much commotion.

II Point: The Faithful Three.

   a. The proclamation had been made, that when the sweet music was heard, all nations and languages were to fall down and worship the golden image.

    b. Shadrach, Meshach and Abed-nego stand up. Nebuchadnezzar says to them, "...who is that God that shall deliver you out of my hands?" (Daniel 3:15). They were men of faith and said, "...our God, whom we serve is able to deliver us from the burning fiery furnace, and he will deliver us out of thine hand, O king." (Daniel 3:17).

    c. The king made sure that the furnace was hot. He made it seven times hotter. The mightiest men were chosen for the task of making the furnace hotter, and they were consumed.

    d. But, there are four men, not three, walking in the fire. The one like the Son of God. (Jesus) The same Jesus who said, "When thou passest through the waters, I will be with thee; and through the rivers, they shall not overflow thee: when thou walkest through the fire, thou shalt not be burned; neither shall the flame kindle upon thee." (Isaiah 43:2).

This was, and still is, His promise. This has been repeated many times, especially during the Roman Empire, and in Russia under the communist reign. I saw the martyr's blood flow. I stood where they stood. Shall I now play with the gospel? God Forbid. To me the gospel is a blood trail. I would rather bleed and die than play.

Conclusion: Once more the king acknowledged the God of Shadrach, Meshach and Abed-nego. But wait! Is his now converted? No! Not yet. We shall see next time what it takes to humble his man. This is a perfect picture of one proud and stubborn heart.

The Prophet Daniel – Part Four

The Prediction of the End of the Times of the Gentiles.

Daniel 4:1-37

Introduction: Last Sunday we saw the moral and religious conditions of the times of the Gentiles. Today we shall see the prediction of the end of the times of the Gentiles.

I Point: Nebuchadnezzar's second dream – The vision of the tree.
   a. It prophesied that he would go mad.
   b. Daniel 4:1-18 are quotations of the King himself after he was restored from his madness.
   c. The fourth chapter therefore is written in the form of a proclamation from the king.
   d. "The Watcher." That means an angel from heaven. We are being watched by angels from heaven, and if there is pride, He is able to abase.

II Point: The interpretation.
   a. Daniel 4:19-27 – This tree applies to the king himself, and to the Gentile rule, or the times of the Gentiles.
   b. The meaning of this is not difficult to find. A great tree in scripture is the symbol of man with great power and influence on the earth. Ezekiel 31:3 "Behold, the Assyrian was a cedar in Lebanon with fair branches, and with a shadowing shroud, and of an high stature; and his top was among the thick boughs."
   Illustration: Israel is spoken of as a vine brought out of Egypt, as per Isaiah 5:7 "For the vineyard of the LORD of hosts is the house of Israel, and the men of Judah his pleasant plant;…"
   c. The interpretation has a warning to the king as well. He might have repented, and perhaps did, but in twelve months all was forgotten. Daniel 4:29-30 "At the end of twelve months he walked in the palace of the kingdom of Babylon. The king spake, and said, Is not this the great Babylon, that I have built for the house of the kingdom by the might of my power, and for the honour of my majesty?" God also keeps His promises. Daniel 4:33 "The same hour was the thing fulfilled upon Nebuchadnezzar:…" He went mad - insane.

d. The spiritual application: This tree tells us of the development of Christendom as a vast earthly institution with power and influence in the earth of Gentile dominion. But it is self-exaltation and pride. This was the great sin of Nebuchadnezzar. PRIDE! Pride is of Satan, and it is distractive to the work of God.
   Let me tell you, judgment will come upon this proud and self-exalting age of the Gentiles, and any self-exalting thought He will punish. He will destroy.

III Point: <u>The seven years of insanity</u>.
   a. After these seven years of insanity Nebuchadnezzar was converted.
   b. That is also the prediction for the Gentile reign till the coming of the Lord. In the seventh year of the tribulation the Lord will come. And as Nebuchadnezzar of old then lifted up his head and began to honour and extol the KING OF KINGS, so shall the Gentiles at the coming of the LORD.

Conclusion: Turn to Him now. Daniel 4:34-37.

The Prophet Daniel – Part Five
Belshazzar's Feast and the Fall of Babylon.
Daniel 5:1-31

Introduction: This took place in 538 B.C. That is 25 years from the day of Nebuchadnezzar's conversion in 563 B.C. after which date we hear no more of him.

During these 25 years we find in the ancient Dynasty that the following kings sat on the throne from 626 B.C. - 539 B.C.
1. Nabu-apla-usur (626 B.C. - 605 B.C.).
2. Nabu-kudurri-usus II (605 B.C. - 562 B.C.). Also known as Nebuchadnezzar II.
3. Amel-Marduk known as Evil Merodach (562 B.C.-560 B.C.)
4. Neriglisser (560 B.C. - 556 B.C.).
5. Labasi – Marduk (556 B.C.)
6. Nabonidus (556 B.C. - 539 B.C.)
7. Belshazzar, the grandson of Nebuchadnezzar, not as ruler, but as second ruler in partnership with his father.

I Point: Belshazzar's Feast.
   a. Belshazzar's princes counseled him to forget his grandfather's proclamation.
   b. Note: The Septuagint Version reads: "And after seven years I gave my soul to prayer, and besought concerning my sins in the presence of the Lord." So, Nebuchadnezzar was truly converted and probably done away with after that, by Evil-Merodach. For 25 years Babylon's kings were just Civil War kings, killing each other, till finally his sin-in-law Nabonidus took the throne, and his son Belshazzar joined him in the reign from years after in 540 B.C. Then Belshazzar got proud and blasphemous and had this feast in 538 B.C. But he was killed that night by Darius the Mede.

II Point: The Interpretation to the writing on the wall.
   a. Years had gone by since Daniel had interpreted Nebuchadnezzar's dream.
   b. Daniel was forgotten by Belshazzar, that blaspheming king.
   c. Here God gets Daniel out again. Listen to his subline words. (Daniel 5:17-23).
      The reading and interpretation of the writing:
      1. MENE, MENE – "Numbered."
      2. TEKEL – "Weighed."
      3. UPHARSIN – "And divided."

Application: The last days of Belshazzar were days of "lust of the flesh, and lust of the eyes," in open defiance and opposition to the God of Israel.

III Point: The fulfillment of the interpretation.

- a. A political power overthrew the literal Babylon.
  Application: And a political power will overthrow the ecclesiastical Babylon.
  Illustration: We are not yet come to the hour, but the material for it is present, for we are living in the days of Laodicea, the days of boasting and vainglory. God will not tolerate this boasting, self-glorying, Christ-blaspheming, and Christ rejecting age forever.
  The material of the final Babylon, the great apostasy, is present with us in our day, and the handwriting is on the wall. The same hand which wrote on the plaster over against the candlestick in Belshazzar's wall, has written the judgment and the doom of apostasy Christendom on the pages of the Bible. There is a MENE-MENE-TEKEL for the present day conditions of Christendom.
- b. MENE, MENE - Numbered. The days are numbered. They cannot extend beyond the time appointed by the God of heaven.
  TEKEL – Weighted and found wanting. Oh, if we, as a Church here, should appear before God, we too, would be found wanting.
- c. Daniel the prophet was set aside. Daniel was 14 years old when God needed him to tell Nebuchadnezzar of God's plan. Now he is 80 years old. He was forgotten, but God gets him out to tell Belshazzar and his generation what God will do to the nation that forgets God.

Conclusion: This moral condition of Babylon is just a foreshadow of the conditions we are now to be found in. It leads to the end, when God once again will cut out the engrafted branches, the Gentiles, and put back Israel upon their own olive tree. Babylon – meaning confusion is all about us; and God wants His people to be separated from that which hates and despiseth the truth.

The Prophet Daniel – Part Six
Darius the Mede
Daniel 6:1-28

Introduction: The last time, we had the feast of Belshazzar, the last king of Babylon, and the invasion of Babylon by King Darius the Mede.

Now today we have the new government under Darius, known as the Medo-Persian Government commencing in 538 B.C. This is the second world empire represented in the dream image of Nebuchadnezzar by the chest and arms of silver. It is therefore inferior to the head of gold "Babylon," and continues in the downward tendency as per the image in the dream.

I Point: The 80 year old prophet.
 a. Daniel was taken to Babylon when he was 14 years old. For 66 years he was in the king's palace, and in all those years he had not broken his promise to his God, when he purposed in his heart not to defile himself.
 b. He prophesied the last night of King Belshazzar, the invasion of Babylon, and the death of the king, by the hand writing on the wall.
 c. King Darius must have heard of this prophesy and set Daniel up as a trust worthy monarch in his kingdom. So Daniel becomes the second ruler in the kingdom of Darius. Daniel 6:1 "It pleased Darius to set over the kingdom an hundred and twenty princes, which should be over the whole kingdom;"

II Point: Envy.
 a. Daniel 6:3 "Then this Daniel was preferred above the presidents and princes, because an excellent spirit was in him; and the king thought to set him over the whole realm." This position was a much desired one by many other lords, so Daniel was greatly envied.
 b. Daniel 6:4 "Then the presidents and princes sought to find occasion against Daniel concerning the kingdom;..." Envy is of the devil, and plans made in envy or jealousy are plans by the serpent.
 c. Daniel 6:4 "...but they could find none occasion nor fault;..." No occasion was found against him. He was a man living a life without reproach. But Satan and his fellows hated him, because of his faith in God.

- d. Daniel 6:7 "All the presidents of the kingdom...have consulted together to establish a royal statute, and to make a firm decree, that whosoever shall ask a petition of any God or man for thirty days, save of thee, O king, he shall be cast into the den of lions." So plans based on lying tongues are set up and these lying men would be exalted. King Darius would appear to be the higher god of any god for 30 days.

III Point: <u>Daniel was undisturbed</u>.

- a. But Daniel was not moved by fear to refrain to neglect his God, nor his prayers to God.
- b. Daniel 6:10 "Now when Daniel knew that the writing was signed, he went into his house; and his windows being open in his chamber toward Jerusalem, he kneeled upon his knees three times a day, and prayed, and gave thanks before his God, as he did aforetime."
Note the steadfastness in verse 10, as before, he makes his prayers; 80 years old, a beautiful walk with God. The devils children around him, to accuse him, see him in sweet communion with his God. What a testimony.
- c. Daniel 6:12 – The decree was signed that any one praying or asking a petition of anyone for 30 days, either God or man, must be cast into the lion's den. This decree was sealed by the ring of the king's signet. Which meant it could not be changed.

IV Point: <u>Daniel in the lion's den</u>.

- a. Note that King Darius blessed Daniel with these words, Daniel 6:16 "...Thy God whom thou servest continually, he will deliver thee."
- b. Daniel 6:18-19 "Then the king went to his palace, and passed the night fasting:..." Darius' sleepless night and his lamentable cry was to Daniel's God.
- c. Daniel's delivery. Daniel 6:22 "My God hath sent his angel, and hath shut the lion's mouths,..."
- d. Daniel 6:23 "...So Daniel was taken up out of the den, and no manner of hurt was found upon him, because he believed in his God."

V Point: <u>Daniel's stand is typical of Christ.</u>
1. <u>Daniel</u> was judged by a king, but the king would have let him go.
   <u>Christ</u> was judged according to the laws of Rome, but the law of Rome would have let him go. However, the people desired His murder.
2. <u>Daniel</u> was cast before lions, as per Psalm 22:21 prophetical of <u>Christ</u>. "Save me from the lion's mouth:"
3. <u>Daniel</u> - "And a stone was brought, and laid upon the mouth of the den; and the king sealed it with his own signet..." (Daniel 6:17).
   <u>Christ's</u> tomb was sealed with Pilot's ring, according to the law of Rome.
4. <u>Daniel</u> was so to speak of, as dead. For never before in history of old was it known that hungry lions would not touch a man. But in the morning Daniel was alive and unhurt. Oh the mighty God of Daniel.
   <u>Christ</u> in 3 days rose from the grave.

VI Point: <u>The proclamation of King Darius</u>.
   a. Daniel 6:26 "I make a decree, That in every dominion of my kingdom men tremble and fear before the God of Daniel: for he is the living God, and stedfast for ever, and his kingdom that which shall not be destroyed, and his dominion shall be even unto the end."
   b. The victory won. The revival was on!
   c. Application: That is the only way we shall see a revival. Only after we, as His people, are willing to go into death with Him, and let the world seal us up for dead.

Conclusion: In every empire we have the same step taken.
1. Nebuchadnezzar took the lead. Worship the image, or you die.
2. Darius said, worship the king, or you die.
3. During the Greco-Macedonian Empire under Antiochus Epiphanies, it was the same.
4. In the Roman Empire we have Herod claiming divine honors.
5. In the Papal power we have the same law, The Pope claims to be divine.
6. In the Communistic rule we have the same, the worship of Lenin in Moscow.
7. All are pointing to the Anti-Christ.

The Prophet Daniel – Part Seven
Daniel's Night Visions
Daniel 7:1-14

Theme: The prophecy of Daniel.

Introduction: The seventh chapter of Daniel takes us back to the first year of Belshazzar's reign. Ever since the insanity of Nebuchadnezzar, Daniel was set aside; till that night when Daniel was called to Belshazzar's feast to interpret the handwriting on the wall (563 B.C. - 538 B.C.). During these years Daniel had wonderful communication with God in dreams and visions.

I Point: <u>Daniel's night visions and their meaning</u>.
   a. In the second chapter we learned that the dream of Nebuchadnezzar was occasioned by the desire of that monarch to know what should come to pass hereafter. The visions of Daniel must have been given to him for a similar reason. He, too, desired knowledge about these great events of the future.
   b. <u>There are four visions in the seventh chapter revealed</u>.
      1. The night vision of the three beasts. (Daniel 7:1-6).
      2. The night vision of the fourth beast with the ten horns and the little horn. (Daniel 7:7-8).
      3. The judgment vision. (Daniel 7:9-12).
      4. The Son of man and His kingdom. (Daniel 7:13-14).
   c. <u>Then follows the divine interpretation of these four visions</u>. This interpretation may be divided into three parts.
      1. A general interpretation. (Daniel 7:15-18).
      2. Daniel's desire to know more about the fourth beast. (Daniel 7:19-22).
      3. The detailed interpretation given. (Daniel 7:23-28).
   d. <u>The first night vision</u>. The prophet saw in his vision the four winds of heaven striving upon the sea. It was a scene of a storm which he beheld. The sea in the word of God is a type of nations. Revelation 17:15 "And he saith unto me, The waters which thou sawest, where the whore sitteth, are peoples, and multitudes, and nations, and tongues."
Also Isaiah 17:12 "Woe to the multitude of many people, which make a noise like the noise of the seas; and to the rushing of nations, that make a rushing like the rushing of mighty waters!"

Illustration: John, the beloved disciple on the isle of Patmos, was alone with God; as Daniel the man greatly beloved, was alone with God. John stood upon the sand of the sea and saw a beast rise up out of the sea. The sand of the sea stands for multitudes of people, while the sea itself presents the people in their agitation.

1st Beast: Daniel 7:4 - It "was like a lion, and had eagles' wings:..."
Illustration: The golden head was the Babylonian Empire in the vision of King Nebuchadnezzar; whereas, the lion was also the Babylonian Empire in Daniel's vision.

2nd Beast: Daniel 7:5 - It was like a bear. The bear stands for the Medo-Persian Empire. In Nebuchadnezzar's vision this power was seen as the chest and arms of silver.
Application: The bear had three ribs in its mouth - the Syrians, Lydia, and Asia Minor had been first conquered by this power.

3rd Beast: Daniel 7:6 - It was like a leopard. Application: The leopard with four wings and four heads is the picture of the Greco-Macedonian Empire, corresponding to the things of brass in the image of Nebuchadnezzar.
Illustration: The four wings denote its swiftness; the four heads are the partition of this empire into the kingdoms of: Syria, Egypt, Macedonia and Asia Minor. It is seen in the next chapter as the rough he goat with a notable horn (Alexander the Great) and the little horn (Antiochus Epiphanies.)

4th Beast: Daniel 7:7 - The Roman World-Empire. It was not seen in the first night vision. Before we turn to the second night vision let me call attention to the fact that in the selection of beasts to represent these world powers who dominion the times of the Gentiles, God tells us that their moral character is beastly.
Illustration: The lion devours; the bear crushes; the leopard springs upon his pray. The next, fourth and last world empire is so beastly that no beast on earth is found to describe its true character.
Illustration: The nations which will be included is the future revival of the Roman Empire in its ten kingdoms aspect will be more fierce than any beast.

Conclusion: Now, this is just the interpretation of the prophetical vision that Daniel saw. Next time we shall take the fourth beast more in detail, which shall point us right to the end of man's power.

The Prophet Daniel – Part Eight
Roman Empire Revived
Daniel 7:7-28

Introduction: Last time we were in Daniel 7:1-7. It was about the four beasts and the fourth beast was of dreadful countenance, and it had ten horns, corresponding to the ten toes of the image Nebuchadnezzar saw in a dream.

I Point: <u>The Little horn</u>.
   a. This is the old Roman Empire revived in the lost days.
   b. Ancient of days. Daniel 7:9 "I beheld till the thrones were cast down, and the Ancient of days did sit, whose garment was white as snow, and the hair of his head like the pure wool: his throne was like the fiery flame, and his wheels as burning fire."
   Illustration: The Holiness of God purged the sin before Him.
   c. This notable great beast, the 4th beast, was given to the burning. Daniel 7:11 "…I beheld even till the beast was slain, and his body destroyed, and given to the burning flame."
   d. Daniel 7:13-14 - But the other beasts were still left alive or (the other governments were kept alive till the Son of Man comes - Jesus Christ's return).

II Point: <u>Scenes of Heaven</u>.
   a. Daniel 7:13-14 - Here we see that God the Father hands over all the kingdoms to the Son, and appoints Him to rule over all people, nations, and languages.
   b. Christ rules for 1000 years on the earth, and then for all eternity.

III Point: <u>Daniel had the intention to seal it all up in his heart.</u>
   a. Daniel 7:28 "…As for me Daniel, my cogitations much troubled me, and my countenance changed in me: but I kept the matter in my heart."
   Illustration: Daniel could not get rid of the thought, just like you and I, sometime, cannot get a thought or a song out of our thinking.
   b. Now in Daniel chapter 8 the Lord sent an interpreter to Daniel and briefly relayed the matter by taking him through another vision recorded in Daniel 8:1-14.
   c. Daniel 7:26-28 - Tells the interpretation and the affect upon Daniel.

Vision of the Seventy Weeks

Daniel 9:1-19

Text: Daniel 9:3 "And I set my face unto the Lord God, to seek by prayer and supplications, with fasting, and sackcloth, and ashes:"

Introduction:
  a. Daniel 9:3-19 – Daniel's prayer and confession.
      1. Daniel 9:3 – He set his face unto the Lord God.
      2. Daniel 9:3 – He seeked the Lord.
      3. Daniel 9:3 – He fasted in sackcloth and ashes.
      4. Daniel 9:4 – He prayed and confessed.
      5. Daniel 9:5 – He confessed his sins.
  b. His prayer was not for himself, but for Jerusalem.
      1. Daniel 9:16-17 – For the Lord's sake.
      2. Daniel 9:19. "O Lord, hear: O Lord, forgive; O Lord, hearken and do; defer not, for thine own sake, O my God: for thy city and thy people are called by thy name."

I Point: God answers.
  a. God reveals His love towards Daniel. Daniel 9:23 "...thou art greatly beloved:..."
  b. God reveals to Daniel that sin must receive its full punishment. Daniel 9:24 "Seventy weeks are determined upon thy people and upon thy Holy city, to finish the transgression, and to make an end of sins, and to make reconciliation for iniquity, and to bring in everlasting righteousness, and to seal up the vision and prophecy, and to anoint the most Holy."
  c. The Seventy Weeks are also pointing out the end of the age.
      1. Till the coming of the Lord at Bethlehem.
      2. Till the coming of the Lord as King.

II Point: The Antichrist.
  a. Daniel 9:27 "And he shall confirm the covenant with many for one week: and in the midst of the week he shall cause the sacrifice and the oblation to cease, and for the overspreading of abominations he shall make it desolation, even until the consummation, and that determined shall be poured upon the desolate."

    b. Daniel 9:27 – He sets up his rule.
       Read: Revelation 17:16-18.
    c. Seven mountains. Revelation 17:9 "…The seven heads are seven mountains, on which the woman sitteth." (Rome)
       The woman is worshiped as the mother of God.
    d. Revelation 17:11 "And the beast that was, and is not, even he is the eighth, and is of the seven, and goeth into perdition." Revelation 17:4-5 and Revelation 17:7-18. (The Woman)

III Point: – <u>The glory of God</u>
    a. Daniel was spoken of as greatly beloved. Daniel 9:23 "…thou art greatly beloved…"
    b. Daniel 10:12-13 – Gabriel announces that he was sent to Daniel, but was hindered by the prince of Persia. (The bear in Daniel 10:13).
    c. Daniel 9:13 - The prince of the children of Israel is Michael, and He reveals that this vision is for the people in the last days.
    d. Daniel 10:20-21 – For his (Daniel's) difference.

IV Point: - <u>The little horn to the end of the book</u>.
    a. Daniel 11:21 "And in his estate shall stand up a vile person, to whom they shall not give the honour of the kingdom: but he shall come in peaceably, and obtain the kingdom by flatteries."

The Time of the End
Daniel 12:1-13

Text: Daniel 12:1-13 also Daniel 10:11-14

Introduction: Read Daniel 11:2-45.

I Point: The Great Tribulation

    a. Revelation 7:14 "…These are they which came out of great tribulation, and have washed their robes, and made them white in the blood of the Lamb."

    b. Daniel 12:1 "And at that time shall Michael stand up, the great prince which standeth for the children of thy people: and there shall be a time of trouble, such as never was since there was a nation even to the same time: and at that time thy people shall be delivered, every one that shall be found written in the book."

II Point: Jacob's Trouble.

    a. Daniel 12:4-7 - The last 3½ years are called "Jacobs Trouble."

    b. Jeremiah 30:7 "Alas! for the day is great, so that none is like it: it is even the time of Jacob's trouble,…"

III Point: The last message to Daniel.

    a. Daniel 12:4 "But thou, O Daniel, shut up the words, and seal the book, even to the time of the end: many shall run to and fro, and knowledge shall be increased."

Daniel 12:8-13 "And I heard, but I understood not: then said I, O my Lord, what shall be the end to these things? And he said, Go thy way, Daniel: for the words are closed up and sealed till the time of the end. Many shall be purified, and made white, and tried; but the wicked shall do wickedly: and none of the wicked shall understand; but the wise shall understand. And from the time that the daily sacrifice shall be taken away, and the abomination that maketh desolate set up, there shall be a thousand two hundred and ninety days. Blessed is he that waiteth, and cometh to the thousand three hundred and five and thirty days. But go thou thy way till the end be: for thou shalt rest, and stand in thy lot at the end to the days."

Sermon Outlines from the Book of Amos

God's Long Suffering and Dealings with His People
Amos 4:6-13

Text: Amos 4:12 "...prepare to meet thy God..."

Introduction: This text suggests that there is a God. Since there is a God, we are assured that we must meet Him. We shall divide our text into four distinct points.

    1. Stop! 2. Look! 3. Listen! 4. Act!

I Point: Stop!
- a. We are living in a fast age. It is hard to come to a stop for sound thinking and sober actions.
- b. What does God say: Jeremiah 6:16 "Thus saith the LORD, Stand ye in the ways, and see, and ask for the old paths, where is the good way, and walk therein, and ye shall find rest for your souls,..."
- c. In other words – Stop! Look for a sign, where you are going. Illustration: Highway signs.
- d. On the way to heaven you will:
    1. Meet death.
    2. Meet God.
    3. Meet judgment.
- e. Hebrews 9:27 "And as it is appointed unto men once to die, but after this the judgment:"
- f. II Corinthians. 5:10 "For we must all appear before the judgment seat of Christ;..."
Therefore, prepare to meet thy God.
- g. You must meet Him.
    1. Either here in this world as your Saviour.
    2. Or after death as your judge.
- h. Let me direct your attention to a man, who was well prepared, but not to meet God. Luke 12:16-21 "And he spake a parable unto them, saying, The ground of a certain rich man brought forth plentifully: And he thought within himself, saying, What shall I do, because I have no room where to bestow my fruits? And he said, This will I do: I will pull down my barns, and build greater; and there will I bestow all my fruits and my goods. And I will say to my soul, Soul, thou hast much goods laid up for many years; take thine ease, eat, drink, and be merry. But God said unto him, Thou fool, this night thy soul shall be required of thee: then whose shall those things be, which thou hast provided?"
- i. Are you lying up for a rainy day?

II Points: Look!

   a. John 1:29 "...Behold the Lamb of God, which taketh away the sin of the world."
   b. Just now, there is life if you look at the crucified one. "Sinner Look!"
   c. This was the cry of Moses, when the people died of the fiery serpents. "Look!" All these people were asked to do is to Look! Not to themselves, nor their own goodness, but to the brazen serpent. (Christ on the Cross.)
   d. John 3:14 "And as Moses lifted up the serpent in the wilderness, even so must the Son of man be lifted up:"

III Point: Listen!

   a. Listen to what or to whom?
      Listen to the Lord. What does he say?
   b. Isaiah 55:1-3 "Ho, every one that thirsteth, come ye to the waters, and he that hath no money; come ye, buy, and eat; yea, come, buy wine and milk without money and without price."
   c. Isaiah 1:18 "Come now, and let us reason together, saith the LORD: though your sins be as scarlet, they shall be as white as snow; though they be red like crimson, they shall be as wool."
   d. II Corinthians 5:21 "For he hath made him to be sin for us, who knew no sin;..."
   e. John 6:37 "...him that cometh to me I will in no wise cast out."

IV Point: Act!

   a. Nothing can be accomplished without actions.
   b. Romans 10:13 "For whosoever shall call upon the name of the Lord shall be saved."
   c. I John 1:9 "If we confess our sins, he is faithful and just to forgive us of our sins, and to cleanse us from all unrighteousness."
   d. Joshua 24:15 "...choose you this day whom ye will serve;..."
   e. Numbers 21 - Look and live!

Sermon Outlines from the Book of Jonah

As God Sees the World
Jonah 1:1-17

Introduction: God looked down from His throne upon Nineveh with great pity. There were 120,000 people in the town without the knowledge of God. Nineveh was up for destruction in one day. God is concerned.

I Point God seeks for a man to save Nineveh.
- a. Revelation 2:18 "...his eyes like unto a flame of fire" sees the man, Jonah. A man fit for the job.
  Application: God still seeks for able men and able women.
- c. When I listen to the reports at the conference on souls being saved, I am convinced we are losing ground at leading souls to Christ. I cry out in agony, "Oh, Lord, what will be the judgment?"

II Point: God's commission to Jonah.
- a. Jonah 1:2 "Arise, go to Nineveh, that great city, and cry against it;..."
  Application: God still gives this commission.
  Illustration: As Jonah of old, we fine excuses, and as Jonah of old, we seek to flee from God's presence.

III Point: Jonah's disobedience.
- a. Jonah 1:3 "But Jonah rose up to flee unto Tarshish from the presence of the LORD,..."
- b. He joined himself to sinners.
- c. He at once was out of fellowship with God.
- d. His heart was hardened. He could sleep, while others around him died without Christ. Jonah 1:5 "Then the mariners were afraid, and cried every man unto his god,...But Jonah was gone down into the sides of the ships and he lay, and was fast asleep."

IV Point: God catches up with Jonah.
- a. Jonah 1:12 "...Take me up, and cast me forth into the sea..."
- b. Jonah 2:1-2 – He repented.
  Application: Hebrews 10:31 "It is a fearful thing to fall into the hands of the living God."

V Point: Jonah prayed.
- a. Jonah 2:1 "Then Jonah prayed unto the LORD his God out of the fish's belly,"

b. And God answered his prayer. Jonah 2:10 "And the LORD spake unto the fish, and it vomited out Jonah upon the dry land."
   Application: Was Jonah pleased with this answer to his prayer? No! He still had to preach.
   c. Jonah 3:1-2 "And the word of the LORD came unto Jonah the second time, saying, Arise, go unto Nineveh, that great city, and preach unto it the preaching that I bid thee."
   d. The message was simple. Jonah 3:4 "...Yet forty days, and Nineveh shall be overthrown."

VI Point: God had mercy towards these people in Nineveh.

   a. Jonah 3:10 "And God saw their works that they turned from their evil way; and God repented of the evil, that he had said that he would do unto them; and he did it not."
   Application: God speaks to us in a remarkable way.

Conclusion: Message for us today.
John 3:7 "...Ye must be born again."
Application: You may find it hard some time in life.
Illustration: Missionary, Frank Miller, lost his wife and three sons in one day, and of whom it is said, "Esther his wife and boys went home, and Frank was left behind to finish the job."
Illustration: You may fear, but like the little girl who was afraid in the dark asked her daddy to let her feel his hands to see if he is the same daddy in the dark as in the light; we need not fear. God is the same today as yesterday and tomorrow.
Illustration: You cannot go through life without leaving marks behind you. There was a miller who went into the bank. His white elbows left marks everywhere and on all the people. You always will leave your mark.

Sermon Outlines from the Book of Malachi

Will a Man Rob God?
Malachi 3:1-12

Introduction: Our text suggests that robbery is the dead downward drag.

Illustration: A man shot a hawk, and after he had shot him, he then saw the reason why that hawk could not fly very high. It was because he had a trap with a chain of about two or three feet on one of his legs. Now there are many Christians, I see just like this. Poor creatures, they have something holding them down, and they can't get very high.

I Point: What is robbery?
   a. Robbery means that we have taken something which is not rightfully our own.
   b. Illustration: In Europe it is very common to find your horses gone in the morning. Or if you have your hammer and ax or something left out, as a rule it will sprout legs overnight.
   c. Robbery, means stealing, does it not?

II Point: How would you judge a thief?
   a. What would you think of a man that steals your goods?
   b. Would you not put him under the law of the land?
   c. Would you not give your voice against a thief? Of course you would.
   d. How many do agree that stealing is sin? Raise your hand.

III Points: What does God say about stealing?
   a. Exodus 20:15 "Thou shalt not steal."
   b. Proverbs 29:24 "Whoso is partner with a thief hateth his own soul:..."
   c. As an illustration to this we take Judas, whom Jesus Himself used as an example. John 12:6 - Judas, "...he was a thief, and had the bag, and bare what was put therein."
   d. I Peter 4:15 "But let none of you suffer as a murderer, or as a thief, or as an evildoer, or as a busybody in other men's matters."
   e. I Corinthians 6:10 "Nor thieves, nor covetous, nor drunkards, nor revilers, nor extortioners, shall inherit the kingdom of God."

IV Point: <u>Now then! Will a man rob God?</u>
   a. What doth God himself say about it? Malachi 3:9 "Ye are cursed with a curse: for ye have robbed me, even this whole nation."

1st Question: How then do we rob God? Malachi 3:8 "...In tithes and offerings."
   a. Malachi 3:10 "Bring ye all the tithes into the storehouse, that there may be meat in mine house,..."
   b. Leviticus 27:30 "And all the tithe of the land, whether of the seed of the land, or of the fruit of the tree, is the LORD'S: it is holy unto the LORD." Leviticus 27:32 "And concerning the tithe of the herd or of the flock, even of whatsoever passeth under the rod, the tenth shall be holy unto the LORD."

2nd Question: Is it then sin if we withhold the tenth part?"
   a. Malachi 3:9 "Ye are cursed with a curse: for ye have robbed me, even this whole nation."

3rd Question: Have we then reason to believe that drought is a curse? Yes, of course! Haggai 1:6 says, "Ye have sown much, and bring in little; ye eat, but ye have not enough; ye drink, but ye are not filled with drink; ye clothe you, but there is none warm; and he that earneth wages earneth wages to put it into a bag with holes."

Why is all this? Because Haggai 1:11 says, "And I (the LORD) called for a drought upon the land, and upon the mountains, and upon the corn, and upon the new wine, and upon the oil, and upon that which the ground bringeth forth, and upon men, and upon cattle, and upon all the labour of the hands."

4th Question: I want you to see that we are under a curse if we keep the things which do not belong to us.

Do you agree with me? If you don't agree with me on these points, it is no use for me to go any farther with it. How many agree that we are under a curse in God's sight if we steal? Would you raise your hand!

V Point: <u>Now then! Will God lift the curse if we repent</u>?
    a. Proverbs 3:9 "Honour the LORD with thy substance, and with the firstfruits of all thine increase:" (and what will happen?) "So shall thy barns be filled with plenty, and thy presses shall burst out with new wine." (Proverbs 3:10).

5th Question: All right would you like to try it?
    Who believes that God means what He says? Raise your hand. Alright, would you now be willing to take God at His own word?

VI Point: <u>Now then! Do you think you are giving something to God if you give Him the tenth?</u>
    a. No, no you're not! You are only paying to Him your debt; that is all.
    b. Illustration: A little girl had been given a new silver dollar. She went to her father and asked him to change it into dimes. "What for? asked the father." "So that I can give the Lord His part," she replied. When in church she dropped her dime in the offering box. Then she dropped in another dime. Her father asked, "Why did you drop in another dime?" "Well," she said, "The first one belonged to the Lord; I can't give Him anything by paying my debt. But the second one I have given to the Lord."
    c. I hope to be able to make you understand that it is a greater sin to rob God than it is to rob man.

VII Point: <u>Does this hold true also for ministers</u>?
    a. Indeed it does. Numbers 18:26 says, "Thus speak unto the Levites, and say unto them, When ye take of the children of Israel the tithes which I have given you from them for your inheritance, then ye shall offer up an heave offering of it for the LORD, even a tenth part of the tithe."
    b. Praise God we are not exempt to laying up treasures in heaven, are we?

Baccalaureate Service

Remember Now Thy Creator in the Day of Thy Youth
Ecclesiastes 12:1

Introduction: Ladies and Gentlemen, Students and Seniors.

I count it a great privilege and honour to speak at this Baccalaureate Service. I do very much realize that I am speaking to seniors. And seniors, of course, do know everything, and moreover, they know that they know everything. Therefore, I shall not even try to tell you new things, but let me only draw your attention to things that you should already know.

I Point: <u>God has a plan</u>.

a. At creation. Genesis 1:1 "In the beginning God created the heaven and the earth."
b. God has a purpose in everything.
c. Even in the up keep of His creation.
   1. Let us take H_2O – water, for example. We know the value of water. Everybody knows that.
   2. But you seniors also will know the weight and substance of water. So you will agree when I say that H_2O is 800 times heavier than air.
   3. Now God in his wise plan sustains the earth. Against gravity God lifts 16,000,000 tons of water each second to water the thirsty earth.
   4. How is it done? Psalm 135:7 answers that, "He causeth the vapours to ascend from the ends of the earth; he maketh lightnings for the rain; he bringeth the wind out of his treasuries."
      i. What is vapour? Little water balloons.
      ii. What has lightning to do with rain? Electrical discharges cause the little molecules of vapor to smite each other into drops.
      iii. What has the wind to do? The wind is the chariot. God has divine guidance in His creation.
d. And God wants to have His guidance in your life. All He asks for is your yieldedness.

II Point: God has a design.
  a. Let us take the caterpillar and the butterfly for instance.
     1. It's just an ugly caterpillar, but when it goes through the process of God's wonderful transformation, what a beautiful flying insect it becomes.
  b. So can God take your life if you are yielded, and transform it into His own image.

III Point: God's design for jewels.
  a. Science tells us that a fiery opal was nothing more than a handful of sand.
  b. God placed it in the bowels of the earth, and applied great heat from beneath and stupendous weight from above, and when men find it, it is a beautiful opal.
  c. Science tells us that an amethyst is nothing more than a handful of clay. God takes that handful of clay and deposits it in the earth and forms it into a beautiful amethyst.
  d. Again science tells us that a diamond is only a piece of black carbon. God takes a handful of black carbon and deposits it in the earth. And from heat and pressure He makes it into a glorious diamond fit for a king's crown.

  How God does it, I don't know; but I do know He can take your drab useless life and transform it into a beautiful jewel fit for His crown.

  Illustration: Dr. Robert G. Lee once called attention to the fact that God takes oxygen and hydrogen, both of them are odorless, tasteless and colorless, and combines them with carbon which is insoluble black and tasteless; and the result is beautiful white sweet sugar.

  How is it done? Take the blood of Jesus Christ and apply it on a black-hearted sinner and God says that he shall be whiter than snow, and a sweet savour unto Him.

  II Corinthians 2:15 "For we are unto God a sweet savour of Christ..."

  "Remember now thy Creator in the day of thy youth..." (Ecclesiastes 12:1).

IV Point: God demands confidence.
  a. Perhaps there are things you cannot understand. Many people cannot understand the Bible. That does not prove that the Bible is wrong. That only proves that they are slow to understand.

- b. People who could not understand the Bible have killed those who could understand, and tried to destroy the Bible. But the Bible shall remain, and will remain to the end.
- c. Many people don't like to read the Bible because the Bible points out their sin. But just because they don't read the Bible does not prove they are not sinners.
  Illustration: Sun rays through a window will reveal dirt and dust.
- d. The Bible is a wonderful Book on Science. Everything ever found in all the Science books is found in the Bible.

"Remember now thy Creator in the days of thy youth..." (Ecclesiastes 12:1)
- a. God has a plan.
- b. God has a purpose
- c. God has a design.
- d. God has a means of transforming you.
- e. All He asks of you is yieldedness on your part.

Conclusion: God demands confidence and faith.

Funeral Service and Burial Rituals at the Graveside

1. **Funeral Program:** Read these scripture verses.

    a. John 11:25-26 "Jesus said unto her, I am the resurrection, and the life: he that believeth in me, though he were dead, yet shall he live: And whosoever liveth and believeth in me shall never die..."
    b. Job 19:25-27 "For I know that my redeemer liveth, and that he shall stand at the latter day upon the earth: And though after my skin worms destroy this body, yet in my flesh shall I see God: Whom I shall see for myself, and mine eyes shall behold, and not another; though my reins be consumed with me."
    c. II Timothy 4:7-8 "I have fought a good fight, I have finished my course, I have kept the faith: Henceforth there is laid up for me a crown of righteousness, which the Lord, the righteous judge, shall give me at that day: and not to me only, but unto all them also that love his appearing."

Psalm 90:1-12
1. "LORD, thou hast been our dwelling place in all generations.
2. Before the mountains were brought forth, or ever thou hadst formed the earth and the world, even from everlasting to everlasting, thou art God.
3. Thou turnest man to destruction; and sayest, Return, ye children of men.
4. For a thousand years in thy sight are but as yesterday when it is past, and as a watch in the night.
5. Thou carriest them away as with a flood; they are as a sleep: in the morning they are like grass which groweth up.
6. In the morning it flourisheth, and groweth up; in the evening it is cut down, and withereth.
7. For we are consumed by thine anger, and by thy wrath are we troubled.
8. Thou hast set our iniquities before thee, our secret sins in the light of thy countenance.
9. For all our days are passed away in thy wrath: we spend our years as a tale that is told.
10. The days of our years are threescore years and ten; and if by reason of strength they be fourscore years, yet is their strength labour and sorrow; for it is soon cut off, and we fly away.
11. Who knoweth the power of thine anger? even according to they fear, so is thy wrath.
12. So teach us to number our days, that we may apply our hearts unto wisdom." (Psalm 90:1-12).

Glory be to the Father and to the Son, and to the Holy Ghost; as it was in the beginning, is now and ever shall be, world without end. Amen.

2. Obituary
3. Prayer
4. Song
5. Scripture
6. Song
7. Message
8. Song
9. The coffin to be opened.
10. The funeral procession goes to the burial grounds.
11. At the graveside.
    a. Job 1:21 "...Naked came I out of my mother's womb, and naked shall I return thither: the LORD gave, and the LORD hath taken away; blessed be the name of the LORD."
    b. Job 14:1-2 "Man that is born of a woman is of few days, and full of trouble. He cometh forth like a flower, and is cut down: he fleeth also as a shadow, and continueth not."
    c. Job 14:5 "Seeing his days are determined, the number of his months are with thee, thou hast appointed his bounds that he cannot pass;"

Revelation 14:13 "And I heard a voice from heaven saying unto me, Write, Blessed are the dead which die in the Lord from henceforth: Yea, saith the Spirit, that they may rest from their labours;...Amen."

For as much as it has please the Almighty God in his wise providence to take out of this world the soul of this loved one, we therefore commit his body to the ground.

        Earth to earth,
        Dust to dust,
        Ashes to ashes.

Looking for the resurrection and the life in the world to come; through our Lord and Saviour Jesus Christ, at whose second coming, in glorious majesty, will judge the world in righteousness. The earth and the sea shall give up their dead and the corruptible bodies of those who sleep in Him shall be changed and made like unto His own glorious body, according to the mighty working whereby He is able to subdue all things unto Himself.

12. Prayer in closing.

Flannel Graph Board Messages

The Creation and the Fall of Man

Genesis 1:1-26

Flannel Graph Board Lesson

*These Scriptures are to be read as I go along with the lesson.
Text: Genesis 1:1-26 - Genesis 2:7 - Genesis 3:15 & 21

I Point: <u>Man was perfect.</u>
- a. Had fellowship with God.
- b. Was clothed with the garment of righteousness.
- c. Had great intelligence.
- d. Then sin entered.
- e. Consequences - Genesis 3:19-20 "In the sweat of thy face shall thou eat bread, till thou return unto the ground; for out of it wast thou taken: for dust thou art, and unto dust shalt thou return."

II Points: <u>Satan's attack.</u>
- a. Genesis 3:1-4
  Their admiration was God till that time.
  Satan promised them to be as gods.
  Genesis 3:4 "And the serpent said unto the woman, Ye shall not surely die:"
- b. Eve looked and coveted.
- c. She partook.
- d. Adam and Eve were stripped of all glory.
  Genesis 3:7 "And the eyes of them both were opened, and they knew that they were naked;..."

III Point: <u>God comes down in judgment</u>.
- a. In the cool of the day.
  Genesis 3:8 "And they heard the voice of the LORD God walking in the garden in the cool of the day: and Adam and his wife hid themselves from the presence of the LORD God amongst the trees of the garden." This can be translated storm tempest and judgment.
- b. God gives room for repentance.
- c. Adam will not take the blame.
  Genesis 3:12 "And the man said, The woman whom thou gavest to be with me, she gave me of the tree, and I did eat."

d. Eve will not take the blame.
      Genesis 3:13 "...And the woman said, The serpent beguiled me, and I did eat."
   e. God gives the promise of the Saviour.
      Genesis 3:15 "And I will put enmity between thee and the woman, and between thy seed and her seed; it shall bruise thy head, and thou shalt bruise his heel."
   f. God shows unto them the Lamb (Christ) slain for their sins.
      Genesis 3:21 "Unto Adam also and to his wife did the LORD God make coats of skins, and clothed them."
   g. The coats of skins are a type of Christ to cover us with the righteousness of God.

Conclusion:
a. Christ the Lamb of God takes the blow.
b. The garments of skin are garments of hope until the Second Coming of Christ.
c. Are you, my friend, looking forward to that day of perfection when the Lord will come?

Moses Hid in the Bulrushes
Exodus 2:1-10
This message was prepared for a
flannel graph board.

I Point: The children of Israel in prosperity.
    a. Exodus 1:7 "And the children of Israel were fruitful, and increased abundantly, and multiplied, and waxed exceeding mighty; and the land was filled with them."
    b. By this time they had lived 350 years in Egypt.
    But they forgot God.
        1. Prosperity was too great.
        2. The young people began to intermarry with the Egyptians.
        3. Sins of modern days were present.
        Illustration: The people liked to feed on the old carcasses of the world.

II Point: Judgment from the Lord.
    a. Exodus 1:11 "...set over them taskmasters..."
    b. Exodus 1:14 "And they made their lives bitter with hard bondage,..."
    c. They killed the male children of the Israelites.
    Illustration: All the riches of this world will fly away on wings. Proverbs 23:5. "Wilt thou set thine eyes upon that which is not? for riches certainly make themselves wings; they fly away as an eagle toward heaven."

III Point: They cried unto God.
    a. God sent a deliverer. But in the form of a little babe.
    b. For 40 years they kept on program, and the boy who was to be there Saviour grew day by day as their prayers grew for 40 long years in slavery.
    c. After 40 years he presents himself as their deliverer, but he was rejected, because he was not according to what they had expected. And they had to wait for another 40 years in the wilderness.
    d. Moses is a type of Christ.
    He came as a deliverer in the form of a babe, and was rejected; but yet, he was the only deliverer the children of Israel could have.
    e. Christ came as a babe, and was rejected; but, He is the only deliverer the world can have.

Conclusion: Your answer to your prayer might be here, but in its infancy. Keep praying.

New Testament
King James Version

Sermon Outlines from the Book of Matthew

Jesus

Matthew 1:18-21

Text: Matthew 1:21 "And she shall bring forth a son, and thou shall call his name JESUS: for he shall save his people from their sins."

Introduction: Let us look at some of the blessings which are associated with the name of "Jesus."

I Point: <u>We have forgiveness in Jesus' name</u>.
    a. Luke 24:47 "And that repentance and remission of sins should be preached in his name among all nations,…"
    b. Acts 10:43 "To him give all the prophets witness, that through his name whosoever believeth in him shall receive remission of sins."
    c. I John 2:12 "I write unto you, little children, because your sins are forgiven you for his name's sake."

II Point: <u>We have salvation in Jesus' name</u>.
    a. John 3:17-18 "For God sent not his Son into the world to condemn the world; but that the world through him might be saved. He that believeth on him is not condemned:…"
    b. Acts 2:21 "And it shall come to pass, that whosoever shall call on the name of the Lord shall be saved."
    c. I Corinthians 6:11 "…but ye are washed, but ye are sanctified, but ye are justified in the name of the Lord Jesus, and by the Spirit of our God.

III Point: <u>We have eternal life in Jesus' name</u>.
    a. I John 5:13 "These things have I written unto you that believe on the name of the Son of God; that ye may know that ye have eternal life, and that ye may believe on the name of the Son of God."
    b. Romans 6:23 "For the wages of sin is death; but the gift of God is eternal life through Jesus Christ our Lord."
    c. John 10:28 "And I give unto them eternal life; and they shall never perish, neither shall any man pluck them out of my hand."
    Application: If my salvation would depend on my name, or on the name of my church, or on the name of my pastor, etc., it would not be very safe.

IV Point: <u>We have access to God in prayer, and a certain answer to our petitions in Jesus' name.</u>
    a. John 14:13-14 "And whatsoever ye shall ask in my name, that will I do, that the Father may be glorified in the Son. If ye shall ask any thing in my name, I will do it."
    b. John 16:23 "...Verily, verily, I say unto you, Whatsoever ye shall ask the Father in my name, he will give it you."

V Point: <u>We worship in Jesus' name</u>.
    a. Matthew 18:20 "For where two or three are gathered together in my name, there am I in the midst of them."
    b. Ephesians 5:20 "Giving thanks always for all things unto God and the Father in the name of our Lord Jesus Christ;"
    c. Colossians 3:17 "And whatsoever ye do in word or deed, do all in the name of the Lord Jesus, giving thanks to God and the Father by him."
    d. Hebrews 13:15 "By him therefore let us offer the sacrifice of praise to God continually, that is, the fruit of our lips giving thanks to his name."

VII Point: <u>Jesus' name is exalted above every other name</u>.
    a. Philippines 2:9-11 "Wherefore God also hath highly exalted him, and given him a name which is above every name: That at the name of Jesus every knee should bow, of things in heaven, and things in earth, and things under the earth; And that every tongue shall confess that Jesus Christ is Lord, to the glory of God the Father."
    a. Jesus has a more excellent name than the angels. Hebrews 1:4 "Being made so much better than the angels, as he hath by inheritance obtained a more excellent name than they."
    b. Revelation: 19:13 & 16 tells us the excellency of His name. Revelation 19:13 "...and his name is called The Word of God." Revelation 19:16 "And he hath on his vesture and on his thigh a name written, KING OF KINGS AND LORD OF LORDS."

Conclusion: The name Jesus is practically the same in all languages. A missionary in the foreign field could not speak the language, but when he prayed, "Jesus help me!" the natives understood having heard the missionary pray in the name of Jesus.

He is a Great God
A Christmas Message
Matthew 1:18 – Matthew 2:1-12

Introduction: On Christmas Day we love to think about a little helpless child lying in the manger; but, instead, I would like to present to you a mighty King. A King of whom it is said, "It is he that sitteth upon the circle of the earth, and the inhabitants thereof are as grasshoppers..." (Isaiah 40:22). I want you to think of Him, who was from the beginning.

I Point: <u>The beginning</u>.
  a. Have you ever thought of the greatness of our Lord?
     i. Let us find His beginning.
     ii. Let us find His end.
     iii. What is eternity?
  b. Isaiah looked 750 years before Christ, and he saw the day you and I call Christmas.
     1. I can hear him cry out aloud: Isaiah 9:6 "For unto us a child is born, unto us a son is given: and the government shall be upon his shoulder: and his name shall be called Wonderful, Counsellor: The mighty God, The everlasting Father, The Prince of Peace."
     2. The prophet Micah looked 700 years before Christ and he writes triumphantly: Micah 5:2 "But thou, Beth-lehem Ephratah, though thou be little among the thousands of Judah, yet out of thee shall he come forth unto me that is to be ruler in Israel; whose goings forth have been from of old, from everlasting."
  c. This is His beginning.

II Points: <u>Your and my beginning</u>.
  a. Matthew 1:21 "And she shall bring forth a son, and thou shalt call his name JESUS: for he shall save his people from their sins."
     1. Hebrews 2:14 "Forasmuch then as the children are partakers of flesh and blood, he also himself likewise took part of the same; that through death he might destroy him that had the power of death, that is, the devil;"
     2. Ephesians 2:19 "Now therefore ye are no more strangers and foreigners, but fellowcitizens with the saints, and of the household of God;"

   b. But let me take one step more, and prove to you that we are more than just children, according to Paul's writing.
      1. Romans 8:16-17 "The Spirit itself beareth witness with our spirit, that we are the children of God: And if children, then heirs; heirs of God, and joint-heirs with Christ; if so be that we suffer with him, that we may be also glorified together."
   c. Let me take just one more step to show to you, beloved, that we are not just heirs; but, kings and priests unto God.
      1. Revelation 1:5-6 "And from Jesus Christ, who is the faithful witness, and the first begotten of the dead, and the prince of the kings of the earth. Unto him that loved us, and washed us from our sins in his own blood. And hath made us kings and priests unto God and his Father; to him be glory and dominion for ever and ever. Amen."

III Point: Your and my job together with Him.
   a. When Christ was on the earth He said, Matthew 23:37 "O Jerusalem, Jerusalem, thou that killest the prophets, and stonest them which are sent unto thee, how often would I have gathered thy children together, even as a hen gathered her chickens under her wings, and ye would not!"
   b. We as joint–heirs must be interested in our kingdom.
      1. When the prophet Jeremiah saw what you and I see, he cried out, "Oh that my head were waters, and mine eyes a fountain of tears, that I might weep day and night for the slain of...my people. (Jeremiah 9:1).
         i. A man in the Russian Revolution lost his eye, yet rejoiced that he could still preach the gospel.
         ii. They realized that they had become the children of a great King, and joint–heirs with Christ.

Conclusion:
   a. I am afraid we are to much like the man who was saved for five years, and his co-workers in the factory had not yet found out that he was a Christian.
   b. Oh, that we were like the girl who got saved and came to P B I. And when she went home, her sister saw her changed life and said, "I don't know what you're got, but I want it."
Application: My dear unsaved soul, if you could only see it; if you could only grasp it; if you could only understand it, you would make this, my King and Saviour, your Saviour, too.

Repentance and Faith

Matthew 4:1-17

Theme: The true nature of gospel repentance.

Text: Matthew 4:17 "From that time Jesus began to preach, and to say, Repent: for the kingdom of heaven is at hand."

Introduction: Repentance is a difficult thing to explain. Repentance, in the Greek, means "to change the mind." As in our word derived from the French, repentance means "To think anew," or "To rethink."

Illustration: The young son said, Matthew 21:29 "...I will not: [go] but afterward he repented (changed his mind) and went."

Again in Luke 15:11-24 - The prodigal son is seen set on going away from his father; then later, he is seen set on going back to his father. This was repentance or change of mind.

This change of mind, and will, is not demanded by the law, but is brought about by the Spirit.

For it is the gift of the risen Saviour.

The preaching of the Gospel, in the power of the Spirit, brings about this change of mind.
Romans 2:4 "...the goodness of God leadeth thee to repentance?"

Repentance is called by various names.
1. Repentance toward God.
2. Repentance unto life.
3. Repentance from dead works.
4. Repentance to salvation.
5. Repentance "Not to be repented of..."
6. Repentance is not a:

I Point: <u>Repentance toward God</u>.
   a. Acts 20:21 "...repentance toward God, and faith toward our Lord Jesus Christ."
   b. We do not ask only that you turn from your sins; but also that you turn to God; otherwise, there would be no hatred for sin.

II Point: <u>Repentance unto life</u>.
   a. Acts 11:18 "...Then hath God also to the Gentiles granted repentance unto life."
   b. Repentance has in view life and salvation.

III Point: <u>Repentance from dead works</u>.
   a. Hebrews 6:1 "...let us go on into perfection; not laying again the foundation of repentance from dead works..."
   b. Dead works must be repented of. The mind must be changed concerning them, so that the heart rejects them.

IV Point: <u>Repentance to salvation</u>.
   a. II Corinthians 7:10 "For godly sorrow worketh repentance to salvation..."

V Point: <u>Repentance "Not to be repented of..."</u>
   a. II Corinthians 7:10 "For godly sorrow worketh repentance to salvation not to be repented of: but the sorrow of the world worketh death."

VI Point: <u>Repentance is not a:</u>
   a. Meritorious Romanists thinking.
   b. Not a remorse or penitence, or penance which is a hateful shame of Rome.

Conclusion: But a plain heart seeking repentance is necessary as per Acts 3:19 "Repent ye therefore, and be converted, that your sins may be blotted out, when the time of refreshing shall come from the presence of the Lord;"

Recognizing Jesus
Matthew 14:15-36

Introduction: The Lord will present Himself in many ways, so that the people may recognize Him as who He is.
1. Matthew 14:15-21 – He stood before them as the provider and sustainer of men.
2. Matthew 14:22-24 – He permits His disciples to go through trials.
3. Matthew 14:25-26 – They go through bewilderment.
4. Matthew 14:25-33 – They were comforted.
5. Matthew 14:33 – He was recognized as the Son of God.
6. Matthew 14:34-36 – He shows His compassion.

I Point: The Provider. (John 6:48).
   a. John 6:58 - He provided for those who remained to listen to His preaching.
   b. John 6:60 - Not all remained. Some reasoned in their own hearts and went home.
   c. Some were so happy for the Word of life they forgot their needs.
   d. For these He provided.
   Application: Matthew 6:33 "But seek ye first the kingdom of God, and his righteousness; and all these things shall be added unto you."

II Point: Trials. (Mathew 14:22-24).
   a. Matthew 14:22 – Jesus constrained his disciples (forced them) to leave Him.
   b. Matthew 14:24 – "...the wind was contrary."
   c. The sky was tossed. The waves were boisterous.
   Illustration: Tell how rough the sea can be.
   d. The night was dark.
   e. They were in the midst of the sea – no escape.
   Application: Fear drives them to wild imaginations.

III Point: Bewilderment. (Matthew 14:25-26).
   a. Matthew 14:25 "...And in the fourth watch of the night, (6 or 7 p.m.) Jesus went unto them, walking on the sea." They see a Spirit, or what they thought was a Spirit.
   b. They cried out in fear.
   c. They felt helpless.
   Application: Tell of the experiences in the rough North Sea.

IV Point: <u>Comfort.</u> (Matthew 14:26-32)
   a. Matthew 14:27 "...Be of good cheer; it is I; be not afraid."
   b. Some just relaxed.
   c. Some get very active. Peter was of this type.
   Matthew 14:28 "And Peter answered him and said, Lord, if it be thou, bid me come unto thee on the water." Peter was always ready of thrills.
   Application: Are you just relaxed in Christ, or are you active in Christ?

V Point: <u>Recognizing.</u>
   a. Matthew 14:33 "...Of a truth thou art the Son of God."
   b. It took all this:
      1. The feeding of the 5000.
      2. The trials at sea.
      3. The bewilderment and fear of perishing.
      4. The personal appearance of Christ.
   c. It took all this before they recognized Him as the Son of God.

VI Point: <u>He shows His compassion.</u> (Matthew 14:34-36).
   a. Are you here tonight open to when Christ hath showed His compassion?
   b. Would you like Him to show His compassion to you?

Conclusion: When you take your eyes off Jesus and look on your circumstances, you will lose footing under you. But if you fix your eyes on Him, you will recognize Him as the Son of God.

The Marriage Feast
Matthew 22:1-14

Text: Matthew 22:4 "...Tell them which are bidden, Behold, I have prepared my dinner: my oxen and my fatlings are killed, and all things are ready: come unto the marriage."

Introduction: Jesus' last sermon on earth was the last invitation to His marriage. Here He pictures unto us, in a parable, how God the Father has prepared a marriage feast for those who will come and partake of it.

I Point: <u>The place</u>
   a. Heaven - most beautiful.
   b. Wedding - a special call.
   c. Friends - a special privilege.
   d. If the call is unheeded, the privilege is lost. (Matthew 22:3-8).

II Point: <u>A far fitted right, and place filled by someone.</u>
   a. Matthew 22:9 "Go ye therefore into the highways..."
   b. All are invited.
   Isaiah 1:18 "Come now, and let us reason together, saith the LORD: though your sins be as scarlet, they shall be as white as snow: though they be red like crimson, they shall be as wool."
   Matthew 11:28 "Come unto me, all ye that labour and are heavy laden, and I will give you rest."
   Revelation 22:17 "The Spirit and the bride say, Come. And let him that heareth say, Come. And let him that is athirst come. And whosoever will, let him take the water of life freely."
   Luke 14:17 "...Come; for all things are now ready."
   Acts 16:31 "Believe on the Lord Jesus Christ, and thou shalt be saved,..."

III Point: <u>The man without the wedding garment.</u>
   a. He did not really like to dress up. He just slipped in to see for curiosity sake.
   b. We have many "so called" Christians, nowadays, who have not the wedding garment on.
   c. You may pass before the rest of the world, but you will not pass before the Master.
   d. The end of such a person without a wedding garment is thus: Matthew 22:13. "Then said the king to the servants, Bind him hand and foot, and take him away, and cast him into outer darkness; there shall be weeping and gnashing of teeth."
   He pasted in the presents of the rest, but he was thrown into hell after all.

The Great Paradox
Matthew 27:35 - 28:1-20

Introduction: In order to get the resurrection story vividly before our eyes we must begin with the death of Christ when He is still on the cross; and so we shall have for our first point:

I Point: <u>He chose to die</u>.
- a. He did not have to die.
  John 18:11 "Then said Jesus unto Peter, Put up thy sword into thy sheath: the cup which my Father hath given me, shall I not drink it?"
- b. He volunteered to go to Calvary.
  John 10:17-18 "Therefore doth my Father love me, because I lay down my life, that I might take it again. No man taketh it from me, but I lay it down of myself. I have power to lay it down, and I have power to take it again. This commandment have I received of my Father."
  Matthew 26:53-54 "Thinketh thou that I cannot now pray to my Father, and he shall presently give me more than twelve legions of angels? But how then shall the scriptures be fulfilled, that thus it must be?"
- c. He did not have to stay on the cross. He chose to die.

II Point: <u>The Resurrection – A sign of Deity and Power.</u>
- a. Romans 1:3-4 "Concerning his Son Jesus Christ our Lord, which was made of the seed of David according to the flesh; And declared to be the Son of God with power, according to the spirit of holiness, by the resurrection from the dead:"
- b. His resurrection is the sign of the great prophet Jonah. It is the sign of Deity.
  They mocked and said, Matthew 27:42 "...If he be the King of Israel, let him now come down from the cross, and we will believed him." But He stayed on the cross and showed His Deity and saved His people.
  Luke 19:10 "For the Son of man is come to seek and to save that which was lost."
  Matthew 18:11 "For the Son of man is come to save that which was lost."
- c. True Christianity is made up of an empty cross, an empty tomb, and a glorified risen Saviour sitting at the right hand of God.

III Point: The Plan.
   a. Luke 24:51 - Redemption was finished; and the twelve legions of angels round about Him, carried Him up to heaven.
   b. Oh, thank God for the empty tomb!
   c. A Lamb in His death, but a Lion in His resurrection.
   Application; I want you to notice that the angel was not at all shy or backward about the opening of the tomb.
   Matthew 28:2 "And, behold, there was a great earthquake: for the angel of the Lord descended from heaven, and came and rolled back the stone from the door, and sat upon it."
   Then note that the keepers were smitten; they "...did shake, and became as dead men." (Matthew 28:4).

IV Point: His Power.
   a. We come back to the first thought where Christ refrained His power. If He but only would beckon His angels:
      1. The earth trembled.
      2. The unsaved shook.
      3. The believers rejoiced.
   b. The fallacy
      1. The fallacy of Roman Catholicism is that it keeps Christ torn and bleeding on the cross. We worship, however, not a dead Jesus, but a living LORD. We go to a throne, not a tomb. Christ could not be holden of death, so He emerged as the Living One. Psalm 16:10 "For thou wilt not leave my soul in hell; neither wilt thou suffer thine Holy One to see corruption."
      Revelation 1:18 "I am he that liveth, and was dead; and, behold, I am alive for evermore, Amen; and have the keys of hell and of death."
   c. All Power.
      1. Matthew 28:18-19 "And Jesus came and spake unto them, saying, All power is given unto me in heaven and in earth. Go ye therefore, and teach all nations, baptizing them in the name of the Father, and of the Son, and of the Holy Ghost:"

Resurrection
Matthew 28:1-10 & Matthew 28:16-20

Introduction: One outstanding account in the procedure of the resurrection is mentioned and dealt with in all four Gospels. And that is the stone which sealed the grave. Let us therefore see what these accounts have to teach us.

I Point: The Stone. (In all four Gospels).
  a. Matthew 28:2 "And behold, there was a great earthquake: for the angel of the Lord descended from heaven, and came and rolled back the stone from the door, and sat upon it."
  b. Mark 16:2-4 "And very early in the morning the first day of the week, they came unto the sepulchre at the rising of the sun. And they said among themselves, Who shall roll us away the stone from the door of the sepulchre? And when they looked, they saw that the stone was rolled away: for it was very great."
  c. Luke 24:1-2 "Now upon the first day of the week, very early in the morning, they came unto the sepulchre, bringing the spices which they had prepared, and certain others with them. And they found the stone rolled away from the sepulchre."
  d. John 20:1 "The first day of the week cometh Mary Magdalene early, when it was yet dark, unto the sepulchre, and seeth the stone taken away from the sepulchre."

II Point: It is this stone that seals sins victims.
  a. Romans 6:23 "For the wages of sin is death;..."
   1. There is not a person here who has not stood at some time in his or her life before this stone which separates and divides us from our loved ones. (The grave).
   2. Here is once when the Omnipresent One was sealed up. It looked as if death had the victory.
   3. For 4000 years no one had ever escaped.
      Since the day of Adam's sin, this stone sealed the doom for death's victims.
   4. It was unknown to Satan that one ever escaped.
      I Corinthians 15:20-21 "But now is Christ risen from the dead, and become the firstfruits of them that slept. For since by man came death, by man came also the resurrection of the dead."

III Point: <u>Sin</u>.
1. Let us see what sin is.
2. The ugliest thing there is, is sin.
3. This worlds suffering is all because of sin.
4. Sorrow of all kind is all because of sin.

Application: Christ hated sin more than death.

a. Look upon Christ! It is not possible to catalogue all the suffering of our Lord.
But to Him any amount of suffering and shame was not to be compared with sin.
He was disallowed, despised, and rejected of men, but this was all better than sin.
He grieved, He groaned, He had nowhere to lay His head.
He was hated, persecuted and oppressed.
He sighed, thirsted, wept with strong crying and tears.
He sweat, as it were, great drops of blood falling down to the ground. But all this was to Him better than sin.
He was taken, bound, led away; accused, afflicted, spat upon, clothed and crowned with thorns; led out, bore the cross, denied, and nailed to the tree.
Crucified, reviled, scarified and made a curse.
He was bruised, broken, and forsaken by God.
He was pierced and poured out His soul unto death.
But all this was to conquer sin.
He, the sinless, suffered all this for your sin and my sin.
Sin had one aim, and that was to put Him behind the stone.

b. Here He is! Dead and buried, and behind the stone.
1. God accepted it.
2. The Lord acknowledged it.
3. Pilate, the representative of man sealed it.

c. Application: Satan's aim. His thought was: "If I could only can get Him behind the stone." It looked as if Satan and death had the victory.
If Christ had remained behind the stone there could have never been salvation.

IV Point: <u>Life behind the stone</u>.

a. This stone can only be rolled away by the life behind the stone.

b. John 12:24 "Verily, verily, I say unto you, Except a corn of wheat fall into the ground and die, it abideth alone: but if it die, it bringeth forth much fruit."
Illustration: Did you ever watch a grain of wheat resurrect?
   i. Look! How it lifts the earth! How is it possible, a little tender blade forcing its way through a rock?
   ii. There is life out of death.
c. John 11:25-26 "Jesus said unto her, I am the resurrection, and the life: he that believeth in me, though he were dead, yet shall he live: And whosoever liveth and believeth in me shall never die."
In other words, I, being in Christ as the scripture says, cannot be kept behind the stone.
d. Here we have the two: The rich man and Lazarus.
   1. Luke 16:19-31 - The account of the rich man and Lazarus. Both died what we call death. But only one remained behind the stone. While Lazarus was in the bosom of Abraham, the rich man pleaded for a drop of cool water. But it was told to him, "...there is a great gulf fixed..." [between us].
e. Death is victory over everyone remaining behind the stone.
f. The wages are paid behind the stone.
Romans 6:23 "For the wages of sin is death;..."
Mark 9:44 "Where their worm dieth not, and the fire is not quenched."
But being in Christ you live.
g. Mark 16:4 "And when they looked, they saw that the stone was rolled away: for it was very great."
Application: You, being in Christ, died with Him on the cross, and therefore, there is no more stone between you and life.

Conclusion: Challenge:
a. There is one thing laid upon you:
Matthew 28:18-20 "And Jesus came and spake unto them, saying, All power is given unto me in heaven and in earth. Go ye therefore, and teach all nations, baptizing them in the name of the Father, and of the Son, and of the Holy Ghost: Teaching them to observe all things whatsoever I have commanded you: and, lo, I am with you alway, even unto the end of the world. Amen."

What Scripture Says About Baptism
Matthew 28:18-20

Introduction: My motto in preaching always was, and always shall be, "Preach the Word." (II Timothy 4:2).

I Point: What must precede baptism? (REPENTANCE).
   a. Matthew 28:19 "Teach" "Preach."
   b. Acts 2:38 "Then Peter said unto them, Repent, and be baptized every one of you in the name of the Jesus Christ…"
   c. Acts 2:41 "Then they that gladly received his word were baptized:…"
   d. Acts 8:12 "But when they believed Philip preaching things concerning the kingdom of God, and the name of Jesus Christ, they were baptized…"
   e. Acts 8:36-37 "…See, here is water; what doth hinder me to be baptized? And Philip said, If thou believest with all thine heart, thou mayest…"
   f. Acts 9:18-19 - After Paul believed he was baptized.
   g. Acts 10:47 - After Cornelius believed he was baptized.
   h. Acts 16:14-15 - After Lydia believed she was baptized.
   i. Acts 16:30-33 – After the Philippian jailor believed he was baptized.
   j. Acts 18:8 – After Crispus believed he was baptized.

II Point Who sets us the example of baptism?
   a. Matthew 3:13-16 – The Lord Jesus Christ Himself.
      i. He was not baptized to become the Son of God, but because He was the Son of God.
         Matthew 3:16 "And Jesus when he was baptized, went up straightway out of the water:…"
      ii. The proclamation of him being the Son of God went forth after he was baptized.
   b. The word baptized means literally translated from the Greek, "dipped under" or "submerged."

III Point: What do we illustrate by Baptism?
   a. Romans 6:1-4 – We show, by faith, the burial and resurrection of Jesus Christ.
   b. Colossians 2:12 "Buried with him in baptism, wherein also ye are risen with him through the faith of the operation of God, who hath raised him from the dead."
   c. Matthew 28:18-20 & Mark 16:15-16.

Conclusion: I have pointed out to you 17 different places in the scripture on baptism. This is just a few. There are many more.

Sermon Outlines from the Book of Mark

Victory Through Love and Unison
Mark 2:1-12

Introduction: A helpless man, a determined faith, a loving Saviour.

I Point: <u>A helpless man</u>.
- a. Mark 2:3 "And they came unto him, bringing one sick of the palsy..."
  Application: A paralytic person; a person outside of Christ, dead in trespasses and sins.
  Application: The condition of the world is paralyzed of sin.

II Point: <u>A determined faith</u>. (Four men brought the palsy man.)
- a. Mark 2:3 "...which was borne of four".
  1. I want you to notice their faith.
  2. Their love for the sick person.
  3. The unison – like minded.
  4. Their testing: Faith without testing is the same as muscles without exercise.
- b. Mark 2:4 – They could not come nigh.
  1. They tried to push through.
     Illustration: Tell of the press of people in large cities: such as New York or Chicago.
- c. They could have felt justified to go on the roof.
- d. Mark 2:4 "...they uncovered the roof...and broke it up."
  Application: Their determined faith pushed forward to prove to the world that Christ is able.

III Point: <u>A loving Saviour</u>.
- a. Mark 2:5 "When Jesus saw their faith..."
  1. Christ did not look upon their recklessness or hard work to uncover the roof, but upon their faith.
  2. Neither did the Lord consider those dignified Pharisees and Scribes sitting there.
  3. Neither did he look upon the man's needs, but on their faith.

Conclusion:
God knows your needs.
He knows your difficulties.
He knows your pain.
He knows the unsaved soul.
He knows your unsaved loved ones.
What He is looking for is your "faith" in His ability to save you and them, and to heal you and them to the uttermost.

Gain the Whole World
Mark 8:27-38

Theme: The gain of the world, and the loss of the soul.

Text: Mark 8:36-37 "For what shall it profit a man, if he shall gain the whole world, and lose his own soul? Or what shall a man give in exchange for his soul?"

Introduction: Those who lose the future do not necessarily get the most out of the present. Nor does it mean that in order to gain the future we must lose the present. For those who gain the future really get the best out of this life, too. They have the best of both worlds.

I Point: What is the world that is to be gained, and the soul that is to be lost?
- a. The World to be gained.
    1. I John 2:15-16 "Love not the world, neither the things that are in the world. If any man love the world, the love of the Father is not in him. For all that is in the world, the lust of the flesh, and lust of the eyes, and the pride of life, is not of the Father, but is of the world." This includes everything in the world that appeals to the senses. "The lust of the flesh, the lust of the eyes, and the pride of life." To gain the world means to get all that it has to give along this line.
- b. The Soul to be lost.
    2. Luke 9:25 "For what is a man advantaged, if he gain the whole world, and lose himself, or be cast away?" The soul means then, the "man himself;" the inner, real manhood and womanhood. To lose the soul means to lose one's self.

II Point: Every person has a soul.
- a. The existence of the soul.
  Genesis 2:7 "And the LORD God formed man of the dust of the ground, and breathed into his nostrils the breath of life; and man became a living soul."
- b. The value of the soul.
  Mark 8:37 "Or what shall a man give in exchange for his soul?"

III Point: <u>Your soul is of infinite value.</u>
1. Because of its divine origin. Genesis 2:7 "And the LORD God formed man of the dust of the ground, and breathed into his nostrils the breath of life; and man became a living soul."
2. Because of the price paid for its redemption.
3. Because of the great contention for its possession.
4. Because of the eternal destiny awaiting it - either heaven or hell.

IV Point: <u>There is great danger of losing one's soul.</u>
 a. There is a sense in which it is already lost.
 b. But there is a final loss that takes place in the future.
 c. How the soul may be forever lost.
  1. By trying to gain the world.
  2. It is only a supposed gain, "IF." Luke 9:25 "For what is a man advantaged, if he gain the whole world, and lose himself, or be cast away?"
  3. It is an uncertain gain. Luke 12:20 "...Thou fool, this night thy soul shall be required of thee: then whose shall those things be, which thou hast provided?"
  4. It is a difficult gain. I Timothy 6:10 "For the love of money is the root of all evil: which while some coveted after, they have erred from the faith, and pierced themselves through with many sorrows."
  5. It is an unsatisfactory gain. Ecclesiastics 1:2 "Vanity of vanities, saith the Preacher, [Solomon] vanity of vanities; all is vanity."
  6. But the loss of the soul is permanent and irreversible. No exchange can save it when once its doom has been pronounced. Luke 12:20 "Thou fool..."

Conclusion: "<u>What shall it profit a man if he gain</u>..." Gain what?
A great deal of money? No!
A position of great influence and power? No!
Our thoughts goes to the extreme limit and pictures a man capturing the whole world; but, "...What shall it profit a man, if he gain the whole world, and lose his own soul?" (Mark 8:36).

Not Ministered Unto, But to Minister

Mark 10:32-45

Introduction: A great fact is here stated concerning the Son of Man. The speaker is our Lord Himself, who in this as in all matters, left us an example that we should follow in His steps.

I Point: <u>The incident</u>.
  a. Mark 10:35-37 – The incident that gave rise to His words is a sad one. Two of His disciples, James and John wanted to be ministered unto.
     Application: What follows? Offence!

II Point: <u>The Master's example</u>.
  a. Mark 10:42-43 – Notice the tenderness and patience.
  b. Mark 10:32-34 – He had been telling his disciples of his cruel suffering and indignity, and the shameful death on the cross that is awaiting Him at Jerusalem.
  c. But they seem unable to think of Him, but begin to quarrel among themselves about as to who is the greatest.
     Application: What a picture of us.
     But Jesus called them unto him and gently quelled the storm.
  d. Mark 10:42-45 – So it shall not be among you. He puts himself as an example.

III Point: <u>Not to be ministered unto</u>.
  a. He, the Son of God, came not to be ministered unto.
  b. What was His purpose? His purpose was to minister unto others.
  c. He loves us. This was His great example to His disciples.
  d. But we, as James and John, too often would like others to minister unto us.
     Application: As Christians of today, we do not realize how much sin and failure, how much vexation and discontent, how much peevishness and irritability, how much discord and unhappiness in our lives is being brought in because we want to be ministered unto, instead of ministering to.

  Illustration: Are we not often cross, vexed, rasped, and indignant. Sometimes we show it by a foolish exhibit of temper. Or you may restrain yourself, but the nasty feeling is planted in your heart.

IV Point: <u>What makes you so cross</u>? Is it because -
  a. You are slighted, ignored, brushed aside. Or your employer does not show you proper consideration. Or your neighbor does not treat you with the respect which is due to your position. You feel it very much; in fact, you are quiet upset about it.
  Why? Is it because you came to minister and were deprived of that privilege? No, indeed not. It is because your importance was not recognized, and you were not ministered unto.
  b. Hence the storm arouses jealousy. That hateful thing called jealousy. What is it? How does it come?
  It all came because you were not ministered unto.
  1. You say – He had no right to ignore me.
  2. He should have praised me.
  3. He should have consulted me.
  4. You feel rubbed the wrong way.

  That may be perfectly true, and we make no excuse for wrong and injustice. But you are a disciple of Jesus Christ, and should minister unto.

V Point: <u>I speak now to ministers and public speakers</u>:

You have been announced to speak on a special occasion. A good audience assembled, and you noticed, with a peculiar satisfaction, that Mr. X, a well-known and influential Christian man was present. You had a great subject and spoke with delight; and at the close you were extremely pleased with yourself. You expected Mr. X to come up and praise you, but instead, he just walked out and said nothing, and you felt like a snuffed-out candle.

Application: That proves that you were not there to minister, but you wanted to be ministered unto.

Broken in the Hands of the Master
Mark 14:1-9

Introduction: Four points are before us here.
1. When to serve the Lord.
2. How to serve the Lord.
3. What to expect from the people when you serve the Lord.
4. What to expect from God when you serve the Lord.

I Point: <u>When to serve the Lord</u>.
- a. Mark 14:1 "...the chief priests and the scribes sought how they might take him by craft, and put him to death."
  Mark 14:3 "...there came a woman having an alabaster box of ointment of spikenard very precious; and she brake the box, and poured it on his head." This woman identified herself with Christ.
- b. When must you serve the Lord?
  Just when everything goes good? Yes, and also when everything goes wrong. You are to serve the Lord in the face of death, when people laugh at you, and mock you, and hate you for Christ's sake.

II Point: <u>How to serve the Lord</u>.
- a. Mark 14:3 "She brake the box..."
  Illustration: What does the alabaster box teach us?
  1. The alabaster box is just the container in which the precious spikenard is filled in.
  2. The spikenard represents the Holy Spirit.
  3. Before the box is filled it is thoroughly cleansed, then filled, and then sealed.

  Comparison: Your body is the vessel, or the container.
  1. You must be cleansed.
  2. You must be filled.
  3. You are sealed by God the Father.

  To whom will it profit? - Anyone before whom your life is broken and poured out for His glory.
- b. She is the purchaser of the alabaster box.
  Christ is your purchaser. I Corinthians 6:20 "For ye are bought with a price..."
- c. The box had to be broken (marred) to make use of the ointment.
  You must be broken before God can use you for his glory.

207

III Point: <u>What to expect from the people (the world) when you serve the Lord.</u>
  a. Mark 14:4 – Your efforts will be counted as waste.
  b. Mark 14:5 – You will be advised to use your gifts in a better (worldly) way.
  c. People will be displeased with you.
  Illustration: What John Taylor said to Hudson Taylor his brother, "Hudson, you are a fool."

IV Point: <u>What to expect from God when you serve the Lord</u>.
  a. Mark 14:6 "Let her alone…"
  b. Mark 14:6 "…she hath wrought a good work for me."
  c. Mark 14:8 "She hath done what she could…"
  d. Mark 14:9 "Verily, I say unto you, Wheresoever this gospel shall be preached throughout the whole world, this also that she hath done shall be spoken of for a memorial of her."

Conclusion:
Your life must be broken in the hands of Christ your purchaser. He calls us to be broken and poured out for Him.

Sermon Outlines from the Book of Luke

Christ – As a Great King
Preached on Christmas Day
Luke 2:1-20

Theme: Christ alone had the right to choose his birth place and parents.

Text: Luke 2:7 "And she brought forth her firstborn son, and wrapped him in swaddling clothes, and laid him in a manger; because there was no room for them in the inn."

Introduction: Today we will look at Christ as the Son of man who is, "...came to seek and to save that which was lost." (Luke 19:10).

I Point: His Birth.
- a. He chose a stable for His palace.
- b. He chose a manger for His cradle.
- c. He chose swaddling clothes for His first garment.

II Point: His Genealogy.
- a. It is traced right down the line of Adam.
- b. He chose to be called "The Son of man."
- c. He chose to lay His glory down.
- d. He who alone had a right to choose.
- e. He chose poverty, humiliation, and utter lowliness. Why did He choose this?
- f. Because He had to become the Son of man.

III Point: His Purpose.
- a. Luke 19:10 "For the Son of man is come to seek and to save that which was lost."
- b. You and I were His possession lost.
- c. We were sold under sin.
- d. He came to pay the price to buy us back again.
  Illustration: A little boy built a boat. He took his boat to the lake to sail it. But the current caught the little boat and took it away. The little boat was lost. Then one day, the little boy walked past a shop, and in the shop window he saw his little boat. He went in and brought it back again, at a great price.
- e. I Corinthians 6:20 "For ye are bought with a price:..."

IV Point: He - The gift of God.
- a. II Corinthians 9:15 "Thanks be unto God for his unspeakable gift."

Conclusion: God emptied heaven to give us the Son of man.

The Humanity of Christ

Luke 2:7

Introduction: It is of utmost importance to hold dearly, and in scripture proportion, the truth of the twofold personality of the Lord Jesus Christ. But we must not let His humanity veil His deity; nor on the other hand, forget that He is a man.

I Point: <u>The humanity of Christ</u>.
- a. By His birth and growth.
    1. Luke 2:7 "And she brought forth her firstborn son,…"
    2. Luke 2:12 "…the babe wrapped in Swaddling clothing, lying in a manger."
    3. Luke 2:40 "And the child grew…"
    4. By His human body.
- c. Hebrews 2:14 - He partook of flesh and blood.
  What does that mean? It has sufferings as, John 11:35 "Jesus wept;" but it also has joy or satisfaction.
- d. John 19:34 - When he died He shed His blood.
  And when he arose from the grave, he came forth in a human body and he went into heaven with a human body.
    1. By His human soul. John 12:27 "Now is my soul troubled;…"
    2. Luke 2:40 "And the child grew, and waxed strong in spirit, filled with wisdom: and the grace of God was upon him."

II Point: <u>The purpose of His incarnation</u>:
- a. To manifest God. John 1:18 "…the only begotten Son, which is in the bosom of the Father, he hath declared him."
- b. To be the King of Israel.
- c. Luke 1:32 - To sit on the throne of David.
- d. Matthew 2:2 "…born King of the Jews?"

III Point: <u>To die for our sins</u>.
- a. I Peter 2:24 "Who his own self bare our sins in his own body on the tree, that we, being dead to sins, should live unto righteousness: by whose stripes ye were healed."
- b. Matthews 26:28 "For this is my blood of the new testament, which is shed for many for the remission of sins."

IV Point: <u>To become our High Priest</u>.
- a. Hebrews 2:17 "Wherefore in all things it behoved him to be made like unto his brethren, that he might be a merciful and faithful high priest in things pertaining to God, to make reconciliation for the sins of the people."
- b. Hebrews 4:15 "For we have not an high priest which cannot be touched with the feeling of our infirmities; but was in all points tempted like as we are, yet without sin."

V Point: <u>To show believers how to live</u>.
- a. I John 2:6 "He that saith he abideth in him ought himself also so to walk, even as he walked."
- b. I Peter 2:21 "For even hereunto were ye called: because Christ also suffered for us, leaving us an example, that ye should follow his steps:"

Come to the Feet of Jesus
Luke 7:36-48

Text: Luke 7:38 "And stood at his feet behind him weeping, and began to wash his feet with tears, and did wipe them with the hairs of her head, and kissed his feet, and anointed them with the ointment."

Introduction: What is your need today, my friend? Take these following characters as your example.

First Character: A sinner.

The Pharisee said to himself, Luke 7:39 "...This man, if he were a prophet, would have known who and what manner of woman this is that touched him: for she is a sinner."
- a. Christ knew it.
- b. The people knew it.
- c. She knew it.
- d. Therefore her request was met.
- e. Luke 7:48 "And he said unto her, Thy sins are forgiven."

Second Character: Without rest.

Luke 8:35 "Then they went out to see what was done; and came to Jesus, and found the man, out of whom the devils were departed, sitting at the feet of Jesus, clothed, and in his right mind:..."
- a. Presence of the devil.
- b. No peace in himself.
- c. No peace for others when he was around.
- d. Without God and without hope in the world.
- e. He meets Jesus, and he takes to the refuge place at the feet of Jesus.

Third Character: Hungered to know Him better.

Luke 10:39 "And she had a sister called Mary, which also sat at Jesus' feet, and heard his word."
- a. Mary knew Him as her Saviour, and therefore she wanted to know Him more.
- b. She took to the same refuge place at his feet.
- c. This is where she learned to know Him better – at the feet of Jesus.

Fourth Character: Needed comfort.
John 11:32 "Then when Mary was come where Jesus was, and saw him, she fell down at his feet, saying unto him, Lord, if thou hadst been here, my brother had not died."
- a. Mary and Martha believed that Jesus could have kept Lazarus alive, but they did not believe that He was able to raise him from the dead.
- b. Illustration: *Under the Red Star* Mark Houseman, p. 114. "Towards evening we entered into the North Sea. Before we could make this entry there was a place known as a lock, in the German, "Kiel." The boat had to wait there for about 45 or 50 minutes, as the waters were too shallow for the boat to pass through. When we came into this lock the shores were higher than our boat, but after its appointed time was up, the boat apparently stood higher than the shores. Let me apply this to our life. Many times it seems if everything goes so fine. The world passes by us in its beauty. But lo, there is a shallow place in life and our little bark adrift cannot go through. Then the good Lord leads us into a lock where we patiently have to wait, perhaps in beds of sickness, perhaps in sorrow. While we wait, the waters of life begin to rise and lift us up. As our little boat shot out on its way again as soon as the gates were opened, so do we launch out once more on our life's journey, having been patiently waiting on the Lord and having taken a refill of fuel in the reading of His precious Word and prayer. We then, too, can face the stormy North Sea of life as we that night faced with our little Baltanik boat the stormy North Sea leading to London, England."

Conclusion: Sometime God has to corner us with sickness, loss of loved ones, lack of home, property, money; or perhaps cripple us, in order to save our soul.

The Price of a Soul

Luke 8:26-39

Text: Luke 8:27 "...there met him out of the city a certain man, which had devils long time..."

<u>In money</u>: - One soul is of more value than all the wealth of the world.
<u>In suffering</u>: - It is better that all the people of the whole world should suffer all their lives on earth, if by their suffering one soul could be saved.
<u>In journeying</u>: - No foreign land is too distant, or any portion of it too inaccessible, for all the people in the whole world to take a journey there, if by so doing one soul could be saved.

There is no trouble too big, no humiliation too deep, no suffering too severe, no love too strong, no labour too hard, and no expense too great, if it is spent in the effort to win a soul.

I Point: <u>Christ's effort to win this poor hell bound man named Legion.</u>
  a. Luke 8:22 – Jesus takes all twelve of His disciples on a missionary trip to save one poor lost soul.
    1. Christ being God knew just exactly what and whom He would meet.
  b. Luke 8:27 "...there met him out of the city a certain man, which had devils long time..." One man and a legion of devils.
  c. Luke 8:28 "...the man said, I beseech thee, torment me not." The demon's trembled.
  d. Luke 8:33 "Then went the devils out of the man, and entered into the swine:..." The demon's fled when they saw Jesus.

II Point: <u>See the contrast between men and animals.</u>
  a. Luke 8:33 - The swine could not resist the devils for one minute; but this man could resist them for a long time.
    Application: Luke 8:28 "When he saw Jesus, he cried out, and fell down before him..."

There are many people nowadays right amongst us who are far worse than Legion was, for when he saw Jesus he ran to Him and fell at His feet. But you unsaved souls here; you will not even bow the knee.

   b. See the change in the man. He was "...clothed, and in his right mind:..." (Luke 8:35).
Application: Any person rejecting Christ is not in his right mind.

   c. What is a soul worth to you? Or what do you value your soul worth?

III Point: <u>The Gadarenes</u>:
   a. Luke 8:37 – They counted wealth worth more than their souls. They said, depart from us.
   b. Christ takes them at their word and leaves.
   c. These Gadarenes owed the Lord a heavy sum for years.
   d. If you don't give to God His share, He will take it.

Conclusion: The unsaved, blinded by Satan, will play around with their soul like a man who plays with his diamond of very great price, and loses it overboard in the sea.

What are you, brother and sister, doing to save the souls of the lost? Are you willing to pay the price?

In Ezekiel 3:18 God said, "When I say unto the wicked, Thou shalt surly die; and thou givest him not warning, nor speakest to warn the wicked from his wicked way, to save his life; the same wicked man shall die in his iniquity; but his blood will I require at thine hand."

Swept and Garnished

Luke 11:14-32

Theme: A heart swept and garnished, but not washed in the blood of the Lamb.

Text: Luke 11:24-25 "When the unclean spirit is gone out of a man, he walketh through dry places, seeking rest; and finding none, he saith, I will return unto my house whence I came out. And when he cometh, he findeth it swept and garnished."

Introduction: It is possible for a person to live a clean garnished life, and yet never been washed in the blood of Christ.

I Point: <u>The unclean spirit retreats</u>.
- a. Luke 11:24 "When the unclean spirit is gone out of a man, he walketh through dry places, seeking rest; and finding none, he saith, I will return unto my house whence I came out…" So he comes back.
- b. He makes you believe you are alright.
- c. He puts your conscious at ease.
- d. He may even help you get rid of some bad habits.
- e. He may make you go to church, give to charity, etc.
- f. He will make a good person out of you.

II Point: <u>You are swept and garnished</u>.
- a. You have cleaned up.
- b. You have become a church member.
- c. People even respect you as such.
- d. And you believe you are alright, and fit for heaven.

III Point: <u>Satan not defiled</u>.
- a. Luke 11:24 "…he saith, I will return unto my house whence I came out."
- b. All your cleaning will not keep him out.
- c. Satan likes to live in a clean house just as well as you do.
- d. It's the goody, goody church member who is the hardest one to lead to Christ.
- e. The out and out sinner knows he is lost.
- f. It is seven times harder for the good to get saved.

IV Point: <u>What will keep the enemy out</u>?
- a. The BLOOD! Exodus 12:13 "...when I see the blood, I will pass over you,..."
- b. I John 1:7 "...the blood of Jesus Christ his Son cleanseth us from all sin."
- c. Revelation: 12:11 "And they overcame him (Satan) by the blood of the Lamb, and by the word of their testimony;..."
- d. Hebrews 9:22 "...without shedding of blood is no remission."

Conclusion: If you are not under the blood of Christ you are yet in your sins. All your righteousness is as filthy rags. Satan holds more souls in his clutches by false churches, than by drunkenness, sin, and vice. Satan is a great church goer.

The Test of Discipleship
Luke 12:35-40

Introduction: The best test of a servant is to observe his conduct in the absence of the master.

As Christians we are under a triple test during the absence of our Lord.

    1st Test – His absence.
    2nd Test – The distance.
    3rd Test – The Silence.

I Point: 1st Test - Absence

    a. Luke 12:35 "Let your loins be girded about, and your lights burning;"
    b. Luke 12:38 "And if he shall come in the second watch, or come in the third watch, and find them so, blessed are those servants."
    c. John 14:2 "...I go to prepare a place for you..."
    Application: Our Lord has been absent nearly two thousand years now. But it is a brief time in God's way of reckoning.
    Illustration: II Peter 3:8 "But, beloved, be not ignorant of this one thing, that one day is with the Lord as a thousand years, and a thousand years as one day."

II Point: 2nd Test - Distance

    a. Acts 1:10-11 "And while they looked stedfastly toward heaven as he went up, behold, two men stood by them in white apparel; Which also said, Ye men of Galilee, why stand ye gazing up into heaven? this same Jesus, which is taken up from you into heaven, shall so come in like manner as ye have seen him go into heaven."
    Application: This is a distance beyond human conception, when we think of light years to the nearest star. They tell us it takes the sunlight 46 years to reach us in a speed like the electricity.
    b. He is going into a far country.
    Colossians 3:1-2 "If ye then be risen with Christ, seek those things which are above, where Christ sitteth on the right hand of God. Set your affection on things above, not on things on the earth."

III Point: 3rd Test - Silence

    a. And here again is the test supreme, which seemingly prolongs beyond endurance.
Illustration: How many people have jumped to conclusions, and how many give up?
But we have His promise. We have His word.
    b. Psalm 50:3 "Our God shall come, and shall not keep silence: a fire shall devour before him, and it shall be very tempestuous round about him."
    c. Luke 12:40 "Be ye therefore ready also for the Son of man cometh at an hour when ye think not."
    d. Jude 1:14 "...Behold, the Lord cometh with ten thousand of his saints."
    e. Revelation 1:7 "Behold, he cometh with clouds; and every eye shall see him,..."
    f. Isaiah 25:9 "And it shall be said in the day, Lo, this is our God; we have waited for him, and he will save us: this is the LORD; we have waited for him, we will be glad and rejoice in his salvation."

Conclusion: He will come, but we need to examine ourselves, beloved, to see if we are standing true to this triple test as faithful servants.

The Long Suffering of God
Luke 13:1-9

Text: Luke 13:8 "And he answering said unto him, Lord, let it alone this year also, till I shall dig about it, and dung it:"

Introduction: I want to speak to you folk just now about the long suffering and patience God has with sinful man.

I Point: <u>The Long suffering of Christ</u>. (Parable Luke 13:6-9).
Luke 13:6 "...A certain man had a fig tree planted in his vineyard; and he came and sought fruit thereon, and found none."
  a. The certain man in the parable is God the Father.
  b. The vineyard is Israel, or the world.
  c. The fig tree is you and I, the Christian.
  d. The dresser is the Lord Jesus Christ.

II Point: <u>The thorough labour of Christ on his children</u>. Isaiah 5:1-4
  a. He fenced it.
  b. Gathered the stones out.
  c. Planted choicest vines.
  d. Built a tower.
  e. Made a winepress therein.
  f. Isaiah 5:2 "...and he looked that it should bring forth grapes..."
  g. Isaiah 5:2 "...and it brought forth wild grapes."
What have you done with your gifts?

III Point: <u>Calling witnesses to the court</u>.
  a. Isaiah 5:3-6 – Judgment - If there is no fruit hew it down.
  b. Luke 13:7 – Judgment - If there is no fruit cut it down.
Application: The fig tree is you and I. How has God found us?
  c. Luke 13:8 – Jesus, our advocate, is pleading your case.
  d. One more year of grace. But, "...My spirit shall not always strive with man,..." (Genesis 6:3).

IV Point: <u>The final judgment</u>.
  a. Repentance is required.
Illustration: There was a man who refused a pardon after the death sentence was pronounced.

Conclusion: You may argue at court all you like, and point out all the good you have done throughout your life, but unless you repent, you are still condemned.

Earth, Heaven and Hell
Luke 15:3-10

Introduction: Three points are to be discussed.
1. Earth and its madness.
2. Heaven and its gladness.
3. Hell and its sadness.

I point: <u>Earth and its madness</u>.
- a. Luke 14:16 "...A certain man made a great supper, and bade many:"
    - i. God bade them.
    - ii. Christ's great supper.
    - iii. His death and resurrection.
- b. Luke 14:17 "...Come; for all things are now ready."
    1. The great invitation.
- c. Note the excuses.
    1. Luke 14:18-20 - Modern excuses.
- d. God's prediction upon these men.
    1. Luke 14:24 "...none...shall taste of my supper."

II Point: <u>Heaven and its gladness</u>.
- a. Luke 15:3-7 - The lost sheep is found. What a joy!
- b. Luke 15:11-24 - The lost son. (Read Luke 15:2-24) Great Joy. These are parables of the joy there is in heaven.

III Point: <u>Hell and its sadness</u>.
- a. Luke 16:19-31 - The rich man and Lazarus.
Illustration: God lifts the lid off hell, so that we can just peek in.
- b. Luke 16:23 "And in hell he lift up his eyes, being in torments,..." Here is a man who had died, but now he lives, talks, sees, and feels.
    1. Torment - Luke 16:24 "...for I am tormented in this flame."
    2. Memories - Luke 16:25 "...remember that thou in thy lifetime receivedst thy good things,..."
    3. Hopelessness - Luke 16:26 "...between us and you there is a great gulf fixed:..."
    4. Dread for others - Luke 16:28 "For I have five brethren; that he may testify unto them, lest they also come into this place of torment."
- c. People still will not listen, nor believe, "...though one rose from the dead." (Luke 16:31).

The Parable of the Lost Son
Luke 15:11-24

Text: Luke 15:18 "I will arise and go to my father,…"

I Point: <u>His earthly home</u>.
- a. A son of a well-to-do home. Luke 15:11 "…A certain man had two sons:" Only two, to inherit the father's property.
- b. An undisciplined home. Luke 15:12 "…Father, give me the portion of goods that falleth to me…" And the father just gives it over.
- c. Luke 15:13 – Will a child be content in an undisciplined home? No! He gathered all together and left home.

II Point: <u>His earthly fun and his gain</u>.
- a. Luke 15:13 - He "…wasted his substance with riotous living."
- b. Untaught, unspanked, lives his own way, and his own will. Luke 15:14 "…he began to be in want…"
- c. His gain - from a rich heir to the hog pen.
  Luke 15:15 "…and he sent him into his fields to feed swine."
- d. He counted himself equal with the swine.
  Luke 15:16 "And he would fain have filled his belly with the husks that the swine did eat:…"
  Illustration: A man raised pigs and taught them to follow him everywhere by dropping peas behind him. Unfortunately, he used the peas to lead them to the slaughter house.

III Point: <u>The lesson he learned</u>.
- a. Luke 15:17 "And when he came to himself,…"
- b. He sees himself a sinner, against God and father.
  Luke 15:18 "…Father, I have sinned against heaven, and before thee."
- c. He sees his depravity. Luke 15:19 "And [I] am no more worthy to be called thy son:…"
- d. He also sees the way out. Luke 15:18 "I will arise and go to my father,…"

IV Point: <u>He repented</u>.
- a. Luke 15:20 "And he arose, and came to his father…"
- b. Luke 15:21 - He humbled himself.
- c. He confesses his sins. Luke 15:21 "…Father, I have sinned against heaven, and in thy sight, and am no more worthy to be called thy son."

V Point: <u>He was accepted</u>.
   a. Luke 15:20 "...But when he was yet a great way off, his father saw him, and had compassion, and ran, and fell on his neck, and kissed him."

VI Point: <u>He was forgiven</u>.
   a. Luke 15:24 "For this my son was dead, and is alive again; he was lost, and is found..."

VII Point: <u>Five things we must know</u>.
   1. We are lost.
   2. We must repent.
   3. There is a Saviour.
   4. We must give ourselves over to Him.
   5. We must believe His Word.

The Two Distinct Natures of Man
Luke 16 19-31

Theme: The material nature and spiritual nature of man.

Introduction: The scripture conclusively proves that man has two distinct natures – a material nature, which is the physical body, and a spiritual nature, which is the soul.

I Point: <u>Scripture recognizes the distinction between the bodily nature and the spiritual nature of man.</u>

   a. Job 32:8 "But there is a spirit in man: and the inspiration of the Almighty giveth them understanding."
The "spirit within man" and the "man" are as distinct as a house and a tenant living within the house.

   b. Job 14:22 "But his flesh upon him shall have pain, and his soul within him shall mourn."
Here the flesh and soul are distinct – The flesh is upon him, it envelops the soul, while the soul is within him, or in the body. These two natures: the flesh without, and the spiritual nature (the soul) within, constitutes the man.

   c. I Corinthians 6:20 "For ye are bought with a price: therefore glorify God in your body, and in your spirit, which are God's."
In this passage, the body and spirit are so closely distinguished that no comment can make it more plain.

   d. Matthew 10:28 "And fear not them which kill the body, but are not able to kill the soul:..."
Here it is evident that the soul is not the body, nor the body the soul; so that, while men are able to kill the body, they are not able to kill the soul.

II Point: <u>Death – Separation of the spiritual nature from the body.</u>

   a. According to the Bible, death is a separation of the spirit from the body.
Ecclesiastes 8:8 "There is no man that hath power over the spirit to retain the spirit; neither hath he power in the day of death:..."

   b. These scriptures further show that death is a separation of the spirit from the body.

    c. Genesis 25:8 "Then Abraham gave up the ghost, and died…"
Genesis 35:29 "And Isaac gave up the ghost, and died,…"
Mark 15:37 "And Jesus cried with a loud voice, and gave up the ghost."
Many other scriptures show that death is a giving up, or that death is a separation of the soul from the body.
    d. What does Paul mean when he said: "…to be absent from the body, and to be present with the Lord." (II Corinthians 5:8).

III Point: <u>What becomes of the departed spirit?</u>
    a. Are they roaming about in space, or do they depart to some definite place? If so, what place?
    b. The Bible makes it clear that there is a definite abode for the departed spirit.
Luke 16:22 "And it came to pass, that the beggar [Lazarus] died, and was carried by the angels into Abraham's bosom:…"
Luke 16:22-23 "…the rich man also died, and was buried; And in hell he lift up his eyes,…"(Hades).
    c. I want you to notice the two places. One up – one down. The angels carried Lazarus, whereas the rich man died and was buried, and in hell he lifted up his eyes, and saw Lazarus afar off.
    d. The place for the departed is found in the Old Testament 65 times. 31 times it is translated hell; 31 times it is translated grave. And three times it is translated the pit.

IV Point: <u>What becomes of the body after the spirit is departed?</u>
    a. Luke 16:22 "…the rich man also died, and was buried;"
    b. John 11:24 "Martha said unto him, I know that he shall rise again in the resurrection at the last day."
The body remains as it fell until the resurrection of the dead.

V Point: <u>Will the unsaved departed suffer as soon as departed?</u>
<u>Will the saved departed enjoy heaven as soon as they are departed?</u>
    a. Luke 16:19-31 - The rich man lifted up his eyes being in torment. This word torment is used in this account 5 times. Lazarus was at once in Abraham's bosom, or in paradise.

VI Point: <u>Where are the saved departed now in the New Testament age?</u>
   a. Ephesians 4:8 "...When he ascended up on high, he led captivity captive, and gave gifts unto men."
   Translation: Christ led the imprisoned out of prison.
   b. The saved that die now are at once in the presence with Christ, where Christ is.
   c. Luke 23:43 "...Verily I say unto thee, Today shalt thou be with me in paradise."
   d. II Corinthians 5:8 "...to be absent from the body, and to be present with the Lord."
   Not any more in hades, but in the third heaven, or paradise, in conscious bliss with Christ.

VII Point: <u>Where is now the abode of the unsaved?</u>
   a. Revelation 20:13 "...death and hell delivered up the dead which were in them:..." This proves that the unrighteous are still going to hades, or hell, in conscious torment as the rich man of Luke 16:22-23 "...the rich man also died, and was buried; and in hell (hades) he lift up his eyes, being in torments,..."

Conclusion: Where are you heading to?

The Questions about Salvation

Luke 18:18-30

Introduction: There are three main references I would like to take up with you dealing on salvation.

1. Luke 13:23 "...are there few that be saved?"
2. Luke 18:26 "...Who then can be saved?"
3. Acts 16:30 "...what must I do to be saved?"

I Point: Luke 13:23 "...are there few that be saved?"

a. Christ was teaching the people the way of salvation, and it seems hard to them. Luke 13:23 "Then said one unto him, Lord are there few that be saved?"
Application: It must have appeared so to an onlooker.

b. Jesus said He was the way, and the only way.
John 10:9 "I am the door: by me if any man enter in, he shall be saved,...."
Then if this poor carpenter of Nazareth was the only way, then there must be few saved.
Application: They did not know Him.

c. And Jesus answered, Luke 13:24 "Strive to enter in at the strait gate: for many, I say unto you, will seek to enter in, and shall not be able."
Matthew 7:14 "...few there be that find it."
Application: It is apparently so now, Christ is still telling the people to strive to enter in.
Matthew 7:13-14 "Enter ye in at the strait gate...Because strait is the gate, and narrow is the way, which leadeth unto life, and few there be that find it."

d. There will be a day when the opportunity will have gone. When the master of the house has shut the door.
Luke 13:25 "When once the master of the house is risen up, and hath shut to the door, and ye begin to stand without, and to knock at the door, saying, Lord, Lord, open unto us; and he shall answer and say unto you, I know you not whence ye are:"
Application: Many empty professors will then find out their mistake. Luke 13:27 "But he shall say, I tell you, I know you not whence ye are; depart from me, all ye workers of iniquity."

II Point: Luke 18:26 "Who then can be saved?"
  a. Luke 18:27 - The story of the rich young ruler.
     Luke 18:18-30 - He was rich, young, moral, religious, and a ruler. What more could be wanted?
     Application: If such a man could not be saved, who then could?
  b. Luke 18:27 "...The things which are impossible with men are possible with God."
     Application: No goodness of man is able to save a soul. Even though it be their very finest.
  c. Jesus gives us here an wonderful illustration:
     1. Luke 18:25 "For it is easier for a camel to go through a needle's eye, than for a rich man to enter into the kingdom of God."

III Point: Act 16:30 "...what must I do to be saved?"
  a. The Philippian jailor asked Acts 16:30 "...what must I do to be saved?
  b. The answer: Acts 16:31 "...Believe on the Lord Jesus Christ, and thou shalt be saved, and thy house."

IV Point: This answer to the Philippian jailer is seven-fold.
  1. Apostolic, therefore authoritative, binding for all time.
  2. Simple – Believe on the Lord Jesus Christ.
  3. Sure - Thou shalt.
  4. Sufficient – Be saved.
  5. Immediate: One minute the jailer was lost, the next minute he was saved, baptized and rejoicing.
  6. Universal: "...and thy house..." What is true for one is true for all.
  7. Personal: "...thou shalt be saved..."

Conclusion: Where do you stand, my friend?

The Facts of Christ's Resurrection
Luke 24:36-53

Introduction: To begin with, we should remember that there is no such thing as a "resurrection" unless it be a bodily resurrection. There is no such thing as the resurrection of a spirit. The spirit never has to be raised from the grave, because it never enters the grave. A spirit can know no resurrection from the dead, because a spirit never dies.

I Point: <u>What was placed in the tomb</u>?
- a. The New Testament continually insists that it was the body which was placed in the tomb.
- b. So it was a body that came forth from the tomb. That which was buried arose. You cannot bury a spirit.
- c. That which arose, could be seen, touched, handled; and identified with the nail prints in Jesus' hands and feet and the spear mark in His side. (Luke 24:39–40 & John 20:24-28).

II Point: <u>What power held Christ in the tomb</u>?
- a. First, there was the power of death.
- b. Second, there were the bindings of large linen cloths wound tightly about Him.
- c. Third, there was the great stone rolled across the mouth of the tomb.
- d. Fourth, there was the seal of the Roman government.
- e. Fifth, there were the soldiers guarding the tomb.
- f. But, on the third day, in spite of all this security, the tomb was found empty!

III Point: <u>The empty tomb</u>.
- a. All scholars agree that the tomb was empty.
- b. 1st The women found it empty.
- c. 2nd The disciples saw it was empty.
- d. 3rd The angel said it was empty.
- e. 4th The guards declared that it was empty.
- f. 5th The Jewish Sanhedrin admitted that it was empty.

How did that tomb become empty? That is the question!

IV Point: <u>The facts of Christ's resurrection</u>.
- a. 1st The resurrection is not a Greek Myth.
- b. 2nd We are not dealing with a story.
- c. 3rd We are dealing with historical facts.

1. Jerusalem was a real city.
2. Jesus was a real man.
3. The crucifixion was a real event.
4. Pontius Pilate was the real Governor of Judaea.
5. The words that Jesus spoke from the cross were truly uttered.
6. Jesus really died.
7. His body was really placed in the tomb.
8. These things are real and truly historic facts.

It is definitely historical then, that the tomb was empty.

V Point: The body is not in the tomb. How did it become empty?
There are only three ways in which the body of Jesus could have made its exit from the tomb.
- a. He had not died, just swooned, and He came out of it and pushed the stone back. (This is impossible.)
- b. The body might have been stolen by his disciples. (This was impossible.)
- c. That He arose in power, He appeared in victory. Furthermore, we should remember that He did not just come out of the tomb and then disappear.
    1. That morning He appeared to Mary Magdalene.
    2. He appeared to the women.
    3. He appeared to Peter.
    4. He appeared to two disciples on the Emmaus road.
    5. He appeared that night in the upper room to ten of His disciples.
    6. A week later He appeared to the eleven disciples.
    7. Sometime later, He appeared to a few of His disciples, early one morning, at the Sea of Galilee.
    8. Once He appeared to about five hundred brethren.
- d. The words that He spoke were those of a man who wanted the disciples to truly believe that He had been raised from the dead. (Luke 24:36-40).

Conclusion: It is the resurrection that gives power to all the churches in the world to preach everywhere, that there is power to save the poor lost soul from hell. Romans 10:9 "That if thou shalt confess with thy mouth the Lord Jesus, and shalt believe in thine heart that God hath raised him from the dead, thou shalt be saved." It was because of the resurrection the disciples in Acts 4:33 could say, "And with great power gave the apostles witness of the resurrection of the Lord Jesus Christ...."

Sermon Outlines from the Book of John

What Christ was Made
John 1:14

1. **Christ was made flesh**.

John 1:14 "And the Word as made flesh, and dwelt among us…"

Romans 1:3 "Concerning his Son Jesus Christ our Lord, which was made of the seed of David according to the flesh;"

Philippians 2:7 "But made himself of no reputation, and took upon him the form of a servant, and was made in the likeness of men:"

2. **Christ was made sin**.

II Corinthians 5:21 "For he hath made him to be sin for us, who knew no sin; that we might be made the righteousness of God in him."

Isaiah 53:6 "All we like sheep have gone astray; we have turned every one to his own way; and the LORD hath laid on him the iniquity of us all."

I Peter 2:24 "Who his own self bare our sins in his own body on the tree, that we, being dead to sins, should live unto righteousness: by whose stripes ye are healed."

3. **Christ was made a curse**.

Galatians 3:13 "Christ hath redeemed us from the curse of the law, being made a curse for us: for it is written, Cursed is every one that hangeth on a tree:"

4. **Christ was made wisdom**.

1 Corinthians 1:30 "But of him are ye in Christ Jesus, who of God is made unto us wisdom, and righteousness, and sanctification, and redemption."

Luke 21:15 "For I will give you a mouth and wisdom, which all your adversaries shall not be able to gainsay nor resist."

Hebrews 10:10 "…we are sanctified through the offering of the body of Jesus Christ once for all."

Ephesians 1:17 "That the God of our Lord Jesus Christ, the Father of glory, may give unto you the spirit of wisdom and revelation in the knowledge of him:"

Christ the Light of the World
John 1:1-14

I Point: <u>What is light? LIGHT IS LIFE.</u>
    a. Light is Life. John 1:4 "In him was life, and the life was the light of men."
    b. Light is one of the first creations. Genesis 1:3 "And God said, Let there be light: and there was light."
    c. John 1:5-9 – Without light all things die.
    d. All things that live must come to the light.
    e. Natural things come to the natural light.
    f. Spiritual things come to the spiritual light.

    Illustration: Spread an old sack on your nice lawn and what will happen?
    Illustration: Spread self-righteousness. Isaiah 64:6 - It is as filthy rags upon your soul.
    Illustration: You may shut yourself out from Christ, but without the Light...?
    Illustration: Take for an example a potato in the cellar. When the spring comes it shots sprouts.

II Point: <u>LIGHT REVEALS</u> - Light will reveal good and bad.
    a. John 3:20-21 "For every one that doeth evil hateth the light, neither cometh to the light, lest his deeds should be reproved. But he that doeth truth cometh to the light, that his deeds may be made manifest, that they are wrought in God."
    Illustration: The sun rays through a window will point out dust, dirt and lint in the room.
    Illustration: Light will also cleanse gray dirty linens.
    Illustration: Light will also darken sheets of white paper.
    b. John 3:17-18 "For God sent not his Son into the world to condemn the world; but that the world through him might be saved. He that believeth on him is not condemned: but he that believeth not is condemned already, because he hath not believed in the name of the only begotten Son of God."

III Point: <u>LIGHT GIVES SIGHT.</u>
   a. A child is born blind both physically and spiritually.
   b. But as soon as light strikes the eye, it sees.
      Illustration: The world is blind because of rejecting the light, Jesus Christ.
      Application: John 9:25 "...one thing I know, that, whereas I was blind, and now I see."
      Illustration: Light will show you the way.
      Application: Tell how I lost my way in a dark night. But when I admitted I was lost, and took light, I found my way home.
   c. The world is lost, but will not admit it is lost.
      Illustration: Tell how the telephone booth works. When you step inside there will be light.

IV Point: One Light superseded the other.
   a. Electric for lamps; Christ for the world.

Conclusion: John 3:21 "But he that doeth truth cometh to the light, that his deeds may be manifest, that they are wrought in God."

The Calls of Christ
John 1:35-51

Introduction: The Lord Jesus has issued three especially important invitations to whosoever will respond.
    1.. John 1:39 and John 1:46 - Come and see.
    2. Matthew 11:28 - Come and unload.
    3. Matthew 16:25 - Come and take.

Let us assume that we, as professing Christians, have responded to that first loving call, and by faith have beheld that "...Lamb of God, which taketh away the sin of the world." (John 1:29).

I Point: Come and See.
- a. John 1:29 - I want you first to visualize the scene here at the shores of Jordan. "...Behold the Lamb of God, which taketh away the sin of the world."
    1. He was pointed out.
    2. He was introduced.
        i. Did you come?
        ii. Did you see?
        iii. Did you realize that He is the Lamb of God?

II Point: Come and Unload.
- a. Matthew 11:28 "Come unto me, all ye that labour and are heavy laden, and I will give you rest."
    Application: You must be emptied first. Nothing can be filled that is already full.
    Illustration: What is there in your life that must be unloaded? Is there something that fills your life?

III Point: Come and Take.
- a. Matthew 16:24 "...take up [your] cross and follow me."
    Application: To take up the cross means to die. I Peter 2:24 "Who his own self bare our sins in his own body on the tree, that we, being dead to sins, should live unto righteousness: by whose stripes ye were healed."
    Illustration: This is the first thing in a Christian's life. You must die. You must carry your own cross up the hill to be nailed there on it.

Conclusion: After you have died with Christ then you can begin to take in the joy of heaven right here on earth, being changed from glory to glory.

II Corinthians 3:18 "But we all, with open face beholding as in a glass the glory of the Lord, are changed into the same image from glory to glory, even as by the Spirit of the Lord."

The Purging of the Temple

John 2:17

Text: John 2:17 "...The zeal of thine house hath eaten me up;"

Introduction: Two kinds of temples are before us to be discussed.
1. The temple where we worship. (The Church or the house of God).
2. The temple which we are. (Our body, the inward man, the place of the Holy Spirit).
   I Corinthians 3:16 "Know ye not that ye are the temple of God, and that the Spirit of God dwelleth in you?"

A.   The temple of worship.

I Point: What Christ found in the temple.
 a. John 2:14 - The temple was filled with earthly things.
    Application: What does Christ find now in the temple?
    1. The churches have become a place of merchandise.
    2. A business man comes to church to be friends with his customers.
    3. The insurance man comes to find customers for his insurance.
    4. The farmer comes to church to find his hired hand.
    5. Young people come to church to make dates with their girl and boy friends.
    6. The church members use the church building as a market place for socials and worldly amusement.

II Point: What Christ did to those people?
 a. John 2:15 "...he drove them all out of the temple,..."
 b. John 2:17 says the same as Psalm 69:9 "For the zeal of thine house hath eaten me up;..."
    Application: What would Christ do if he should walk into our churches today? I tell you, you would be embarrassed.
    1. Some would be driven out with a scourge.
    2. Your oxen, horses, cattle, sheep and tractors, which take the place of Christ, would be openly revealed and overthrown.
    3. Your money, which is your god, would be poured out, and overthrown.

B. The second temple which is your body.

III Point: <u>What Christ expects to find in this temple.</u>
1. Psalm 29:9 "...in his temple doth every one speak of his glory."
2. Isaiah 6:1 "...his train filled the temple."
3. I Corinthians 3:16 "Know ye not that ye are the temple of God, and that the Spirit of God dwelleth in you?"
4. I Corinthians 6:19 "What? know ye not that your body is the temple of the Holy Ghost which is in you, which ye have of God, and ye are not your own?"
5. II Corinthians 6:16 "And what agreement hath the temple of God with idols? for ye are the temple of the living God; as God hath said, I will dwell in them, and walk in them; and I will be their God, and they shall be my people."

IV Point: <u>What has He found in your heart?</u>
1. Instead of His glory being spoken in you; He finds a profane language were the name of the Lord is being used in vain.
2. Instead of his train filling the temple; He finds Satan and his lusts being on the throne.
3. Instead of the Spirit of God dwelling in you; you have smoked Him out and cursed Him out.
4. Instead of having the Holy Ghost as our guide, and our lives in His hand; you are your own boss, and are also trying to lose the Holy Ghost.
5. Instead of having God dwell among us and walk with us; you have given your members of your body to Satan that he may profane his lust there with.
6. Instead of being God's children; you have become the children of the devil.

Conclusion:
1. Christ was crucified.
2. Satan was dethroned.
3. The judgment of God fell. (Hosea 8:14).

Analysis of John 3:16

John 3:1-16

Text: John 3:16 "For God so loved the world, that he gave his only begotten Son, that whosoever believeth in him should not perish, but have everlasting life."

I Point: The analysis of John 3:16
  i. For God...........................The greatest person.
  ii. So loved..........................The greatest love.
  iii. The world.........................The greatest company.
  iv. That He gave...................The greatest act.
  v. His only begotten Son.....The greatest gift.
  vi. That whosoever...............The greatest opportunity.
  vii. Believeth in Him............The greatest simplicity.
  viii. Should not perish...........The greatest promise.
  ix. But.................................The greatest difference.
  x. Have everlasting life.......The greatest possession.

II Point: <u>God's love in Christ</u>
  a. People say, "All our love is wrapped up in our child." The love of God is all wrapped up in His Son, Jesus Christ.
  Matthew 3:17 "...This is my beloved Son, in whom I am well pleased."
  b. The love of God in Christ from eternity. (John 17:20-24).

III Point: <u>God's love toward men</u>.
  a. This love was handed down to men through Christ on the cross.
  b. John 19:30 "...It is finished:"
  c. Luke 21:28 "And when these things begin to come to pass, then look up, and lift up your heads; for your redemption draweth nigh."

IV Point: <u>God expects love from men</u>.
  a. The greatest expression we can produce is in Psalm 111:10 "The fear of the LORD is the beginning of wisdom..."
  b. Where there is fear of the Lord there also will be expression of his love toward mankind. Matthew 25:40 "...Verily I say unto you, Inasmuch as ye have done it unto one of the least of these my brethren, ye have done it unto me."

V Point: <u>The Five Tragedies</u>.
1. A face without eyes.
2. A desert without water.
3. A sky without stars.
4. A heart without Christ.
5. A nation without God.

Application: If you have Christ in your heart you will try to express your love for Him.

Illustration: Are you proud of being a Christian? Tell the story of how the girl was proud of her parents.

Conclusion: There is nothing more precious than a child kneeing at a mother's knees in prayer, and learning the love of God from her lips. A godly mother is the most important person in the world.

Mothers, are you teaching your children the love of God?

What are you doing with the love of God that He wants you to plant in the heart of your children?

Illustration: A little boy sat on his mother's lap and asked her why her hands were so ugly, when her face was so pretty and young looking. The mother answered, "Because when you were a baby the house caught on fire. I ran upstairs to your bedroom and took you out of your crib, but the fire burnt my hands. That is why my hands look so ugly." The little boy held his mother's hands and said, "Oh mommy, they are the most beautiful hands in the world."

New Birth

John 3:1-21

Text: John 3:7 "Marvel not that I said unto thee, Ye must be born again."

Introduction: Perhaps some of you have been wondering what is meant when we say, "Ye must be born again."

Proposition:
    1. Is it baptism?
    2. Is it reformation?
    3. Is it conformation?
    4. Is it joining the Church?
    5. It is being good?

I Point: New Birth.
    a. Galatians 6:15 "For in Christ Jesus neither circumcision availeth any thing, nor uncircumcision, but a new creature."
    b. John 3:6 "That which is born of the flesh is flesh; and that which is born of the Spirit is spirit."
    Application: You simply cannot reform the old flesh.
    c. Jeremiah 13:23 "Can the Ethiopian change his skin, or the leopard his spots? then may ye also do good, that are accustomed to do evil."
    Application: It actually means what it says, "Ye must be born again."
    d. II Corinthians 5:17 "Therefore if any man be in Christ, he is a new creature: old things are passed away; behold, all things are become new."
    Application: To be born of the Spirit is a birth contrary to the natural birth.

II Point: Born of water and born of Spirit.
    a. Water always represents cleansing.
    Application: In the Old Testament water stands for the Messiah (Christ). Wash in pure water, or wash in Christ the Messiah.
    b. John 3:8 "The wind bloweth where it listeth, and thou hearest the sound thereof, but canst not tell whence it cometh, and whither it goeth: so is every one that is born of the Spirit."

Application: The wind carries the very essence of life. And yet what a nuisance a strong wind can be. But you take the wind out of the world and no man can live. Now, take the Christian out of the world, and the world cannot exist.

This cannot be understood with the natural mind.
- c. John 3:9 "...How can these things be?"
   Illustration: Explain how a kernel of wheat falls into the ground and dies; and then it brings forth the blade.
   Romans 10:9-10 "...If thou shalt confess with thy mouth the Lord Jesus, and shalt believe in thine heart that God hath raised him from the dead, thou shalt be saved."

III Point: Is this new birth of absolute necessity?
- a. Yes. John 3:5 "Jesus answered, Verily, verily, I say unto thee, Except a man be born of water and of the Spirit, he cannot enter into the kingdom of God."
- b. Do people see its necessity? No, not at all.
   Example – The woman at the well. (John 4:6-39).
- c. Why don't people see its necessity?
   1. Because people love to work out their own salvation.

Conclusion: Titus 3:5 "Not by works of righteousness which we have done, but according to his mercy he saved us, by the washing of regeneration, and renewing of the Holy Ghost."

Application: The new birth is a gift. It must be received as a gift. Ephesians 2:8-9 "For by grace are ye saved through faith; and that not of yourselves: it is the gift of God: Not of works, lest any man should boast."

Illustration: Tell the story of the man who was condemned to die and refused a pardon. A pardon is no sooner a pardon until it is accepted and acknowledged as a pardon.

You must accept Christ's gift.

Jesus and the Samaritan Woman
John 4:1-42

Introduction: We shall look into this blessed portion of God's word tonight and see these things:

1. John 4:4 -- Christ's compassion.
2. John 4:7 -- Christ's appeal to men.
3. John 4:11 – Men's rejection.
4. John 4:15 – The woman's accepting.
5. John 4:19 – Her confession of sin.
6. John 4:28 - Her labour for Christ.
7. John 4:35 – Her result in her service.

I Point: His Compassion.
   a. John 4:4 "And he must needs go through Samaria."
   b. Christ saw a sinner who knew she was a sinner.
   c. He saw a seeking soul.
   d. He saw an opportunity to lead her to salvation.
   e. He saw a servant in her.

II Point: Christ's appeal to men.
   a. John 4:7 "...Jesus saith unto her, Give me to drink."
   b. Christ wants you to give Him something.
   c. Your life to Christ is as great a blessing to Him as a cool drink of water to a thirsting man.

III Point: Men's rejection.
   a. John 4:11 "...Sir, thou hast nothing to draw with, and the well is deep: from whence then hast thou that living water?"
   b. Doubt, they cannot see through it, so they reject it.
   c. She was caught in sin.
   d. Startled in surprise.
   e. Convicted by the Holy Spirit.

IV Point: The woman's accepting.
   a. John 4:15 "The woman saith unto him, Sir, give me this water, that I thirst not, neither come hither to draw."
   b. John 4:17-18 - She was willing to accept the gift of God, but not willing to confess her sins.
   c. Christ points out her sins.

V Point: <u>Her confession of sin.</u>
   a. John 4:19 "…Sir, I perceive that thou art a prophet."
   b. Trying to justify herself.
   c. John 4:20-21 - We got the right stuff.
   d. Persuaded. John 4:26 "Jesus saith unto her, I that speak unto thee am he."

VI Point: <u>Her labor for Christ</u>.
   a. John 4:28 – She "…went her way into the city,…"
   b. John 4:28-29 "…and saith to the men, Come, see a man, which told me all things that ever I did: is not this the Christ?"
   c. She became a witness.

VII Point: <u>Her result in service for the Lord.</u>
   a. John 4:35 "Say not ye, There are yet four months, and then cometh harvest? behold, I say unto you, Lift up your eyes, and look on the fields; for they are white already to harvest."
   b. Witness
   c. Bring others to Christ.

Conclusion: Where are you standing just now?

The Great Divide
John 7:37-43

Text: John 7:43 "So there was a division among the people because of him."

Introduction: Three great divisions are outlined to us in John's Gospel alone.
1. John 7:43 - The people are divided in the opinion of what He was.
2. John 10:19 - There is a division therefore of what He said.
3. John 9:16 – There is a division because of what He did.

I Point: <u>Christ the Great Divide.</u>
- a. John 7:37-43.
    1. Darkness and Light.
    2. Life and death.
- b. There must be a division between Christian and non-Christian.
  Exodus 8:23 "And I will put a division between my people and thy people…"
- c. Luke 12:51 – Christ says, "Suppose ye that I am come to give peace on earth? I tell you, Nay; but rather division:"
- d. John 7:43 "So there was a division among the people because of him."

II Point: <u>There was a division because of what He did.</u>
- a. John 9:1-16 – The blind man.
    1. Why was there a division because of what He did?
- b. We notice the blind man was born blind.
- c. He was tired of his blindness.
- d. He accepted healing regardless by whatever method.
- e. He was completely changed.
- f. He was born again.
    2. This was the cause of the division.

Illustration: Tell about the great divide in the British Columbia Mountains.

Application: Unsaved people cannot feel comfortable in the presence of Christ. They do not feel comfortable around Christians.

Likewise, a Christian also should not feel comfortable in the world.

Illustration: Put a live chick under a dead hen, and you have the illustration.

This blind man was kept out of the synagogue the next day because he was in touch with Christ.

It was his testimony that caused the division.

The world rejoices when you fall.

III Point: There was a division because of what he had said.
 a. John 10:9 "I am the door, by me if any man enter in, he shall be saved,…"
 b. John 10:14 "I am the good shepherd, and know my sheep, and am known of mine."
 c. John 10:19 "There was division therefore again among the Jews for these saying.

Conclusion: On which side are you tonight? If you love the Lord enough to follow Him you divide yourself from the world. You become a child of the King.

Repentance and Faith
John 5:1-17

Text: John 5:6 "...Wilt thou be made whole?"

Introduction: This story illustrates the nature of true repentance.

<u>The nature of true repentance is three fold</u>.
1. A word to the <u>will</u>.
   John 5:6 "...Wilt thou be make whole?"
2. A word to the <u>faith</u>.
   John 5:8 "...Rise, take up thy bed, and walk."
3. A word to the <u>conscience</u>.
   John 5:14 "...sin no more, lest a worse thing come unto thee."

I Point: <u>John 5:6 "...Wilt thou be made whole?"</u>
- a. Repentance by the will.
  Application: Nothing need keep the sinner from salvation. Sin has been dealt with, but you must deal with your will.
  Illustration: John 5:40 "And ye will not come unto me, that ye might have life."
  The will that keeps on saying, "I will not;" must say, "I will!"

II Point: <u>John 5:8 "...Rise, take up thy bed, and walk."</u>
- a. To the willing repentant soul the Lord speaks a word of faith.
  1. Fear.
  2. Act.
- b. You may say, "I can't!" but God says, "Act!" As the attempt is made the power of God will come.
- c. Illustration:
  1. The Ten lepers.
     As they went they were cleansed.
  2. The woman whom Satan had bound.
     She could not lift herself.
     Luke 13:12 - Jesus said, "...Woman thou art loosed from thine infirmity." And she did the impossible.
  3. The man with the withered arm.
     He could not stretch it out, but when Jesus bade him do it, he did.

III Point: <u>John 8:11 "...Go, and sin no more."</u>
- a. This third word has its place in every true Christian.
- b. It is the word to the conscience.
- c. That is how we become a Christian. We REPENT, believe in Jesus, and quit sinning.
- d. John 5:14 "...lest a worse thing come unto thee."
  Application: The worse thing means, a person who really never received a change of heart, but only a "so called" imagination.

The Resurrection of Lazarus
John 11:1-7

Introduction: Three Points I see in this portion of scripture.
1. Faith was needed.
2. Repentance was needed.
3. Obedience was needed.

I Point: <u>The family life before they knew Jesus</u>.
- a. Just three common people in the world: Lazarus, Mary, and Martha.
    1. John 11:2 - They were sinners.
    2. Just living for self.
- b. After they learned to know Jesus.
    1. They were cleansed.
    2. They became His friends. John 11:3 "...he whom thou lovest..."
    3. God uses them in testings.

II Point: <u>Testings</u>.
- a. Sickness, death.
- b. They could do nothing.
- c. Faith was needed.

III Point: <u>Faith</u>.
- a. The Lord could not help her until she had faith in Him. John 11:22 "But I know, that even now, whatsoever thou wilt ask of God, God will give it thee."
- b. The Lord is trying to convince her that Lazarus will live again. John 11:23 "...Thy brother shall rise again."
- c. No faith. John 11:24 "...I know that he shall rise again in the resurrection at the last day."
- d. He asked her to believe, and the Lord begins to show her His power of resurrection. John 11:25 "...I am the resurrection, and the life: he that believeth on me, though he were dead, yet shall he live:"

IV Point: <u>Repentance</u>.
- a. John 11:32 - Mary repented.
  No doubt Mary, as well as Martha, had been hurt by Him because He had lingered, and did not come at their call.
- b. John 11:32 – Mary "...fell down at his feet,..."
- c. Immediately Jesus asked her, "...Where have ye laid him?" (John 11:34).

Application: Christ is at your side to help you as soon as you are willing to confess your faults to Him. As soon as we are willing to line-up with the Lord, we too shall see, a resurrection of the dead – dead in Spirit.

V Point: <u>Obedience</u>.
  a. <u>First command</u> - John 11:39 "Jesus said, Take ye away the stone." A command to his own.
  Application: Christ will not do the things that you and I can do ourselves.
  There are stones in-between the dead and Christ, the life and resurrection.
  b. And you will see the resurrection.
  John 11:43 "And when he thus had spoken he cried with a loud voice, Lazarus come forth."
  c. <u>Second commend</u> - John 11:44 "...Loose him and let him go."
  Illustration: When the unsaved are resurrected from the power of death and sin, they came forth, with habits bound by past sins, "Loose them and let them go."

Conclusion: Show them how to live a Christian life.
If someone tells me that he is saved, I never doubt that; but, I say to him or her, "I shall be looking for fruit now."
Matthew 7:20 "Wherefore by their fruits ye shall know them."
Unsaved folks, too, like to show fruit, but it is corrupt and not accepted.
Matthew 7:17 "Even so every good tree bringeth forth good fruit; but a corrupt tree bringeth forth evil fruit."

The Heroic Life of Our Lord
John 12:12-33

Introduction: Speaking of Him as heroic, let us first give His side of meekness.

I Point: Meekness
  a. We saw Him as the feet washer, a servant to men.
  b. He came to wash away man's sins.
  c. He came to be set at naught.
  d. He came riding on an ass's colt. Not on a princely horse as a hero of war.
  e. Not with an army of soldiers before him.
   1. But with children with palm branches in their hands.
   2. This is our meek and lowly Jesus.

II Point: In this Spirit.
  a. He set off a fire in this world.
  b. Not to consume the earth like an atomic bomb; but instead, to burn like Moses' bush did burn.
  c. At this Palm Sunday entry of our Lord, He set the world on fire with the gospel.
  d. As the children sang, "Hosanna to the King" and the people that loved Him thronged Him; or, as Moses turned and looked on that burning bush, so must you and I turn and look and take orders of Him that speaks to us, "Go ye into the world."
  Application: John 12:19 "...behold, the world is gone after him." The world and the devil could not prevail against this fire that was turned lose.

III Point: Paul is the great pattern of Christianity.
  a. He set a fire lose when he said, "For to me to live is Christ, and to die is gain." (Philippians 1:21).
  b. Thousands of other men and women counted death gain, rather than to live for the devil and the world.
  c. This Spirit was set lose by the meek and lowly Jesus. Not by a hero. John 12:21 "...Sir, we would see Jesus."
  d. It is because of this conquering Hero, the meek and lowly one, that the world stands today.
  Illustration: Take the second coming of Christ. You take the Christians out, and the world would crumble. Now, may I ask, "Are you willing to follow this lowly Jesus, or are you awaiting judgment?"

The Triumphant Entry into Jerusalem

John 12:12-36

Introduction: First, I want you to get the vision of a King entering into a country.
Illustration: Think of when the King of England came through Canada.
Next, what I want you to see are the witnesses.

I Point: <u>The King</u>.
- a. John 12:15 "Fear not, daughter of Sion; behold, thy King cometh, sitting on an ass's colt." This was prophesied by the prophet Zechariah 487 years before Christ was born.
- b. Zechariah 9:9 "Rejoice greatly, O daughter of Zion; shout, O daughter of Jerusalem: behold, thy King cometh unto thee: he is just, and having salvation; lowly, and riding upon an ass, and upon a colt the foal of an ass."
- c. The expectation of the people.
- d. The Holy Spirit's complete control of the people.

II Point: <u>The witnesses of Him being a King</u>.
- a. John 12:13 – "Took branches of palm trees, and went forth to meet him, and cried, Hosanna: and Blessed is the King of Israel that cometh in the name of the Lord."
- b. The best way we can know anything is true is by witnesses.

Seven Witnesses
1. <u>1st Witness</u> – <u>God</u>.
   Matthew 3:17 "And lo a voice from heaven, saying, This is my beloved Son, in whom I am well pleased."
2. <u>2nd Witness</u> – <u>John</u>.
   John 1:34 "And I saw, and bare record that this is the Son of God."
3. <u>3rd Witness</u> – <u>Nathanael</u>.
   John 1:49 "Nathanael answered and saith unto him, Rabbi, thou art the Son of God: thou art the King of Israel."
4. <u>4th Witness</u> – <u>The people</u>.
   Matthew 14:33 "Then they that were in the ship came and worshiped him, saying, Of a truth thou art the Son of God."

5. 5th Witness – <u>Babes and sucklings</u>.
   Matthew 21:16 "And said unto him, Hearst thou what these say? And Jesus saith unto them, Yea; have ye never heard, Out of the mouth of babes and sucklings thou hast perfected praise?"
6. 6th Witness – <u>The disciples</u>.
   Luke 19:40 "…I tell you that, if these should hold their peace, the stones would immediately cry out."
7. 7th Witness – <u>The heavenly host</u>.
   Revelation 5:11-12 "…and I heard the voices of many angels saying with a loud voice, Worthy is the Lamb that was slain to receive power, and riches, and wisdom, and strength, and honour, and glory, and blessing."

Conclusion:
Here we have seven witnesses, these are only a very few.

<u>Now you are my witnesses</u>.
1. Romans 10:9-10 "That if thou shall confess with thy mouth the Lord Jesus, and shalt believe in thine heart that God hath raised him from the dead, thou shalt be saved."
2. Matthew 10:32 "Whosoever therefore shall confess me before men, him will I confess also before my Father which is in heaven."
3. Philippians 2:11 "And that every tongue shall confess that Jesus Christ is Lord, to the glory of God the Father."
4. I John 4:2 "Hereby know ye the Spirit of God: Every spirit that confesseth that Jesus Christ is come in the flesh is of God."

Love for His Own
John 13:1-20

Text: John 13:1 "...having loved his own which were in the world, he loved them unto the end."

Introduction: Love to the end means to love always or to love all the way through.

I Point: His manifestation of love.
  a. John 13:4-8 – As a servant.
  b. He showed them love one for another. Not another ordinance, such as the Lord's Supper or baptism, but how to express love one for another.

II Point: The misunderstanding of Peter.
  a. Peter said, "...Thou shalt never wash my feet...." (John 13:8).
  Peter wanted to teach his fellow disciples good manners, not to permit the Lord to wash his feet. But he did not take the towel of the Lord to help him.
  Illustration: We love to tell others how to pray and how to love the Lord, but we don't like to show them by His example of washing feet.
  Application: John 13:7-8 "Jesus answered and saith unto him, What I do thou knowest not now, but thou shalt know hereafter. Peter saith unto him, Thou shalt never wash my feet. Jesus answered him, If I wash thee not, thou hast no part with me."
  Christ will not fellowship with people who have unclean feet. (Unconfessed sin.) He washes them first.
  Illustration: A drunkard said to his pastor, "I never will touch alcohol again." But the pastor replied, "You don't know the power of the devil."
  Application: Like Peter of old, we do not realize the power of the devil.
  b. A little girl was asked by her mother, when she came home from Sunday school, "What have you been studying today?" The little girl said, "Just as if." The mother asked her to explain. The little girl read John 13:10 "...ye are clean," just as if you never sinned. You have been born again and need not be born over, but you need daily your feet to be washed.

Conclusion: It is an example, not an ordinance. It is in remembrance of Him, in the name of the Father, Son and Holy Spirit. As one to another, help and comfort where needed.

God's Promises

John 14:1-6

Text: John 14:14 "If ye shall ask any thing in my name, I will do it."

Introduction: John 16:24 "Hitherto have ye asked nothing in my name: ask, and ye shall receive, that your joy may be full."

Many and precious are the promises which God gives to His praying children. He tells us that as we pray and receive, our joy shall be full.

John 14:1-3 "Let not your heart be trouble: ye believe in God, believe also in me. In my Father's house are many mansions: if it were not so, I would have told you. I go to prepare a place for you. And if I go and prepare a place for you, I will come again, and receive you unto myself; that where I am, there ye may be also."

I Point: John 14:1 "Let not your heart be troubled: ye believe in God, believe also in me."

   a. The most standing promise for today.
   b. Hearts are failing today.
   c. Even hearts of people who believe in God.

II Point: John 14:2 "In my Father's house are many mansions: if it were not so, I would have told you. I go to prepare a place for you."

   a. We are troubled as to our living places here on earth, but are we troubled as to our heavenly home?

III Point: John 14:3 "And if I go and prepare a place for you, I will come again, and receive you unto myself; that where I am, there ye may be also."

Conclusion: These are God's promises.
John 14:14 "If ye shall ask any thing in my name, I will do it."

The Holy Spirit
John 14:13-27

Text: John 14:26 "But the Comforter, which is the Holy Ghost, whom the Father will send in my name, he shall teach you all things, and bring all things to your remembrance, whatsoever I have said unto you."

Introduction: Many people think the Holy Spirit is an influence, on emanation, or manifestation.

I Point: What is He?
   a. Him, He. John 14:17 "Even the Spirit of truth; whom the world cannot receive, because it seeth him not, neither knoweth him: but ye know him; for he dwelleth with you, and shall be in you."
   Application: A person.
   b. John 15:26 and 16:14 "...He shall teach you all things,..."
   c. Matthew 28:19 "Go ye therefore, and teach all nations, baptizing them in the name of the Father, and of the Son, and of the Holy Ghost:" (He is the third person in the Trinity.)
   Application: Here we see that He has a name, not just an influence. But a person after whose image we were created. Genesis 1:26 "Let us make man in our image..."

II Point: Who is He?
   a. Acts 28:25 "...Well spake the Holy Ghost by Esaias the prophet unto our fathers,"
   b. Acts 5:3 "...why has Satan filled thine heart to lie to the Holy Ghost,..."
   Application: He is here known as the Holy Ghost, and as God.
   c. John 3:5 "Jesus answered, Verily, verily, I say unto thee, Except a man be born of water and the spirit, he cannot enter into the kingdom of God." Where we have water, meaning Messiah or Christ, it is the Holy Spirit.
   d. Omnipotent. Genesis 1:2 "...And the Spirit of God moved upon the face of the waters."
   e. Omnipresent. Psalm 139:7-8 "Whither shall I go from thy spirit? or whither shall I flee from thy presence? If I ascend up into heaven, thou art there: if I make my bed in hell, behold, thou art there."
   f. Omniscient. Isaiah 40:13 "Who hath directed the Spirit of the LORD, or being his counsellor hath taught him?"

III Point: What is His work?
   a. He convicts men of sin, or righteousness, of judgment. (John 16:7-11).
   b. He regenerates. (John 3:5).
   c. He seals. (Ephesians 1:13 -14).
   d. He baptizes into one body. (I Corinthians 12:13).
   e. He indwells. (John 14:17).
   f. He imparts gifts. (I Corinthians 12:1-10 & Ephesians 4:8).
   g. He outflows. (John 7:38-39).
   h. He comforts. (John 14:16).
   i. He teaches. (John 14:26).
   j. He guides. (John 16:13).
   k. He manifests Himself in power. (Acts 1:8).

All this is the work of the same blessed Holy Spirit.

IV Point: He can be grieved.
   a. Ephesians 4:30 "And grieve not the Holy Spirit of God, whereby ye are sealed unto the day of redemption."
   b. I Thessalonians 5:19 "Quench not the Spirit."

Conclusion: God wants us to walk in the Spirit (Galatians 5:16), and be led by the Spirit. (Galatians 5:18).

Abiding in Christ
John 15:1-27

Text: John 15:7 "If ye abide in me, and my words abide in you, ye shall ask what ye will, and it shall be done unto you."

Introduction: Today, I would like to take you through three points out of John 15:1-27.
1. Abiding in Christ.
2. Bringing forth much fruit.
3. Withered branches for the fire.

I Point: <u>Abiding in Christ</u>.
- a. What is it to abide in Christ?
- b. Christ uses here a parable.
    1. John 15:1 "I AM the true vine, and my Father is the husbandman." Here is pronounced a great truth. There is a Living Vine-Christ; and living branches-Christians.
- c. A vine cannot exist without a husbandman, and a husbandman could not exist without the vine. And the branch, of course, cannot exist without both of these.
- d. The vine could live without the branches, but the branches could not live without the vine. The very life of the branch is the vine. But neither the vine nor the branches could bear fruit of itself alone.
- e. To abide in Christ, the vine, I then must rename my independence and draw my sustenance from Christ the vine.
- f. If I draw my life from Christ, then:
    1. My prayers are His prayers.
    2. My desires are His desires.
    3. My will is His will.
    4. My life and my all is His.
- g. If it is so with you then you may use the authority laid down in John 15:7 "...ye shall ask what ye well, and it shall be done unto you."
- h. How may we abide in Him?
    1. We must live in His Word - The Bible.
    2. Joshua 1:8 "This book of the law shall not depart out of thy mouth; but thou shalt meditate therein day and night, that thou mayest observe to do according to all that is written therein: for then thou shalt make thy way prosperous, and then thou shalt have good success."

3. Psalm 119:11 "Thy word have I hid in mine heart, that I might not sin against thee."
   This is the only method to abide in Christ.
   John 15:7 "If ye abide in me, and my words abide in you, ye shall ask what ye will, and it shall be done unto you."

i. It is vain to expect an answer to our prayer except we meditate much upon the word of God. It is by feeding on His word day by day as the branches feed on the vine that we will grow and bear much fruit.

j. Our difficulty of not seeing fruit is all because we, as His branches, do not feed enough on the word.

II Point: <u>Bring forth much fruit.</u>

a. John 15:5 "I am the vine ye are the branches: He that abideth in me, and I in him, the same bringeth forth much fruit: for without me ye can do nothing."

b. If we abide in Christ and feed on His word we then will feel a burden for the lost.
   Just remember, when you pray for a revival it will cost you plenty. There is a cost for revival.

III Point: <u>What is a revival?</u>

a. It is a time of quickening or visitation of the Lord upon His own people. At such time we all get a new love for the lost. The Holy Spirit imparts new life to His own people.

b.. All the squabbles in church and the looking for respect and honor from others just simply goes. You don't see the Christians standing and fighting or disagreeing among themselves. The preacher does not need to go around and pat some of his members on the back in order to keep them on his side. They are on the Lord's side and do not look for glory over it.

c. In time of revival Christians snap out of worldliness, such as: playing cards, dancing, going to theaters, smoking, drinking, etc. A new Spirit of prayer and sacrifice enters into them.

d. The prayer meetings are no longer drudgery, but a joy and a privilege.

e. The conversation on the street when you meet someone is no more about the weather and politics, but about Christ, salvation, revival, heaven and hell.

- f. Revivals are very bad for saloon keepers, dance halls, and theaters.
- g. All this interest will come when Christians will start reading the Bible every day and praying every day without fail.
  This is what happens when there is true revival.
- h. Unfortunately, most Christians do not spend more than five minutes each day in prayer. Time yourself next time and see if this is true of you.

IV Point: <u>Withered Branches</u>.

- a. John 15:6 "If a man abide not in me, he is cast forth as a branch, and is withered; and men gather them, and cast them into the fire, and they are burned."
- b. A withered branch is no good except for fuel.

Conclusion: You may put up complaint and say the people do not listen to me.

Illustration: A young man came to Moody and told him that the people do not listen to him. Moody asked him, "Have they spit on you yet?" "No," the young man answered. "Then go back and preach until they do."

The love of God
John 17:1-26

Introduction: The extreme depravity of the heart of man brought out the love of God which not only cuts out sin by the roots; but transforms the sinner into a new creature in Christ Jesus.

1. **What is the measure of love?**
   John 17:23 Thou "...hast loved them, as thou hast loved me."

   Breadth–John 3:15-16 "That whosoever believeth in him should not perish, but have eternal life. For God so loved the world, that he gave his only begotten Son, that whosoever believeth in him should not perish, but have everlasting life."

   Length–Jeremiah 31:3 "The LORD hath appeared of old unto me, saying, Yea, I have loved thee with an everlasting love: therefore with lovingkindness have I drawn thee."

   Depth – Galatians 2:20 "I am crucified with Christ: nevertheless I live; yet not I, but Christ liveth in me: and the life which I now live in the flesh I live by the faith of the Son of God, who loved me, and gave himself for me."

   Height –Ephesians 2:6 "And hath raised us up together, and made us sit together in heavenly places in Christ Jesus:"

2. **Who is the object of God's love?**
   a. John 3:16 "For God so loved the world, that he gave his only begotten Son, that whosoever believeth in him should not perish, but have everlasting life."
   b. Ephesians 2:4-5 "But God, who is rich in mercy, for his great rich love wherewith he loved us, Even when we were dead in sins, hath quickened us together with Christ, (by grace ye are saved:)
   c. Galatians 2:20 "...who loved me, and gave himself for me."

3. **How does God love me?**
   a.. Hosea 14:4 "...I will love them freely:..."
   b. John 16:27 "For the Father himself loveth you, because ye have loved me, and have believed that I came out from God."
   c. John 13:1 "...having loved his own which were in the world, he loved them unto the end."

4. **What has God's love done for you?**
   a. I John 4:10 "Herein is love, not that we loved God, but that he loved us, and sent his Son to be the propitiation for our sins."

   Propitiation is the appeasing between the wrath of God and man.
   b. Revelation: 1:5 "...Unto him that loved us, and washed us from our sins in his own blood."
   c. Titus 3:5 "Not by works of righteousness which we have done, but according to his mercy he saved us, by the washing of regeneration, and renewing of the Holy Ghost;"
   d.. Ephesians 2:6 "And hath raised us up together, and made us sit together in heavenly places in Christ Jesus:"
   e. II Thessalonians 2:16-17 "Now our Lord Jesus Christ himself, and God, even our Father, which hath loved us, and hath given us everlasting consolation and good hope through grace, Comfort your hearts, and stablish you in every good word and work."
5. **What will God's love do for us?**
   a. Ephesians 5:27 "That he might present it to himself a glorious church, not having spot, or wrinkle, or any such thing; but that it should be holy and without blemish."
   b. Jude 1:24 "Now unto him that is able to keep you from falling, and to present you faultless before the presence of his glory with exceeding joy."
   c. Romans 8:38 "For I am persuaded, that neither death, nor life, nor angels, nor principalities, nor powers, nor things present, nor things to come, Nor height, nor depth, nor any other creature, shall be able to separate us from the love of God, which is in Christ Jesus our Lord."
   d. Hebrews 12:6 "For whom the Lord loveth he chasteneth,..."

Sanctification
John 17:1-26

Text: John 17:17-19 "Sanctify them through thy truth: thy word is truth. As thou hast sent me into the world, even so have I also sent them in the world. And for their sakes I sanctify myself, that they also might be sanctified through the truth."

I Point: Sanctification, like many other words of the scripture, is threefold in meaning.

First - The believer is being sanctified the very moment he or she accepts the shed blood of Jesus Christ as a covering for sin.
  a. Hebrews 10:9-10 "Then said he, Lo, I come to do thy will, O God. He taketh away the first, that he may establish the second. By the which will we are sanctified through the offering of the body of Jesus Christ once for all."
  b. I John 1:7 "...the blood of Jesus Christ his Son cleanseth us from all sin."

Second – In experience the believer is being sanctified by the work of the Holy Spirit, through the Word of God, day by day from the dominion of sin.
  a. Romans 6:14 "For sin shall not have dominion over you: for ye are not under the law, but under grace."
  b. John 17:17-19 "Sanctify them through thy truth: thy word is truth. As thou hast sent me into the world, even so have I also sent them in the world. And for their sakes I sanctify myself, that they also might be sanctified through the truth."

Third – The believer will be completely sanctified at the second coming of Christ.
  a. I Thessalonians 5:23 "And the very God of peace sanctify you wholly; and I pray God your whole spirit and soul and body be preserved blameless unto the coming of our Lord Jesus Christ."
  b. I John 3:2 "Beloved, now are we the sons of God, and it doth not yet appear what we shall be; but we know that, when he shall appear, we shall be like him; for we shall see him as he is."

II Point: In these three great factors of sanctification there are seven distinct divisions, by whom, and through whom, and in whom, we are being sanctified.

Seven Distinct Divisions:
We are sanctified:
1. By God the Father.
2. In Jesus Christ.
3. By the Holy Spirit.
4. By faith.
5. By the blood.
6. By truth.
7. Wholly sanctified.

1st Division: We are sanctified by God the Father.
   a. Jude 1:1 "Jude, the servant of Jesus Christ, and brother of James, to them that are sanctified by God the Father, and preserved in Jesus Christ, and called:"
   b. Ephesians 1:4 "According as he hath chosen us in him before the foundation of the world, that we should be holy and without blame before him in love:"
   c. I Peter 1:15-16 "But as he which hath called you is holy, so be ye holy in all manner of conversation; Because it is written, Be ye holy; for I am holy."

2nd Division: We are sanctified in Christ Jesus.
   a. I Corinthians 1:2 "...to them that are sanctified in Christ Jesus, called to be saints, with all that in every place call upon the name of Jesus Christ our Lord, both their's and our's:"
   b. I Corinthians 1:30 "But of him are ye in Christ Jesus, who of God is made unto us wisdom, and righteousness, and sanctification, and redemption:"
   c. Hebrews 10:10 "By the which will we are sanctified through the offering of the body of Jesus Christ once for all."

3rd Division: We are sanctified through and by the Holy Spirit.
   a. Romans 15:16 - That they "...might be acceptable, being sanctified by the Holy Ghost."
   b. I Corinthians 6:11 "And such were some of you: but ye are washed, but ye are sanctified, but ye are justified in the name of the Lord Jesus, and by the Spirit of God."
   How does this all take place? What must you and I do?

4th Division: <u>We are sanctified by faith</u>.
  a. Acts 26:18 "…that they may receive forgiveness of sins, and inheritance among them which are sanctified by faith that is in me."
  b. Acts 15:9 "And put no difference between us and them, purifying their hearts by faith."
  c. I John 5:4 "For whatsoever is born of God overcometh the world: and this is the victory that overcometh the world, even our faith."
  The greatest thing to remember that gives us faith to overcome is to remember that we have been sanctified by the blood of Christ.

5th Division: <u>We are sanctified by the blood of Christ.</u>
  a. Hebrews 13:12 "Wherefore Jesus also, that he might sanctify the people with his own blood suffered without the gate." (Calvary.)
  b. Hebrews 9:14 "How much more shall the blood of Christ, who through the eternal Spirit offered himself without spot to God, purge your conscience from dead works to serve the living God?"
  c. I John 1:7 "…the blood of Jesus Christ his Son cleanseth us from all sin."

6th Division: <u>We are sanctified by the truth</u>.
  a. John 17:17-19 "Sanctify them through thy truth: thy word is truth. As thou hast sent me into the world, even so have I also sent them in the world. And for their sakes I sanctify myself, that they also might be sanctified through the truth."

7th Division: <u>We ought to be wholly sanctified.</u>
  a. I Thessalonians 5:23 "And the very God of peace sanctify you wholly; and I pray God your whole spirit and soul and body be preserved blameless unto the coming of our Lord Jesus Christ."
  b. I Peter 3:15 "But sanctify the Lord God in your hearts: and be ready always to give an answer to every man that asketh you a reason of the hope that is in you with meekness and fear:"

Conclusion: Some children are cleaned up always, and yet they are always dirty. Some children are cleaned up and they stay clean. Repentance is no sooner repentance; unless you quit doing the sin you repented of.

It Is Finished
John 19:1-42

Theme: Christ died according to the scripture.

Introduction: We shall try to see what Christ meant by the cry on the cross, "It is finished."

I point: <u>God's plan of salvation, before the world was</u>.
   a. Revelation 13:8 "...the Lamb slain from the foundation of the world."
   b. <u>To Satan</u> - Genesis 3:15 "I will put enmity between thee and the woman, and between thy seed and her seed; it shall bruise thy head, and thou shalt bruise his heel."

II Point: <u>God's plan of salvation revealed unto men by object lessons.</u>
   a. <u>To Adam</u> - Genesis 3:21 "Unto Adam also and to his wife did the LORD God make coats of skins, and clothed them."
   b. <u>To Noah</u> - Genesis 6:14 "Make thee an ark..." the Ark was a type of Christ as a refuge for His people.
   c. <u>To Abraham</u> - Genesis 22:2 "...Take now thy son, thine only son Isaac, whom thou lovest,..."
   d. <u>To Israel</u> - Exodus 12:13 "...when I see the blood, I will pass over you..."

III Point: <u>God's plan of salvation revealed unto men by prophecy.</u>
   a. <u>To Isaiah</u> - Isaiah 9:6 "For unto us a child is born, unto us a son is given: and the government shall be upon his shoulder: and his name shall be called Wonderful, Counsellor, The almighty God, The everlasting Father, The Prince of Peace."
   b. Isaiah 53:1-10 "...as a lamb to the slaughter..." (Isaiah 53:7).
   c. <u>To Micah</u> - Micah 5:2 "But thou, Beth-lehem Ephratah, though thou be little among the thousands of Judah, yet out of thee shall he come forth unto me that is to be ruler in Israel; whose goings forth have been from of old, from everlasting."

IV Point: <u>God's plan of salvation revealed unto men according to scripture in the Person of Jesus Christ.</u>
   a. Matthew 1:21 "And she shall bring forth a son, and thou shalt call his name JESUS: for he shall save his people from their sins."

- b. John 1:29 "...Behold the Lamb of God, which taketh away the sin of the world."
- c. John 11:25 "...I am the resurrection, and the life: he that believeth in me, though he were dead, yet shall he live:"

V Point: God's plan of salvation finished.
- a. Galatians 4:4 "But when the fullness of the time was come, God sent forth his Son, made of a woman, made under the law."
- b. Matthew 27:1 "When the morning was come, all the chief priests and elders of the people took counsel against Jesus to put him to death:"
- c. John 19:28 "After this, Jesus knowing that all things were now accomplished, that the scripture might be fulfilled, saith, I thirst."
    1. John 19:29-30 "Now there was set a vessel full of vinegar: and they filled a spunge with vinegar, and put it upon hyssop, and put it to his mouth. When Jesus therefore had received the vinegar, he said, It is finished: and he bowed his head, and gave up the ghost."

Conclusion:
1. It is finished.
2. It is free.
3. It is simple.
4. It is precious.

However, this is hard to understand for many people still trying to work out their own salvation. Nevertheless, God's word says, "For by grace are ye saved through faith; and that not of yourselves: it is the gift of God: not of works, lest any man should boast." (Ephesians 2:8-9).

Sermon Outlines from the Book of Acts

The Ascension of Christ
Acts 1:1-14

Introduction:
1. First, I want you to see His walk on earth in bodily form. (Luke 24:36-53).
2. Next, I want you to take to heart the great commission He left with his disciples. (Matthew 28:16-20).
3. Now, I want you to see the promise given of His return. (Acts 1:10-11).

I Point: His Present Work.
   a. Romans 8:34 "Who is he that condemneth? It is Christ that died, yea rather, that is risen again, who is even at the right hand of God, who also maketh intercession for us."
   b. I John 2:1-2 "...And if any man sin, we have an advocate with the Father, Jesus Christ the righteous: And he is the propitiation for our sins:..."

II Point: His Return.
   Read: I Thessalonians 4:13-18; and Acts 1:10-11.

1st Event: The resurrection of the body of the believer - (The Rapture.)
   a. Philippians 3:21 "Who shall change our vile body, that it may be fashioned like unto his glorious body..."
   b. I Corinthians 15:51-52 "Behold, I shew you a mystery; We shall not all sleep, but we shall be changed, In a moment, in the twinkling of an eye, at the last trump: for the trumpet shall sound, and the dead shall be raised incorruptible, and we shall be changed."

2nd Event: Rewarding of the Saints.
   a. II Corinthians 5:10 "For we must all appear before the judgment seat of Christ; that every one may receive the things done in his body, according to that he hath done, whether it be good or bad."
   b. Rewards have nothing to do with salvation.

3rd Event: Revolution on the earth - (The Great Tribulation).
   a. Satan - II Thessalonians 2:4 "Who opposeth and exalteth himself above all that is called God, or that is worshipped; so that he as God sitteth in the temple of God, shewing himself that he is God."

- b. Psalm 2:2-3 "The kings of the earth set themselves, and the rulers take counsel together, against the LORD, and against his anointed, saying, Let us break their bands asunder, and cast away their cords from us."
- c. Matthew 24:21 "For then shall be great tribulation, such as was not since the beginning of the world to this time, no, nor ever shall be." (Armageddon).

4th Event: The Return of Christ in Glory with His saints.
- a. Revelation 20:1-3 "And I saw an angel come down from heaven, having the key of the bottomless pit and a great chain in his hand. And he laid hold on the dragon, that old serpent, which is the Devil, and Satan, and bound him a thousand years. And cast him into the bottomless pit, and shut him up, and set a seal upon him, that he should deceive the nations no more, till the thousand years should be fulfilled: and after that he must be loosed a little season."
- b. The Millennium. Christ reigns with his saints for a thousand years.

5th Event: The Releasing of Satan.
- a. This release of Satan is granted to give all the people, then living on the earth for a thousand years in peace, who have not had an opportunity to reveal their wicked heart, to choose to follow God or Satan.

Reference to this is found in:
- a. Revelation 20:7-9 "And when the thousand years are expired, Satan shall be loosed out of his prison, And shall go out to deceive the nations which are in the four quarters of the earth, Gog, and Magog, to gather them together to battle: the number of whom is as the sand of the sea. And they went up on the breadth of the earth, and compassed the camp of the saints about, and the beloved city: and fire came down from God out to heaven, and devoured them."
- b. Ezekiel 38:1-4 "And the word of the LORD came unto me, saying, Son of man, set thy face against Gog, [Russia] the land of Magog, the chief prince of Meshech [Moscow] and Tubal, [Tobolsk] and prophesy against him, And say, Thus saith the Lord GOD; Behold, I am against thee, O Gog, the chief prince of Meshech and Tubal: And I will turn thee

  back, and put hooks into thy jaws, and I will bring thee forth, and all thine army, horses and horseman, all of them clothed with all sorts of armour, even a great company with bucklers and shields, all of them handling swords:"

c. This is the day when the Lord will stand on the Mount of Olives and shall smite the nations. Zechariah 14:3-4 "Then shall the LORD go forth, and fight against those nations, as when he fought in the day of battle. And his feet shall stand in that day upon the Mount of Olives…"

6th Event: The White Throne Judgment.

a. Revelation: 20:12-15 "And I saw the dead, small and great, stand before God; and the books were opened: and another book was opened, which is the book of life: and the dead were judged out of those things which were written in the books, according to their works. And the sea gave up the dead which were in it; and death and hell delivered up the dead which were in them: and they were judged every man according to their works. And death and hell were cast into the lake of fire. This is the second death. And whosoever was not found written in the book of life was cast into the lake of fire."

b. Mark 9:44 "Where their worm dieth not, and the fire is not quenched."

7th Event: Reconstruction of the earth; A new heaven and a new earth.

a. Revelation 21:1 "And I saw a new heaven and a new earth; for the first heaven and first earth were passed away; and there was no more sea."

Revival - Part II
Acts 5:1-16

Theme: When is revival to be expected?

Text: Acts 5:11 "And great fear came upon all the church, and upon as many as heard these things."

I Point: When can we look for a revival?

1. When wickedness grieves, humbles, and distresses Christians.
   a. The story of Ananias and Sapphira. (Acts 5:1-11).
      Application: It was the sin of lying that grieved Peter. Peter knew what it meant to tell lies.
   b. In the Old Testament we fine a humbling of His people.
      II Kings 19:1 "And it came to pass, when king Hezekiah heard it, that he rent his clothes, and covered himself with sackcloth, and went into the house of the LORD."
      Application: The blasphemy of Assyria grieved the people and drove them to a revival. And the Lord saved His people. Sometimes Christians do not seem to mind the wickedness around them, and if they talk about it, it is in a cold, indifferent, unfeeling way.

II Point: When can we look for a revival?

2. When Christians pray as if their hearts were set upon revival. A deep, continual, earnest desire for the salvation of sinners will surely bring a revival, unless the Spirit is grieved away by sin. If Christians will only be humbled and pray, they will soon see God's arm in a revival.
   a. Luke 24:49 "And, behold, I send the promise of my Father upon you: but tarry ye in the city of Jerusalem, until ye be endured with power from on high."
   b. Matthew 18:19 "Again I say unto you, That if two of you shall agree on earth as touching any thing that they shall ask, it shall be done for them of my Father which is in heaven."
   c. Acts 2:1 "And when the day of Pentecost was fully come, they were all with one accord in one place." Praying.

III Point: <u>When can we look for a revival?</u>

3. When Christians confess their sins one to another.
    a. James 5:16 "Confess your faults one to another, and pray one for another, that ye may be healed. The effectual fervent prayer of a righteous man availeth much."
    b. Matthew 18:15 "Moreover if thy brother shall trespass against thee, go and tell him his fault between thee and him alone:..."
    c. Proverbs 28:13 "He that covereth his sins shall not prosper: but whoso confesseth and forsaketh them shall have mercy." Application: If the Christians would begin to confess their sin: sins of commission and sins of omission, there would be revival. Instead of this, we look for an excuse. We blame the weather, blame the road, blame the car, blame the children, and blame others, but not ourselves who is the guilty party. Instead of the city needing the revival, we need to say; "I" need a revival.

IV Point: <u>When can we look for a revival?</u>

4. When Christians are willing to make a sacrifice to carry it out. They must be willing to sacrifice their feelings, their business, their time, and to help forward the work.
    a. II Corinthians 8:12 "For if there be first a willing mind, it is accepted according to that a man hath, and not according to that he hath not."
    b. II Corinthians 9:6-7 "But this I say, He which soweth sparingly shall reap also sparingly; and he which soweth bountifully shall reap also bountifully. Every man according as he purposeth in his heart, so let him give; not grudgingly, or of necessity: for God loveth a cheerful giver."
    c. I Thessalonians 1:9 "...how ye turned to God from idols to serve the living and true God;"
    Application: Idolatry need not only apply to the heathen idol, but to our self worldly.

V Point: <u>When can we look for a revival</u>?

5. When preachers in their preaching aim at the conversion of the lost.
    a. James 5:19-20 "Brethren, if any of you do err from the truth, and one convert him; Let him know, that he which converteth the sinner from the error of his way shall save a soul from death, and shall hide a multitude of sins."
    b. Daniel 12:3 "And they that be wise shall shine as the brightness of the firmament; and they that turn many to righteousness as the stars for ever and ever."

VI Point: <u>When can we look for a revival</u>?

6. When ministers and Christians are willing to have God promote it by any instrument as He pleases.
    a. I Corinthians 1:27 "But God hath chosen the foolish things of the world to confound the wise; and God hath chosen the weak things of the world to confound the things which are mighty;"
    I Corinthians 1:29 "That no flesh should glory in his presence."
    b. Exodus 7:19 - God chose a rod for Moses. And in Samson's time He chose the jaw bone of an ass.
    c. So He may choose you and me.

Conclusion: Psalm 51:1 "Have mercy upon me, O God, according to thy lovingkindness: according unto the multitude of thy tender mercies blot out my transgressions."

*This is Part II of the Revival Series:
  Part I - Isaiah 44:22, page 133.
  Part II - Acts 5:1-16, page 271.
  Part III – Psalm 42:1-11, page 112.

The First Martyr

Acts 7:44-60

Text: Acts 7:55 "But he, being full of the Holy Ghost, looked up stedfastly into heaven, and saw the glory of God and Jesus standing on the right hand of God."

Introduction: Tell briefly the story of Stephen. (Acts 7:54-60).

I Point: <u>The condition of Jerusalem.</u>

- a. Time: 33 A. D. Just after the crucifixion of Christ.
- b. The first church.
- c. The first deacons.
  Acts 6:5 "...and they chose Stephen, a man full of faith and of the Holy Ghost,..."
- d. Acts 6:8 "And Stephen full of faith and power, did great wonders and miracles among the people."

II Point: <u>The persecution of the Church.</u>

- a. Acts 6:9 – They arose against the Church.
- b. Acts 6:10 "And they were not able to resist the wisdom and the spirit by which he [Stephen] spoke."
- c. His face was as of an angel. Acts 6:15 "And all that sat in the council, looking stedfast on him, saw his face as it had been the face of an angel."

III Point: <u>Stephen before the Council.</u>

- a. Acts 7:51 "Ye stiffnecked and uncircumcised in heart and ears, ye do always resist the Holy Ghost: as your fathers did, so do ye."
- b. Acts 7:59 "And they stoned Stephen, [while he was] calling upon God, and saying, Lord Jesus, receive my spirit."
- c. The testimony he bore.
- d. The wisdom he manifested.
- e. The glow on his face.
- f. His steadfastness unto death.
  What an example!

IV Point: <u>How he died and what he accomplished at death.</u>
    a. He died praying for his murderers. Acts 7:60 "And he kneeled down, and cried with a loud voice, Lord, lay not this sin to their charge. And when he had said this, he fell asleep."
    b. He fell asleep in Jesus.
    c. But through his death, Saul (later known as Paul), was convicted.

Conclusion:
1. We are in need of men like Stephen.
2. We are in need of a persecution.
3. The blood of the martyrs is the seed of the Church.
4. Tell the story of John and Betty Stam in china.
John and Betty Stam were American Christian missionaries to China during the Chinese Civil War. This missionary couple was murdered by the Communist Chinese soldiers in 1934 for their faith.

The Conversion of Saul of Tarsus

Acts 9:1-25

Text: Acts 9:15 "...he is a chosen vessel unto me, to bear my name..."

Introduction: Last Sunday we saw Saul standing with the slayers of Stephen. Today we see him smitten down to the ground before the Lord.

I Point: <u>A mighty man</u>.
- a. Acts 9:1-2 - He had the authority to slay and to bind men and women. Acts 9:14 "And here he hath authority from the chief priests to bind all that call on thy name."
(Acts 22:1-5 and Acts 26:10-11).
- b. Saul was a mighty man.
He was a well-bred man.
He was a learned man.
He was a man with a great initiative and zeal toward God.
Application: Where are you, my friend, standing today among the up and up?
Do you think you could do something for God?
Saul thought he could, with a great zeal.

II Point: <u>Saul became a broken man.</u>
- a. He fell to the ground. Acts 9:4 "And he fell to the earth, and heard a voice saying unto him, Saul, Saul, why persecutest thou me?"
- b. His eyes closed as to the worldly glory. Acts 9:8 "And Saul arose from the earth; and when his eyes were opened, he saw no man:...."
- c. He began to pray. And God spoke to Ananias and told him to go to "...one called Saul, of Tarsus: for, behold, he prayeth," (Acts 9:11).
- d. Acts 9:12 - He also had others to pray for him.
Application: Oh, sinner, my friend, have you been knocked down from your high horse? Are your eyes closed as to the glory of self and the world? Are you praying?

III Point: <u>He is a chosen vessel</u>.
- a. Acts 9:15 - The Lord said, "...he is a chosen vessel unto me, to bear my name...".
  1. Before the Gentiles.
  2. Before kings.
  3. Before the children of Israel.
- b. God began to pour Saul from vessel to vessel.
- c. He was blind for three days. Acts 9:9 "And he was three days without sight, and neither did eat nor drink."
  Application: In those three days Saul became the Apostle Paul.
- d. He was filled with the Holy Ghost. Ananias said, Acts 9:17 "...Brother Saul, the Lord, even Jesus, that appeared unto thee in the way as thou camest, hath sent me, that thou mightiest receive thy sight, and be filled with the Holy Ghost."
- e. He was baptized. Acts 9:18 "...he received sight forthwith, and arose, and was baptized."
- f. Acts 9:20 "And straightway he preached Christ..."
- g. Acts 9:22 - He confounded the Jews.

Conclusion:
Acts 9:22 - As his testimony he recounts his conversion.
Acts 26:9 – He is not ashamed of Christ.
Romans 1:16 "For I am not ashamed of the gospel of Christ: for it is the power of God unto Salvation to every one that believeth;..."

Perfect Liberty Gives Perfect Victory

Acts 12:1-19

Introduction: We shall, in an expository manner, go through Acts 12:1-19, and see why and how Peter enjoyed such victory.

I Point: Acts 12:1 "Now about that time…"
    a. About what time? Acts 12:1 "…Herod the king stretched forth his hands to vex certain of the church."
    b. About the time of great doings for the Lord.
        Illustration: If you hinder Satan, he won't leave you alone.
        1. Christian persecution. Acts 12:2 "He killed James the brother of John…"

II point: Acts 12:3 "And because he saw it pleased the Jews, he proceeded further to take Peter…"
    a. Whom do the Jews represent?
    b. In our day they represent the so called "religious folks."
        Illustration: If there is nothing being done here by you, they will be your friends; but, you just begin to do things for God, then woe is you.

III Point: Acts 12:4 "…he put him [Peter] in prison.
    a. The world saw Peter bound.
    b. The world thinks you are bound.
    c. But Peter had liberty.
    d. Peter was in need of a rest.
    e. He was kept in prison.
    f. Acts 12:6 "…Peter was sleeping,…"
    g. He had peace in his heart.
    h. He had peace around him the body guards provided.

IV Point: While you and I rest in Christ, God works.
    a. Acts 12:7 "And, behold, the angel of the Lord came upon him…and raised him up, saying, Arise up quickly…"
    b. Peter gets the vision.
    c. He receives a command.
    d. Acts 12:8 "and the angel said unto him, Gird thyself;…"
    e. The Lord foresees the attack of Satan.
        Illustration: Ephesians 6:10-19 (Spiritual warfare).
    f. Acts 12:8 - And the angel said, "… follow Me." We would love to go ahead, but God's order and plan is to follow Him.

V Point: <u>God's plans perfectly times day, hour, and second.</u>
   a. Acts 12:9 "And he went out, and followed him, and wist not that it was true which was done by the angel; but thought he saw a vision."
   b. Acts 12:9-10 - The guards were blinded.
   c. The iron gates opened.

VI Point: <u>Acts 12:11 "And when Peter was come to himself, he said,</u> Now I know of a surety, that the Lord hath sent his angel, and hath delivered me out of the hand of Herod,..."
   a. If you really follow the Lord you will forget yourself.
   b. You then will learn the reason of it all. (Acts 12:12).
   c. You will find it was not you at all.

VII Point: <u>Acts 12:14 - The Lord reveals the faithful one amongst those that had prayed.</u>
   a. Acts 12:15 – They had been praying for Peter's release, but when Rhoda came to them and said that Peter was standing at the door, they did not believe, but said, "Thou art mad."
   b. Peter rebuked their unbelief and, Acts 12:17 "...declared unto them how the Lord had brought him out of the prison..."

Conclusion: I wonder just how many of us are Rhoda's. She never opened the door.
James 5:16 "...The effectual fervent prayer of a righteous man availeth much."

The Unknown God
Acts 17:1-23

Text: Acts 17:23 "For as I passed by, and beheld your devotions, I found on altar with this inscription, TO THE UNKNOWN GOD. Whom therefore ye ignorantly worship, him declare I unto you."

Introduction:
Acts 17:2-3 - Paul's manner.
Acts 17:4 – Greeks' response.
Acts 17:5 & 13 – Jew's response.

Application: Our manner: or our aim in preaching to you the gospel.
1. The response of the people who are not religious.
2. The response of the people who are religious.

Illustration: It is the "so called" religious folk who give us the round up.
Acts 17:5 - They "...gathered a company, and set all the city in a uproar,..."

I Point: Paul at Athens.
   a. Acts 17:16 "...his spirit was stirred in him, when he saw the city wholly given to idolatry."

   Application: I have wondered many times why people would be so foolish as to worship idols; but, I discovered that idol worship is the most common thing in our country, in our town, and in every one of your homes.
   b. An idol is an image, and is derived from the imagination of your mind.
   c. Your idols and my idols are:
     1. Self.
     2. Good works.
     3. Your place.
     4. Your face.
     5. Your grace.
     6. Your church.
   d. Among all of these you mix the name of God.
   Application: Acts 17:15-21 – In verse 21 I see our young folks: Acts 17:21 "...there spent their time in nothing else, but either to tell, or to hear some new thing." A thoughtless, aimless generation.

II Point: <u>The Unknown God</u>.

a. Acts 17:22-23 – Compare the sight of Athens with the sight of United States.
   1. You cannot worship God until you know Him.
   2. You cannot even love or respect a person until you have learned to know Him.
   3. You might be a faithful friend to others, but God says you could not be faithful to me until you know me.
   4. You might be a faithful church goer and church loving person, but you can't serve or love the Lord until you know Him.
   5. You might be the very best man or woman, but that cannot give you any credit. You must know Him personally.
   6. You perhaps did a lot of good, for this country or even gave all your goods away to feed the poor, but it profits you nothing unless you know Him.
   7. Read I Corinthians 13:1-3.

b. Paul says - Acts 17: 23 "For as I passed by, and beheld your devotions, I found an altar with the inscription, TO THE UNKNOWN GOD. Whom therefore ye ignorantly worship, him declare I unto you."

Beloved, it is this friend of mine, my Father, my Saviour; Him I declare unto you.

III Point: <u>How to know Him</u>.

a. John 3:7 "Marvel not that I said unto thee, Ye must be born again."
You must be born of Him! You must be bone of His bone, and flesh of His flesh. "Ye must be born again."

b. I Corinthians 2:14 "But the natural man receiveth not the things of the Spirit of God: for they are foolishness unto him: neither can he know them, because they are spiritually discerned."

c. I Corinthians 1:18 "For the preaching of the cross is to them that perish foolishness;..."

d. II Corinthians 4:3-4 "But if our gospel be hid, it is hid to them that are lost: In whom the god of this world (Satan) hath blinded the minds of them which believe not, lest the light of the glorious gospel of Christ, who is the image of God, should shine unto them."

Application: Your way and your good works, all you can name before the Lord, may be perfectly good; but, God says, "There is a way which seemeth right unto a man, but the end thereof are the ways of death." (Proverbs 14:12).

It seems right to general folk to go on and do the best you can, and go to church, etc.; but, if you don't know God personally as your Saviour and friend you are no better off than the Athenians were.

The Athenians were very zealous. They had all kinds of gods to make sure they got them all. They even put up an altar to the unknown God. But what good did all that do for them? They still did not know Him.

Conclusion:
Do you know this God?
Would you like to get acquainted with Him?

Salvation or Religion
Acts 28:16-37

Introduction: It is possible to be religious and still be unsaved. The world has many man-made or woman-made religions, but there is only one glorious plan of salvation offered by God.

Even the Apostle Paul before his conversion had very much religion, and even persecuted the true church of God. But let us now meditate upon how the Word of God treats the subject under the heading salvation or religion.

Of course, when we think of religion we naturally think of these as a means to get to heaven, or getting favor with God. But looking through the Bible we find nowhere that religion would give any such confidence as salvation here outlined.

I Point: What salvation gives to men.
1. Joy – Psalm 35:9 "And my soul shall be joyful in the LORD: it shall rejoice in his salvation."
2. The Rock – Psalm 95:1 "O COME, let us sing unto the LORD: let us make a joyful noise to the rock of our salvation."
3. The Cup – Psalm 116:13 "I will take the cup of salvation, and call upon the name of the LORD."
4. Everlasting – Isaiah 45:17 "But Israel shall be saved in the LORD with an everlasting salvation: ye shall not be ashamed nor confounded world without end."
5. Salvation of our God – Isaiah 52:10 "The LORD hath made bare his holy arm in the eyes of all the nations; and all the ends of the earth shall see the salvation of our God."
6. Garments of salvation – Isaiah 61:10 "I will greatly rejoice in the LORD, my soul shall be joyful in my God; for he hath clothed me with the garments of salvation, he hath covered me with the robe of righteousness, as a bridegroom decketh himself with ornaments, and as a bride adorneth herself with her jewels."

II Point: The New Testament evidences of salvation.
1. Knowledge of salvation – Luke 1:77 "To give knowledge of salvation unto his people by the remission of their sins."
2. No other salvation – Acts 4:12 "Neither is there salvation in any other: for there is none other name under heaven given among men, whereby we must be saved."

3. <u>The word of salvation</u> – Acts 13:26 "Men and brethren, children of the stock of Abraham, and whosoever among you feareth God, to you is the word of this salvation sent."
4. <u>The way of salvation</u> – Acts 16:17 "...These men are the servants of the most high God, which shew unto us the way of salvation."
5. <u>The day of salvation</u> – II Corinthians 6:2 "(For he saith, I have heard thee in a time accepted, and in the day of salvation have I succoured thee: behold, now is the accepted time; behold, now is the day of salvation.)"
6. <u>The token of salvation</u> – Philippians 1:28 "And in nothing terrified by your adversaries: which is to them an evident token of perdition, but to you of salvation, and that of God."

III Point: What are we? What have we?
1. <u>Heirs of salvation</u> – Hebrews 1:14 "Are they not all ministering spirits, sent forth to minister for them who shall be heirs of salvation?"
2. <u>Author of salvation</u> – Hebrews 5:9 "And being made perfect, he became the author of eternal salvation unto all them that obey him;"
3. <u>Gospel of salvation</u> – Ephesians 1:13 "In whom ye also trusted, after that ye heard the word of truth, the gospel of your salvation: in whom also after that ye believed, ye were sealed with that holy Spirit of promise,"
4. <u>Faith unto salvation</u> – I Peter 1:5 "Who are kept by the power of God through faith unto salvation ready to be revealed in the last time."
5. <u>Unmerited salvation</u> – Titus 2:11 "For the grace of God that bringeth salvation hath appeared to all men."
6. <u>Blood-bought salvation</u> – Acts 20:28 "Take heed therefore unto yourselves, and to all the flock, over the which the Holy Ghost hath made you overseers, to feed the church of God, which he hath purchased with his own blood."
7. <u>A soul-saving salvation</u> – I Peter 1:9 "Receiving the end of your faith, even the salvation of your souls."

Conclusion: After seeing all these references pointing to what salvation has brought, no wonder Paul says in Hebrews 2:3 "How shall we escape, if we neglect so great a salvation;..."

Sermon Outlines from the Book of Romans

I am a Debtor
Romans 1:1-16

Preached to a Youth Group

Text: Romans 1:14 "I am debtor both to the Greeks, and to the Barbarians; both to the wise, and to the unwise."

I Point: <u>You are a debtor to God for your life</u>.
- a. Were you never born you would not have had a chance to be born again and fit for heaven.
- b. You are a debtor to God for the fact that you were born in the very enlightened dispensation of grace.
- c. You are a debtor to God for the fact that you are living in America, a free country. Not Russia as I was.
- d. You are a debtor to God if you were born to Christian parents.
- e. You are a debtor to God if you were brought up in a Christian home.

II Point: <u>Some are unthankful</u>.
- a. Illustration: I will tell you of my own unthankfulness.
  1. Forgetting my covenant to God and the promise to my godly mother to be a preacher.
  2. Reaching out to earthly success.
  3. Forgetting God's intervening hand in my time of searching.

III Point: <u>We are all debtors</u>.
- a. We are all debtors to God for his love and grace to us.
- b. We are debtors to God for His great salvation.

Conclusion: Be thankful to God and dedicate your life to Him.

The Guilty World
Romans 1:1-18

I Point: The wrath of God.
   a. Romans 1:18 "For the wrath of God is..."
      1. Revealed against ungodliness.
      2. Against unrighteousness.
      3. Hypocrisy: They know the truth, but practice ungodliness.

II Point: Without excuse.
   a. Romans 1:19-20 - Because God reveals:
      1. Romans 1:19 – Himself to all men.
      2. Romans 1:20 - Even through nature.

III Point: They become foolish and darkened.
   a. Romans 1:21 "...their foolish heart was darkened."
      1. Unthankful.
      2. Became vain.
      3. Became superstitious and foolish.
      4. Yet thinking themselves to be wise.
   b. Their heart cried out to worship something, so they followed superstitious corruptible things as in Romans 1:23 "And changed the glory of the uncorruptible God into an image made like to corruptible man, and to birds, and fourfooted beasts, and creeping things."

IV Point: The result.
   a. Romans 1:24 "Wherefore God also gave them up..."
   b. Romans 1:24-32 – He gave them up to:
      1. Uncleanness.
      2. Lusts.
      3. Their bodies dishonoured.
      4. Vile affections.
      5. Reprobate minds. (Romans 1:28).
   c. Romans 1:29-31 "Being filled with all unrighteousness, fornication, wickedness, covetousness, maliciousness; full of envy, murder, debate, deceit, malignity; whisperers, Backbiters, haters of God, despiteful, proud, boasters, inventors of evil things, disobedient to parents, Without understanding, covenantbreakers, without natural affection, implacable, unmerciful:"

Conclusion:
a. Romans 1:32 "Who knowing the judgment of God, that they which commit such things are worthy of death, not only do the same, but have pleasure in them that do them."
b. They know their ways are worthy of death; but yet, have pleasure in them and lead others in the same condemnation.

The Fact of Sin
Romans 5:1-21

Text: Romans 5:12 "Wherefore, as by one man sin entered into the world, and death by sin; and so death passed upon all men, for that all have sinned:"

Introduction: Romans 5:12 shall be presented to you under three distinct headings:
1. The fact of sin.
2. The penalty of sin.
3. The clear title for sin.

I Point: The fact of sin.
   a. Romans 5:12 – The fact of sin is demonstrated to us by death.
   b. Death is universal. All die, the good and the bad.

   Since we see that death is universal, even upon little children, therefore, there must be a universal cause for it, and that cause is sin.

   Genesis 2:17 "...for in the day that thou eatest thereof thou shalt surely die."

   Romans 5:12 "Wherefore, as by one man sin entered into the world, and death by sin; and so death passed upon all men, for that all have sinned:"

   Jeremiah 17:9 "The heart is deceitful above all things, and desperately wicked: who can know it?"

   Job 15:16 "How much more abominable and filthy is man, which drinketh iniquity like water?"

   John 3:18 "...he that believeth not is condemned already..."

II Point: The penalty of sin.
   a. We shall now discuss what penalty you and I must pay for our sin. Romans 6:23 "For the wages of sin is death,..."
   Ezekiel 18:20 "The soul that sinneth, it shall die..."
   b. God will take II Thessalonians 1:8 "...vengeance on them that know not God, and that obey not the gospel of our Lord Jesus Christ:"
   Application: When God is taking vengeance on sin, do you have a clear title to show to Him that your sins are paid for?

III Point: <u>The clear title for sin</u>.
    a. The penalty God demands is eternal death, and eternal damnation.
Hebrews 9:27 "And as it is appointed unto men once to die, but after this the judgment:"
Hebrews 2:3 "How shall we escape, if we neglect so great salvation;…"
Application: There is no escape. Sin must be paid for. If one judge would let off men who are guilty to die, we would not think very much of that judge. So neither can God let any go without a clear title from sin.
    b. The clear title is the blood of Jesus Christ.
I John 1:7 "…the blood of Jesus Christ his Son cleanseth us from all sin."
Exodus 12:13 "…when I see the blood, I will pass over you…"
Application: Some say, "I cannot see it so. I live and let live." But, if that would save a person, then God made a very foolish move when He sent Christ to the earth to redeem us.

Conclusion:
John 6:37 "All that the Father giveth me shall come to me, and him that cometh to me I will in no wise cast out."
Romans 10:13 "For whosoever shall call upon the name of the Lord shall be saved."
Romans 5:1 "THEREFORE being justified by faith, we have peace with God through our Lord Jesus Christ:"

Justification – Part I
Romans 5:1-21

Text: Romans 5:1 "THEREFORE being justified by faith, we have peace with God through our Lord Jesus Christ:"

Introduction: Let me take you to Romans for a little while. For in just one more week we shall have Baptismal services. But before I speak on baptism I would like to preach on justification.

I Point: <u>What the word of God says about sin.</u>
1. Romans 3:10 "...There is none righteous, no, not one:"
2. Romans 3:11 "There is none that understandeth, there is none that seeketh after God."
3. Romans 10:23 "For all have sinned, and come short of the glory of God;"
4. Ezekiel 18:4 "...the soul that sinneth, it shall die."
5. Jeremiah 17:9 "The heart is deceitful above all things, and desperately wicked: who can know it?"

We are justified:
1. By God.
2. By grace.
3. By blood.
4. By resurrection.
5. By faith.
6. By words.
7. By works.

II Point: <u>Justification by God.</u>
   a. Romans 8:33 "...It is God that justifieth."
   b. Justification is the legal aspect of the believer's relation to God as judge of all the earth.
   c. God must be righteous, and righteousness always demands a price. Yet, He justifies, and that the ungodly, when he believes in Jesus. Romans 3:26 "...that he might be just, and the justifier of him which believeth in Jesus."

III Point: <u>Justification by grace.</u>
   a. Romans 3:24 "Being justified freely by his grace through the redemption that is in Christ Jesus:"
   b. Note the word "freely." It means gratuitously. Grace acted without any merit or constraint on man's part, and the gift of salvation is free.

IV Point: <u>Justification by blood</u>.
  a. Romans 5:9 "...being now justified by his blood, we shall be saved from wrath through him."
  b. A judge cannot forgive. He must be satisfied.
  c. The cross satisfied the judge of all the earth. He can now acquit the believer.
  d. Romans 3:26 - Without the cross God could not forgive and remain just. But in the cross he found a ground upon which he could be just, and the justifier of him that believeth in Jesus.

V Point: <u>Justification by resurrection</u>.
  a. Romans 4:25 "...raised again for our justification."
  b. Resurrection only justifies in that it shows that the sacrifice has been accepted.
  c. The work of Christ is complete by the resurrection.

VI Point: <u>Justification by faith</u>.
  a. Romans 5:1 "Therefore being justified by faith, we have peace with God through our Lord Jesus Christ."
  b. Faith identifies us with Christ, so that His death is reckoned our death.
  c. In Him we died, and he that died is justified.

VII Point: <u>Justification by words</u>.
  a. Matthew 12:37 "For by thy words shalt thou be justified..."
  b. The evidence of justification is from the lips of those who make confession to His name. Romans 10:9 "That if thou shalt confess with thy mouth the Lord Jesus..."
  c. A man's word discloses what is in him.
  d. Matthew 12:34 "...for out of the abundance of the heart the mouth speaketh."

VIII Point: <u>Justification by works</u>.
  a. James 2:24 "Ye see then how that by works a man is justified, and not by faith only."
  b. Just as words evidence it, so good works are fruit of it.
  c. Just as love is not love if it shows no kindness, so faith is not faith if it produces no works.

*This is Part I of Justification.
The II Part of Justification - Romans 8:28-39, page 300.

Baptism
Romans 6:1-23

Text: Romans 6:4 "Therefore we are buried with him by baptism into death:...."

Introduction: What saith the scripture about baptism?

There are three questions that I am sure every thoughtful inquirer would like to have answered concerning baptism.
- 1st - What constitutes baptism? It is sprinkling, pouring, or immersion?
- 2nd - What precedes baptism, or who may be baptized and under what conditions?
- 3rd – What is the meaning or symbolism of baptism?

Is it just a senseless church requirement, or is there some good reason for it? There is only one way we may find out. Let us turn to the scripture.

I Point: What constitutes baptism?
    a. Is it sprinkling, pouring or emersion?
       1. Jesus went <u>into the Jordan River</u>.
       2. Acts 8:38 - The Ethiopian went down <u>into the water</u>.
       3. Baptism is <u>immersion</u>.

II Point: What precedes baptism?
    a. Romans 6:1-4 – Death unto sin precedes baptism; Or, in other words, salvation.
    b. Acts 2:47 "...And the Lord added to the church daily such as should be saved."
    Application: How were they added unto the church?
    c. Acts 2:40-41 "Then they that gladly received his word were baptized:...."
    d. Acts 8:12 "But when they believed Philip preaching the things concerning the kingdom of God, and the name of Jesus Christ, they were baptized, both men and women."

    1. The story of Philip and the Ethiopian eunuch.
       As soon as he believed in Christ he was baptized.
       Acts 8:36-37 "...See here is water; what doth hinder me to be baptized? And Philip said, If thou believest with all thine heart, thou mayest. And he answered and said, I believe that Jesus Christ is the Son of God."
       Acts 8:38 "...and they went down both into the water...and he baptized him..."

2. The story of the apostle Paul.
   Acts 9:18 "And immediately there fell from his eyes as it had been scales: and he received sight forthwith, and arose, and was baptized."

3. The story of Cornelius.
   Acts 10:47 "Can any man forbid water, that these should not be baptized, which have received the Holy Ghost as well as we?"

4. The story of the Philippian jailor.
   Acts 16:33 "And he took them the same hour of the night, and washed their stripes; and was baptized, he and all his, straightway."
   Illustration: In Russia, when someone accepted Christ in the winter time, they made a hole in the ice and baptized them at once.

III Point: What is the symbolism of baptism?
   a. Romans 6:4 "Therefore we are buried with him by baptism into death: that like as Christ was raise up from the dead by the glory of the Father, even so we also should walk in newness of life."
   b. Baptism is a symbol of Christ's death and resurrection.
   c. It is simply an act of living in obedience to Christ.
   d. Matthew 28:19-20 "Go ye therefore, and teach all nations, baptizing them in the name of the Father, and of the Son, and of the Holy Ghost: Teaching them to observe all things whatsoever I have commanded you: and lo, I am with you alway, even unto the end of the world. Amen."

What the Resurrection Guarantees
Romans 6:1-23

Introduction: Many events in the world have blest us. But there is no single event known in all the history of the human race which brought about such enormous change and revelation than the resurrection of our Lord Jesus Christ.

I Point: What His resurrection proves.
- a. There has been one Man whom death could not hold.
- b. The power of death has been broken by this Man.
- c. The earth could not keep, within its dark soil, the precious body of the Man from heaven.
- d. The power of death snapped, and Christ conquered death.

II Point: What His resurrection means to us.
- a. He proves His ability to raise us from the dead by delivering Himself from death.
- b. His death was as real as our death will ever be, and our deliverance will be as glorious as was His.
- c. By coming out of the tomb and fulfilling that promise, He assured us that all of His other words are equally true, and He is equally capable of fulfilling them.
- d. This means that when He said His blood was shed for the remission of sins, God forgives our sins through faith in His blood.
- e. This means that when He said He come down from heaven, He did indeed come down from heaven.
- f. This means that when He came to seek and to save that which was lost, He is able to save sinners unto the uttermost.
- g. This means that when He said He would come again and receive us unto Himself, that He actually will come again.
- h. The empty tomb is the seal and assurance of the reality of all Christ said, of all Christ did, and all of all Jesus is.

III Point: We are now to live a heavenly life.
- a. At the beginning, though none lived on the earth, He did have communion with heaven.
- b. As proof – the Son of God became the Son of Man. But as the Son of Man He was ever in communion with heaven. And yet, He lived a perfect human life while on earth. In other words, Christ lived on earth a heavenly life.

c. Therefore we are to "Set our affections on things above, not on things of the earth. (Colossians 3:2).
d. Our Father is in heaven. His children are to walk on earth as citizens of that heavenly country. (Hebrews 11:16, Philippians 3:20).
e. All these heavenly realities Christ has assured to us by His breaking off death's power over us. Through His resurrection, we have the guarantee of a like resurrection.
f. We have the guarantee of His life, of His Spirit, of His holiness, of His peace, and of His joy to be and to share with Him through all eternity.
e. I John 3:1-3 "BEHOLD, what manner of love the Father hath bestowed upon us, that we should be called the sons of God: therefore the world knoweth us not, because it knew him not. Beloved, now are we the sons of God, and it doth not yet appear what we shall be: but we know that, when he shall appear, we shall be like him; for we shall see him as He is. And every man that hath this hope in him purifieth himself, even as he is pure."

To Conquer the Capital "I"

Romans 7:1-25

Text: Romans 7:24 "O wretched man that I am! who shall deliver me from the body of this death?"

Introduction: To conquer self, to put capital "I" in its right place, is the problem we are all up against. And it is no new problem. It is as old as mankind.

With all our modern civilization, we have not changed a bit. Jerimiah 17:9 "The heart is deceitful above all things, and desperately wicked: who can know it?"

I Point: O wretched man.

    a. The apostle Paul realized his wretchedness.
    b. Romans 7:24 "O wretched man that I am!"
       He finds the wretchedness in himself.
    c. Romans 7:24 "...who shall deliver me?..."
       He realized his need for a deliverer.
    d. Romans 7:24 "...who shall deliver me from this body of death?" Or from this dead body?
       Illustration: In those days it was the custom that if someone had murdered a person, he then was tied to the dead body until he died with it.
       Ephesians 2:1 "And you hath he quickened who were dead in trespasses and sins."
    e. Romans 7:24 – According to God's Word you have that corruptible capital "I." That dead body of yours is hung around your neck starring you in the face at every turn in your walk.

II Point: How can I conquer this wretched man the capital "I".

    a. Romans 7:25 - Thanks be to God, who delivers me through Jesus Christ our Lord.
    b. The only remedy that will overcome the capital "I" is: I John 1:7 "...the blood of Jesus Christ his Son cleanseth us from all sin."

III Point: In contrast, if you like to be miserable, follow this:

How to be Perfectly Miserable by C. J. Sodergren.

1. Think about yourself.
2. Talk about yourself.
3. Use "I" as often as possible.
4. Mirror yourself continually in the opinion of others.
5. Listen greedily to what people say about you.
6. Expect to be appreciated.
7. Be suspicious.
8. Be jealous and envious.
9. Be sensitive to slights.
10. Never forgive a criticism.
11. Trust nobody but yourself.
12. Insist on consideration and respect.
13. Demand agreement with your own view on everything.
14. Sulk if people are not grateful to you for favors shown.
15. Never forget a service you may have rendered.
16. Be on the look-out for a good time for yourself.
17. Shirk your duties if you can.
18. Do as little as possible for others.
19. Love yourself supremely.
20. Be selfish.

And you will be perfectly miserable.

Conclusion: To not be miserable get right with God.

Romans 7:24-25 "O wretched man that I am! who shall deliver me from the body of this death? I thank God through Jesus Christ our Lord…"

The Spirit of Leadership
Romans 8:14-17

Text: Romans 8:14 "For as many as are led by the Spirit of God, they are the sons of God."

Introduction: Moses provides our first illustration of divinely imputed leadership mentioned in the scripture.

I Point: <u>Leadership is a gift</u>.
- a. Exodus 3:10 "Come now therefore, and I will send thee unto Pharaoh, that thou mayest bring forth my people the children of Israel out of Egypt."
  Application: What do we hear Moses say?
  Exodus 4:10 "And Moses said unto the LORD, O my Lord, I am not eloquent, neither heretofore, nor since thou hast spoken unto thy servant: but I am slow of speech, and of a slow tongue."
- b. Moses had no natural gift of leadership. He was rejected in his first effort to champion Israel.
- c. God gives His spirit of leadership.
  Exodus 4:2 "And the LORD said unto him, What is that in thine hand? And he said, A rod."
  Application: God uses what you have in your hand: a book, a saw, a hammer, a pot, a child, a pen, or whatever it may be, God will say to you, "What is that in your hand?"

II Point: <u>The Spirit of God comes upon leaders</u>.
- a. The Spirit is mentioned as coming upon certain individuals and they become leaders.

  1. <u>Gideon</u>:
     Judges 6:34 "But the Spirit of the LORD came upon Gideon, and he blew a trumpet:..." When he then blew the trumpet, all the children of Israel gathered together. And again when he blew the trumpet the victory was won.

  2. <u>David</u>:
     The Spirit of the Lord came mightily upon David and he led Israel to victory. He never lost a battle before or after he became King.

3. <u>The Prophets</u>.
   The Prophets were led by the Spirit as what to say and do.

4. <u>Philip</u>:
   The Spirit led Philip to the eunuch just when the time was ripe to lead him to Christ.
   Acts 8:26 "And the angel of the Lord spake unto Philip, saying, Arise, and go toward the south unto the way that goeth down from Jerusalem unto Gaza, which is desert."
   Application: Philip could have objected to go to a desert, because he was at that time preaching the gospel.

5. <u>Peter:</u>
   Acts 12:5-17 - In prison Peter was led by the Spirit out of prison.

6. <u>Even our Lord</u>:
   Matthew 4:1 "THEN was Jesus led up of the Spirit into the wilderness to be tempted of the devil."

Conclusion: Oh that this Spirit would come upon us as a church. Oh that this same Spirit would come upon us individually. What a difference that would be in our lives and ministry for Christ.
Romans 8:14 "For as many as are led by the Spirit of God, they are the sons of God."

Justification – Part II
Romans 8:28-39

Text: Romans 8:33 "Who shall lay anything to the charge of God's elect? It is God that justifieth."

Introduction: There are seven points on justification.

1. Justification by whom?
2. The source of justification.
3. The ground of justification.
4. The price of justification.
5. How to appropriate justification.
6. What is the proof of justification?
7. What is the fruit of justification?

I Point: Justification by whom? – God.
   a. Romans 8:33 "...It is God that justifieth."
      Believers are justified by Him who rules the universe.
      Illustration: The Supreme Court.
   b. Who is to be justified?
      i. The sinner.
      ii. The sinner that believes.
      iii. The sinner that accepts the justification.

II Point: The source of justification – Grace.
   a. Romans 3:24 "Being justified freely by his grace through the redemption that is in Christ Jesus."
   b. Ephesians 2:8-9 "For by grace are ye saved through faith; and that not of yourselves: it is a gift of God: Not of works, lest any man should boast."
   c. Titus 3:7 "That being justified by his grace, we should be made heirs according to the hope of eternal life."
      Application: That is why so many people reject salvation, because it is a gift. They want to earn it.

III Point: The ground of justification – Obedience.
   a. Romans 5:19 "For as by one man's disobedience many were made sinners, so by the obedience of one shall many be made righteous."
   b. Obedience unto death. Philippians 2:8 "And being found in fashion as a man, he humbled himself, and became obedient unto death, even the death of the cross."
      Application: The ground of condemnation is disobedience. The ground of justification is obedience. How much sorrow comes from disobedience.

IV Point: <u>The price of justification – Christ's blood</u>.
   a. Romans 5:9 "Much more then, being now justified by his blood, we shall be saved from wrath through him."
   b. Ephesians 1:7 "In whom we have redemption through his blood, the forgiveness of sins, according to the riches of his grace;"
   c. Ephesians 2:9 "Not of works, lest any man should boast." But how people try to do it on their own.

V Point: <u>How to appropriate justification - By faith</u>.
   a. Romans 5:1 "THEREFORE being justified by faith, we have peace with God through our Lord Jesus Christ:"
   b. Galatians 2:16 "Knowing that a man is not justified by the works of the law, but by the faith of Jesus Christ,..."
   c. Acts 13:39 "And by him all that believe are justified from all things,..."

VI Point: <u>What is the proof of my justification? -The Resurrection</u>.
   a. Romans 4:25 "Who was delivered for our offences, and was raised again for our justification."
   b. Romans 6:9 "Knowing that Christ being raised from the dead dieth no more; death hath no more dominion over him."
   c. There is no salvation to anyone unless he believes in the resurrection of Jesus Christ.

VII Point: <u>What is the fruit of justification? – Works</u>.
   a. James 2:20 "...faith without works is dead?"
   b. Matthew 5:16 "Let your light so shine before men, that they may see your good works, and glorify your Father which is in heaven."
   c. Titus 3:8 "...they which have believed in God might be careful to maintain good works. These things are good and profitable unto men."

*This is Part II of Justification.
Part I of Justification - Romans 5:1-21, page 290.

The Five Principles of Discipleship
Romans 10:1-15

Text: Romans 10:13 "For whosoever shall call upon the name of the Lord shall be saved."

Introduction:
- 1st God's purpose.
- 2nd God's plan.
- 3rd God's provision.
- 4th God's power.
- 5th God's price.

I Point: <u>God's Purpose</u>.
- a. God's purpose and heart's desire is that all men should be saved.
  Romans 10:13 "For whosoever shall call upon the name of the Lord shall be saved."
  II Peter 3:9 "The Lord is not slack concerning his promise, as some men count slackness; but is longsuffering to us-ward, not willing that any should perish, but that all should come to repentance."
- b. People are not saved just for show.
  1. God does not save a business man just to show that He can save a business man.
  2. Neither does he save a college student just to make him or her an exhibition to the other college students.
  3. If that would be the case, then, that would be like training a soldier for battle, and then send him home.
  4. God's purpose is to hold you, brother and sister, responsible for the unsaved around you.
- c. The challenge to us Christians.
  1. Romans 10:14 "How then shall they call on him in whom they have not believed? and how shall they believe in him of whom they have not heard? and how shall they hear without a preacher?"
  2. God's promises – Acts 1:8 "But ye shall receive power, after that the Holy Ghost is come upon you: and ye shall be witnesses unto me both in Jerusalem, and in all Judaea, and in Samaria, and unto the uttermost part of the earth."
  3. Application: God expects that the gospel should go out from us as living water goes out of the fountain.

4. If you don't give out, you soon become as a stagnant pool or a dead church.
5. God's purpose for you folks here is that you may see the need around you.
d. Let us just for a moment look around, and what do we see?
1. There are unsaved everywhere. There are whole towns and villages without a born again person in them.
Illustration: Little boys and girls ask, "You are cursing when you say the name of Christ?"
2. Now shall we look a little farther into the foreign lands, and what do we see?
There are millions upon millions of them who have never heard these sweet words in Romans 10:13 "For whosoever shall call upon the name of the Lord shall be saved."
3. Let me give you a few figures which were given 3 years ago.
1st There are 300,000,000 benighted in superstition confusions and demon haunted.
2nd There are 210,000,000 swept in idolatry and Hinduism.
3rd There are 300,000,000 who are crowding the sorrowful temples of Buddha.
4th There are 220,000,000 in the ugly grip of Mohamedism.
5th There are 25,000,000 falling down before the shrine of Shintoism.
6th There are 158,000,000 groping in the fear hunted darkness of fetishism. (A Portuguese idol).
7th And there are 270,000,000 shadowing beneath the sinister cloak of Catholicism.
8th There are 300,000,000 weeping widows in India, alas, little girls from the age of six years and up. These helpless little children are being blamed for the death of their old husbands. They would bury them alive with their old dead husband or burn them at the stake.
9th There are 200,000,000 incurable lepers in Nigeria.
10th There are 65,000 blind people in Nigeria alone.
11th There are 12,000,000 Jews shattered through the world, who as yet, reject Christ as their Messiah. Yet, it is God's purpose and heart's desire that all should be saved.

Mark 16:15 "...Go ye into all the world, and preach the gospel to every creature."
4. Do you realize that there are 250,000 people dying every day? (That is 3 per second).
5. Oh, believer, we are before God with blood dripping from our hands.
God said in Ezekiel 33:8 "When I say unto the wicked, O wicked man, thou shalt surely die; if thou dost not speak to warn that wicked from his ways, that wicked man shall die in his iniquity; but his blood will I require at thine hand."

II Point: God's Plan.

a. To His disciples He said - Mark 1:17 "...Come ye after me, and I will make you to become fishers of men."
b. To Moses He said - Exodus 3:10 "Come now therefore, and I will send thee unto Pharaoh, that thou mayest bring forth my people the children of Israel out of Egypt."
c. To Joshua He said - Joshua 1:2 "...arise, go over this Jordan, thou and all this people, unto the land which I do give unto them, even to the children of Israel."
d. To Gideon He said - Judges 6:12 "...The LORD is with thee, thou mighty man of valour." Judges 6:14 "...Go in this thy might, and thou shalt save Israel from the hand of the Midianites: have not I sent thee?"

Application: If God gives an unusual order, He also has the plan to see you through.

III Point: God's Provision.

a. Philippians 4:13 "I can do all things through Christ which strengtheneth me."
b. Philippians 4:19 "But my God shall supply all your need according to his riches in glory by Christ Jesus."
c. Matthew 28:18-20 "...All power is given into me in heaven and in the earth. Go ye therefore, and teach all nations, baptizing them in the name of the Father, and of the Son, and of the Holy Ghost: Teaching them to observe all things whatsoever I have commanded you: and, lo, I am with you alway, even unto the end of the world. Amen."

IV Point: God's Power.

    a. Daniel 11:32 "...but the people that do know their God shall be strong, and do exploits."

    b. All these did exploits for God: Abel, Enoch, Noah, Abraham, Sara, Isaac, Jacob, Joseph, Moses, Joshua Gideon, David.

V Point: God's Price.

    a. John 12:24 "Verily, verily, I say unto you, Except a corn of wheat fall into the ground and die, it abideth alone: but if it die, it bringeth forth much fruit."

    b. God's price demands not a creed, not a church, not a method, but a life unto death.

    c. Romans 12:1-2 "I BESEECH you therefore, brethren, by the mercies of God, that ye present your bodies a living sacrifice, holy, acceptable unto God, which is your reasonable service. And be not conformed to this world: but be ye transformed by the renewing of your mind, that ye may prove what is that good, and acceptable, and perfect, will of God."

The Living Sacrifice
Romans 12 1-2

Introduction: The book of Romans from the very first chapter teaches us that there is nothing good in us: that is in the flesh. I therefore believe that Romans is one of the most helpful books in the Bible, for we cannot be a living sacrifice unto God until we have learned the fact that there is no good thing in us. As long as we think we are somebody, when we are nothing, we are deceived, and of no help to anybody.

I Point: Living Sacrifice.

a. I beseech you therefore:

1. Why therefore? It is "therefore" because, there is no other way.
2. Now, a living sacrifice is a peculiar sacrifice. A living sacrifice is one that has been sacrificed once and raised again.
3. II Corinthians 7:1-3 - It has died and been made alive.
Paul said to the Corinthian Church, II Corinthians 7:3 "...ye are in our hearts to die and live with you." He is coming to die and live with them. He did not say he was going to live and die with them, but I am coming over that we are all going to die and then live together.
4. Here is a living sacrifice, a sacrifice that has died and been brought alive again.
5. In other words, Romans 12:1 "I BECEECH you therefore, brethren, (who have died and been made alive again) by the mercies of God, that ye present your bodies a living sacrifice, holy, acceptable unto God, which is your reasonable service."
6. We are to be a life that is scarified with Christ and has the resurrected life in Christ.
7. Galatians 2:20 "I am crucified with Christ: nevertheless I live; yet not I, but Christ liveth in me: and the life which I now live in the flesh I live by the faith of the Son of God, who loved me, and gave himself for me."

II Point: Resolutions.

    a. Good resolutions made in the flesh are no more than eyewash. There is nothing to them, and they don't last at all.
    b. Good natural gifts, such as leadership gifts are a gift of great power. Some people have power in their words. Some people have a personality to sway, to draw, and to entice others. By these gifts they can present themselves good, and respectable before men; and, in a spiritual realm, they can lead people to Christ as far as they have gone themselves.
    c. But what God wants is a living sacrifice, one that died to self, and to all natural powers and abilities, and is now living in Christ.
    d. A dead offering cannot be presented. The Lord will not give His gifts to men that have not as yet died and been resurrected with Christ.
        ii. First, is your death to self?
        iii. Second, is your life with Christ in His resurrection?
        iv. Third, what is your sacrifice?
        v. Forth, what is your reasonable service?

III Point: Transformed.

    a. First, you must be conformed into Christ's death.
    b. Unless you are made conformable into His death you cannot be transformed into His life. A transformation comes after resurrection, and a resurrection only follows a death and burial.
    c. It seems as if we naturally are born conformed to this world, and Christians can again go back to this world's conformity. Paul therefore warns us: "And be not conformed to this world: but be ye transformed by the renewing of your mind, that ye may prove what is that good, and acceptable, and perfect, will of God." (Romans 12:2). A Christian's life is not much of a life until you begin to enter into the blessings of that life. Until you begin to receive the things that are yours.
    d. You were made conformable to the death of Christ; but now, by ye transformed

1. In other words, be not again conformed to the schemes of this world. The world is full of schemes.
2. Romans 8:1 "THERE is therefore now no condemnation to them which are in Christ Jesus, who walk not after the flesh, but after the Spirit."
3. So, we have an obligation not to think more highly of ourselves than we ought to think, but think soberly about this because it is an important matter.
4. Souls are at stake! The Lord is coming again soon! You and I have an obligation to face. Honestly, say, "Lord, I want to enter into that place. I want to have my life transfigured. I am tired of trying to reform it. I want it transformed as Christ was on the mountain of Transfiguration." All kinds of public attractions to bring people to church are not a substitute for God's way, as when you and I are being transfigured before the world as these who have been with Christ.

Sermon Outlines for the Book of I Corinthians

Christians, What are you building?
I Corinthians 3:1-10

Introduction: We want not merely Christians, but healthy, strong, happy, well-established and well instructed Christians. Our aim is that they may be presented perfect in Christ Jesus.

Illustration A great bell tower, after standing for many years, cracked and fell. It was later found out that shady materials had been built in where it could not be seen. What a lesson to us Christians.

What kind of materials are you using to build upon this foundation which is Christ Jesus? We don't build the foundation. Jesus Christ is the foundation - The Rock. We just build upon that Rock.

I Corinthians 3:12 "Now if any man build upon this foundation gold, silver, precious stones, wood, hay, stubble;"

I Point: The foundation.
  a. I Corinthians 3:11 "For other foundation can no man lay than that is laid, which is Jesus Christ."
The construction goes on. The foundation is laid. The material is at your disposal. Just help yourself.
I Corinthians 3:12 says you can pick from, gold, silver, precious stones, or wood, hay, and stubble. Which material would you like to build with?
Your time to build is measured out to you from the day that you accepted Christ until the day you die. Your structure then remains standing till that day.
I Corinthians 3:13 "Every man's work shall be made manifest: for the day shall declare it, because it shall be revealed by fire; and the fire shall try every man's work of what sort it is."

  b. The day of settlement.
I Corinthians 3:14-15 "If any man's works abide which he hath built thereupon, he shall receive a reward. If any man's work shall be burned, he shall suffer loss: but he himself shall be saved; yet so as by fire."
    1. Salvation is free.
    2. Rewards are earned.
    3. Salvation is present.
    4. Rewards are future.

II Point: <u>The structure then fitted together</u>.
- a. We are the temple of God. I Corinthians 3:16 "Know ye not that ye are the temple of God, and that the Spirit of God dwelleth in you?"
  Illustration: After we have been tried in the fire, we than will fit into the great structure as a block prepared and polished to fit in firmly, fitted together to a holy habitation of our Lord.
  Ephesians 2:21-22 "In whom all the building fitly framed together groweth unto an holy temple in the Lord: In whom ye also are builded together for an habitation of God through the Spirit."
- b. The Holy Spirit takes these polished and tried blocks and fitly forms them together.
  There is no more hammering, no more chiseling or pounding heard in the process of the building. They are fitly framed together by the Holy Spirit.

Conclusion:
1. Are you one of this construction crew?
2. Are you building on the foundation Christ Jesus?
3. What materials are you using?
   - a. Gold, silver, and precious stones? Or wood, hay and stubble?
   - b. The day will declare it. You choose!

Purge Out the Old Leaven
I Corinthians 5:1-8

Theme: I Corinthians 5:7 "Purge out therefore the old leaven, that ye may be a new lump…"

Introduction: This chapter, as we all know, talks of the gross sins such as immorality. I do not mean thereby that that particular sin is present among us just because I chose to preach from this chapter and text; but let us see if there is not even in us a little of old leaven that would spoil our sweetness with Christ.

I Point: Uncovers sin.
   a. I Corinthians 5:1 - Goes down to the reported sin of fornication.
   b. He associates this awful sin with pride. I Corinthians 5:2 "…ye are puffed up,…"
   c. I Corinthians 5:3 – He proves to them that the whole church is in sympathy with this sin.
   Application: If you are in sympathy with someone that has sinned, and try to hide or cover him, you then are equal with the sinner.

II Point: Judgment upon the sinner and Church.
   a. I Corinthians 5:5 "To deliver such an one unto Satan for the destruction of the flesh, that the spirit may be saved in the day of the Lord Jesus."
   Application: Many people suffer untold agonies because of some sin.
   1. Remember Jacob of old. (Genesis 32:24-3).
   2. Remember Samson. (Judges 16:21).
   3. Remember Nebuchadnezzar, how for seven years he had to be a beast. (Daniel 4:28-37).

III Point: God's challenge
   a. I Corinthians 5:7 "Purge out therefore the old leaven, that ye may be a new lump…"
   Application: They were not to spare either son or daughter, but "Purge out."
   b. Why have we so much trouble in our churches today? Because we, as a church, compromise and excuse sin in our own self and in our loved ones.

   Illustration: The leaven puffs up the dough, but when the baker gives it a punch, down it goes.

   Illustration: A man shot a bird because it could not fly very high and afterward found out it had a chain on its foot to hold him back.

Conclusion: So it is in your life?

Covet the Best Gifts
I Corinthians 12:1-31

Text: I Corinthians 12:31 "But covet earnestly the best gifts: and yet shew I unto you a more excellent way."

Introduction: With many Christians it is the lack of a real desire for the outpouring of the Holy Spirit. They are satisfied with a barren, cold, fruitless, dry, worldly, sickly, unyielded and defeated Christian life.

I Point: <u>Will God pour out the Holy Spirit on anybody? No!</u>
   a. A person first must be saved.
   b. He must be living the life of a Christian.
   c. He must have a desire for the person of the Holy Spirit.
   d. He must covet this better gift.
   e. He must, as it were, thirst for the infilling of the Holy Spirit.
   Application: John 7:37 "In the last day, that great day of the feast, Jesus stood and cried, saying, If any man thirst, let him come unto me, and drink."
   Illustration: Mary sat at the feet of Jesus.
   Luke 10:42 "...Mary hath chosen that good part, which shall not be taken away from her."
   Application: When you and I sit down at the feet of Jesus, it is then that you will feel the filling.

II Point: <u>Will God give the Holy Spirit to Christians who have left all for Jesus sake? Yes!</u>
   a. Psalm 84:11 "...no good thing will he withhold from them that walk uprightly."
   Illustration: The giving of the Holy Spirit is, in other words, that our "will" will be given over to the guidance of the Holy Spirit.
   b. Why is it then that so many Christians have not the filling of the Holy Spirit?
   Application: Simply because there is something in their life they will not give up.
   Application: You may be a minister and hold a large church; or, you even might be a missionary having forsaken all: home, country etc.; Or you may be a very fine person in the community; and yet, if there is something the Holy Spirit points His finger at for you to give up, unless you give it up, you will be one of the most miserable people in the world, and your life is barren.

c. No desire or thirst will there be in a life that has not cut the shore lines, even though you may be a wonderful person.
Application: The daily condemnation you feel in your heart will drown the desires to covet the best gifts.

III Point: <u>May I suggest a few simple rules for receiving such an outpouring of the Holy Spirit.</u>
1. Be sure you are saved.
2. Make a complete surrender.
3. Ask for the cleansing by the blood of Jesus Christ upon all your life, from all your sins.
   Illustration: The priests had to have the blood on their right ear, thumb and great toe.
   That meant that they had to listen to God's commandments, (ear); act according to the wishes of the Holy Spirit; (thumb); and walk in His way, (great toe).
4. Ask for the Holy Spirit to come upon you.
   Matthew 7:11 "…how much more shall your Father which is in heaven give good things to them that ask him?"
   " Ye have not because ye ask not." (James 4:2).
5. Believing and expecting God's blessings are conditional upon expectant faith.
   Illustration: Tell the story of the Christian lad that was told what a wonderful system the telegraph would be to receive answers the same day you ask.
   "When the wires in Shetland were being erected, a Christian boy stood looking at the wires on the poles, and a shrewd man of business said to the boy, "What a wonderful thing! When the wires are finished you will be able to send a message two hundred miles or more, and get an answer within an hour."
   "Nothing very wonderful about that." said the lad.
   "Why," said the keen man of the world, "Do you know anything more wonderful?"
   I should think I do." answered the lad.
   "What is it?" asked the man.
   "Did you ever hear of people getting an answer before they send it?" The lad said,
   "What do you mean?" asked the man.
   "I only mean that Isaiah 65:24 says, 'And it shall come to pass, that before they call, I will answer; and while they are yet speaking, I will hear.'" (Unknown)
   John 15:8 "Herein is my Father glorified, that ye bear much fruit…"
   I Corinthians 12:31 "But covet earnestly the best gifts: and yet shew I unto you a more excellent way."

True Love
I Corinthians 13:1-13

Introduction: In the thirteenth chapter of I Corinthians, Paul gives us this relationship of love to Christian life and service. This is especially true because the term love is used in so many different ways and often so misused. Let us practice "heavenly love" upon this divine gift of love.

I Point: <u>Charity – (Love)</u>. (I Corinthians 13:1-3).
  a. "Though I speak with the tongues of men and of angels, and have not charity (love), I am become as sounding brass, or a tinkling cymbal.
  And though I have the gift of prophecy, and understand all mysteries, and all knowledge; and though I have all faith, so that I could remove mountains, and have not charity (love), I am nothing.
  And though I bestow all my goods to feed the poor, and though I give my body to be burned, and have not charity (love), it profiteth me nothing."
  b. <u>The Lover's Love</u>.
  This love is intense and dazzling, surmounted with an halo dimming all others around about. This is known as the most selfish love of all natures of love.
  c. <u>The Friendship Love</u>.
  This love supplies understanding and sympathy as well as help in time of need.
  d. <u>Family Love</u>.
  This is an expanding love, a growing love, a sharing love. Regardless how many children there are born into the family there is an equal love for them all. Yet not reaching to the love of man and wife.
  e. <u>Enemies Love</u>.
  The principal element in this love is a concern for their eternal welfare. It is the most meager of all loves.
  f. <u>The Love of God</u>.
  This is the love of a heavenly Father for His children, inspiring in us that trustful love for Him. We are most secure when in His care.
  The love of the bridegroom is mentioned in His love for the church. Ephesians 5:25 "...even as Christ also loved the church, and gave himself for it;"

His love is Proverbs 18:24 "...a friend that sticketh closer than a brother."

He loved His enemies enough to die for them.

Romans 5:6 "For when we were yet without strength, in due time Christ died for the ungodly."

The expression "the love of God" becomes more clear. Romans 8:38-39 "For I am persuaded, that neither death, nor life, nor angels, nor principalities, nor powers, nor things present, nor things to come, Nor height, nor depth, nor any other creature, shall be able to separate us from the love of God, which is in Christ Jesus our Lord."

All true love is sent from God. I John 4:10 "Herein is love, not that we loved God, but that he loved us,..."

g. <u>True Love</u>.

All true love must have confidence and trust in the one loved.

True love has a desire to serve. Where love is true, we have a deep longing to serve.

h. <u>Sacrificial love</u>.

John 15:13 "Greater love hath no man than this, that a man lay down his life for his friends."

The Christians' Circle of Testimony
I Corinthians 15:1-6

Introduction: There are five circles that we would like to look at; from the border-line Christians to the very bosom Christians. There seem to be a great number of border-line Christians, but oh so few bosom Christians.

I Point: The Five Hundred: (I Corinthians 15:1-6).
I Corinthians 15:6 "After that, he was seen of about five hundred brethren at once;..." The five hundred were "brethren" that had followed Him when He was on the earth. They were believers in Christ, and enjoyed the blessing they received from His hands.
Application: They represent that large body of the redeemed.

II Point: The Seventy: (Luke 10:1-11).
Luke 10:1 "After these things the Lord appointed other seventy also, and sent them two and two before his face into every city and place, whither he himself would come." These were appointed by our Lord for certain work and fully instructed for it. So these are of the circle of the large body, but, oh, so few out of the total flock. Only 70 out of 500 will do any kind of work for the master.
Illustration: Charles Haddon Spurgeon said one time when asked of his success. He said, "Do not give me the credit, I have 100 evangelists in my church, who are busy every day of the week, bringing people to the services and then praying them through."

III Point: The twelve: Mark 3:13-19).
Mark 3:14 "And he ordained twelve, that they should be with him, and that he might send them forth to preach." These were selected to be with our Lord and to preach the Word. They were those on whom He could depend and could use, and with whom He could have a close fellowship, a circle of fellowship in time of trials. These are they that would take beatings and imprisonment for Christ.
Illustration: Moody sent out a young man to preach the gospel. However, he came back and said, "They do not listen to me." Moody asked, "Have they spit on you yet?" "No!" answered the young man. "Then go out and preach until they do."

IV Point: <u>The Three: Matthew 17:19</u>).

Matthew 17:1-2 "And after six days Jesus taketh Peter, James, and John his brother, and bringeth them up into an high mountain apart. And was transfigured before them: and his face did shine as the sun, and his raiment was white as the light." Out of the twelve were chosen three for a still closer fellowship. These three accompanied our Lord to the place where He manifested His deity – at the transfiguration. What a privilege.

Application: Can God trust you to a close fellowship with Him, or are you just a border-line Christian? Just living for the loaves and fishes, but not having any close fellowship with Christ.

V Point: <u>The Bosom Christian</u>:

John 13:23 "Now there was leaning on Jesus' bosom one of his disciples, whom Jesus loved." The bosom Christian is one that shows unto us that inner circle of love. When our Lord was arrested, all fled, but the Apostle John. We need not wonder why we find 24 times the word love is mentioned in the fourth chapter of the 1st Epistle of John. It was he whose head rested on our Saviour's bosom.

Conclusion: Have you allowed the Holy Spirit to strip your life bare of the false satisfaction of pious pretense? In what circle do you find yourself, my friend?

In Vain

I Corinthians 15:1-21

Introduction: - It is a solemn fact that much that passes for religion, devotion, and faith is in vain.

I Point: Believing in vain - if:
  a. I Corinthians 15:2 "By which also ye are saved, if ye keep in memory what I preached unto you, unless ye have believed in vain." Where the foundations are destroyed, we have no rest for our faith.
  b. Faith in our own opinion is in vain.
  c. We must have the Word of God (Christ). We cannot build on men's ideas, or it is in vain.
  d. James 2:2 – Faith must be a living principle.

II Points: Christ died in vain - if:
  a. Galatians 2:21 "I do not frustrate the grace of God: for if righteousness come by the law, then Christ is dead in vain."
  b. This is an awful thought. Is Calvary of no avail?
  c. No, not in the least.

III Point: Grace received in vain - if:
  a. II Corinthians 6:1 "... ye receive not the grace of God in vain."
  b. Those who profess to be saved by grace and continue in sin have received the grace of God in vain.
  c. Those who rejoice in grace and show none to others have received the grace of God in vain.
  d. That would be like the servant who was forgiven by the king, but then went out and refused to forgive a fellow servant. (Matthew 18:23-35).

IV Point: Worship in vain - if:
  a. Matthew 15:9 "But in vain they do worship me, teaching for doctrines the commandments of men."
  b. Worship must be in Spirit and in truth.
  c. Men like to set a doctrine of their own and then teach it as a commandment of God.
  But God puts it as rebellion and labour done in vain.
  Illustration: The idolater worship, such as Romanism, or any other formality, it is worship done in vain.

The Firstfruits of the Resurrection
I Corinthians 15:1-23

Text: I Corinthians 15:20 "But now is Christ risen from the dead, and become the firstfruits of them that slept."
I Corinthians 15:23 "But every man in his own order: Christ the firstfruits; afterward they that are Christ's at his coming."

Introduction: Easter is not known by many people why or what took place on this particular day.

I Point: Christ died and rose again.

- a. I Corinthians 15:3-4 "For I delivered unto you first of all that which I also received, how that Christ died for our sins according to the scripture; And that he was buried, and that he rose again the third day according to scripture."
  Application: For 4000 years it was the grave that had the victory. No one ever come out, when once in the grave.
  Application: Satan's only aim was to get his victims into the grave. It was never known to him that any could escape.
- b. Christ was the firstfruits of the resurrection. (The first resurrected from the grave.)

II Point: Without the resurrection of Christ there is no hope for mankind.

- a. I Corinthians 15:17 "And if Christ be not raised, your faith is vain; ye are yet in your sins."
    1. I Peter 1:3 "Blessed be the God and Father of our Lord Jesus Christ, which according to his abundant mercy hath begotten us again unto a lively hope by the resurrection of Jesus Christ from the dead."
    2. Romans 10:9 "That if thou shalt confess with thy mouth the Lord Jesus, and shalt believe in thine heart that God hath raised him from the dead, thou shalt be saved."
    3. John 11:25 "...I am the resurrection, and the life: he that believeth in me, though he were dead, yet shall he live:" Christ the firstfruits of the resurrection.
- b. His resurrection is necessary for our security.
    1. Romans 8:34 "Who is he that condemneth? It is Christ that died, yea, rather, that is risen again, who is even at the right hand of God, who also maketh intercession for us."

      2. Hebrews 7:25 "Wherefore he is able also to save them to the uttermost that come unto God by him, seeing he ever liveth to make intersession for them."
      3. I John 2:1-2 "...if any man sin, we have an advocate with the Father, Jesus Christ the righteous: And he is the propitiation for our sins:..."
  c. His resurrection is necessary for our resurrection.
      1. I Thessalonians 4:14 "For if we believe that Jesus died and rose again, even so them also which sleep in Jesus will God bring with him."

Conclusion: Christ the firstfruits of the resurrection.
1. If Christ were not risen there would be no salvation.
2. If Christ were not risen there would be no safety on earth.
3. If Christ were not risen there would be no resurrection for us.

The Glorified Resurrected Body
I Corinthians 15:51-53

Text: I Corinthians 15:51-52 "Behold, I shew you a mystery; We shall not all sleep, but we shall all be changed, In a moment, in the twinkling of an eye, at the last trump:..."

I Point: <u>The Rapture.</u>
- a. I Thessalonians 4:13-18
    - i. I Thessalonians 4:16 "...the dead in Christ shall rise first."
    - ii. I Thessalonians 4:17 "Then we which are alive and remain shall be caught up together with them in the clouds, to meet the Lord in the air:..."

II Point: <u>What will the resurrected or raptured body be like?</u>
- a. Resurrected means the "rising of that which is fallen."
    - i. I Corinthians 15:37 "And that which thou sowest, thou soweth not that body that shall be,..."
    I Corinthians 15:42 "...It is sown in corruption; it is raised in incorruption:"
    - ii. Died mortal and raised immortal.
    I Corinthians 15:44 "It is sown a natural body; it is raised a spiritual body."
    - iii. I Corinthians 15:40 - Sown terrestrial (Earthly).
    Raised celestial (Heavenly).
- b. There is a great difference between eternal existence and eternal life and immortality.
All people have an eternal existence, but only the saved ones have eternal life.

III Point: <u>What will be the appearance of these bodies?</u>
- a. Incorruptible
Immortal
Glorified
In Power
- b. Like the resurrected glorified body of Christ.
- c. That is, it will have the like attributes, and the like characteristics as Christ's resurrected body had.
Philippians 3:21 "Who shall change our vile body, that it may be fashioned like unto his glorious body, according to the working whereby he is able even to subdue all things unto himself."

- d. I John 3:2 "Beloved, now are we the sons of God, and it doth not yet appear what we shall be: but we know that, when he shall appear, we shall be like him; for we shall see him as he is."
    Psalm 17:15 "As for me, I will behold thy face in righteousness: I shall be satisfied, when I awake, with thy likeness."
- e. What was Christ's body like?
    1. John 1:14 "And the Word was made flesh,..." It was a real body.
- f. Christ appeared after the resurrection 10 times.
    1. Matthew 28:9-10 "And as they went to tell his disciples, behold, Jesus met them, saying, All hail. And they came and held him by the feet, and worshipped him. Then said Jesus unto them, Be not afraid: go tell my brethren that they go into Galilee, and there shall they see me."
- g. Christ's was recognized.
    John 20:16 "Jesus saith unto her, Mary. She turned herself, and saith unto him, Rabboni; which is to say, Master."
    John 20:28 "And Thomas answered and said unto him, My Lord and my God."
    Luke 24:41-43 "...he said unto them, Have ye here any meat? And they gave him a piece of a broiled fish, and of an honeycomb. And he took it, and did eat before them."
    There is no blood recorded. The blood is the earthly life.
    There is no blood needed in a glorified body.

IV Point: What ages of people are entitled to the glorified bodies?
- a. Luke 20:36 – All ages. "Neither can they die any more: for they are equal unto the angels; and are the children of God, being the children of the resurrection."
    There is nowhere in the Bible that there is any difference between man and woman. There is no marriage in heaven.
- b. All infants that have died will be resurrected. All the infants not born and who died in the womb will be resurrected in power.

Conclusion: Are your looking forward to the glorified body?

Sermon Outlines from the Book of II Corinthians

The Face of Jesus
II Corinthians 4:1-7

Text: II Corinthians 4:6 "For God, who commanded the light to shine out of darkness, hath shined in our hearts, to give the light of the knowledge of the glory of God in the face of Jesus Christ."

Introduction: The Bible gives us the most vivid photograph of the face of Jesus, than any other picture ever seen, of some individual.

We read that in the art galleries of Rome in the palace of the Vatican, there are walls of inspiring pictures on either side and on all sides. It is to be said, "Wonder of Wonders." For days you could stand and look at the faces and expression painted by the world's greatest artists who tried to picture for us the face of Christ the Lord.

But when you begin to look in the Bible and draw your own conclusion of His face, you will find more "Wonder of Wonders" than in the galleries of the Vatican.

I Point: <u>A Sad face</u>.
- a. Yes, the face of Jesus was a sad face, sometimes.
    - i. Sad because of man's deafness to His Word.
    - ii. Sad because of man's ungratefulness.
    - iii. Sad because of unresponsiveness.
    - iv. Sad because of blindness to the beauty of His life.
    - v. Sad because of the fact that He knew that "The heart is deceitful above all things, and desperately wicked: who can know it?" (Jeremiah 17:9).
    - vi. His face was not a sad face that testified to his own hurt, but sad for others.

II Point: <u>A shining Face</u>.
- a. Yes, the face of Jesus was a shining face, sometimes.
  Matthew 17:1-2 "And after six days Jesus taketh Peter, James, and John his brother, and bringeth them up into an high mountain apart, And was transfigured before them: and His face did shine as the sun, and his raiment was white as the light."
- b. This mountain of transfiguration was 9,200 feet above sea level, and there he showed to the disciples the express image of his person. Hebrews 1:3 "Who being the brightness of his glory, and the express image of his person, and upholding all things by the word of his power,..."
- c. Revelation 1:1-18 - We see, through John on the isle of Patmos, the face of Jesus. Revelation 1:16 "...and his countenance was as the sun shineth in his strength."

d. And again we see the face revealed unto us by the Apostle Paul. Acts 9:3-5 "...suddenly there shined round about him a light from heaven: And he fell to the earth, and heard a voice saying unto him, Saul, Saul, why persecutest thou me? And he said, Who art thou, Lord? And the Lord said, I am Jesus whom thou persecutest:..."

III Point: <u>A stained face.</u>
   a. Yes, the face of Jesus was a stained face.
   In Bethany we see the face stained with tears when He saw Martha and Mary weeping over the death of Lazarus their brother. John 11:35 "Jesus wept."
   b. Also we see Jesus weeping when he looks over Jerusalem. Luke 19:41 "And when he was come near, he beheld the city, and wept over it,"
   c. Again we see Jesus weeping in the garden of Gethsemane. Luke 22:44 "And being in an agony he prayed more earnestly: and his sweat was as it were great drops of blood falling down to the ground."
   d. We see His loving face stained with tears, stained with blood, and stained with spit. Mark 15:19 "And they smote him on the head with a reed, and did spit upon him,..." Isaiah 50:6 "...I hid not my face from shame and spitting."

IV Point: <u>A smitten face.</u>
   a. Yes, the face of Jesus was a smitten face.
   The oldest prophet, Isaiah, 800 years before the birth of Christ wrote, Isaiah 50:6 "I gave my back to the smiters, and my cheeks to them that plucked off the hair: I hid not my face from shame and spitting."
   b. No wonder in Isaiah 52 we find these words: Isaiah 52:14 "...his visage was so marred more than any man,..."

V Point: <u>A set face.</u>
   a. Jesus set his face "like a flint" toward the cross of Calvary, where he was to give His body to the nail.
   b. Isaiah 53:10 "...make his soul an offering of sin,..."
   c. Isaiah 50:7 "...therefore have I set my face like a flint, and I know that I shall not be ashamed."
   d. Isaiah 53:10 "Yet it pleased the LORD to bruise him; he hath put him to grief: when thou shalt make his soul an offering for sin,..."

VI Point: <u>A scorching face.</u>
   a. Matthew 16:13 "...Whom do men say that I the Son of man am?"
   b. With this same scorching expression of his face he drove the sellers out of the temple.
   c. John 2:15 "And when he had made a scourge of small cords, he drove them all out of the temple,..."
   d. And one day He will send all the abominable to hell with that same scorched face.

VII Point: <u>A seen face.</u>
   a. I John 3:2 "...it doth not yet appear what we shall be: but we know that, when he shall appear, we shall be like him; for we shall see him as he is."
   b. Revelation 1:7 "Behold, he cometh with clouds; and every eye shall see him,..."
   c. Psalm 17:15 "As for me, I will behold thy face in righteousness: I shall be satisfied, when I awake, with thy likeness."

The Authority of the Believer
II Corinthians 4:7
My Humanity & My Divinity

Introduction: Can a born again Christian say that they are divine? If so, upon whose authority? The answer is: Christ Jesus the divine person living in you reflects divinity through you. Therefore, you and your life can be divine, in as much as you would permit Christ to live and act in and through you. You cannot be divine without Christ.

We shall therefore take 9 different points of <u>humanity</u>, and run them parallel with 9 different points of <u>divinity,</u> and thus by God's Word see if we have any right to believe that we have divinity in our possession.

My Humanity
I Point: II Corinthians 4:7 "…in earthen vessels,…"
- a. 1st Thought: Genesis 2:7 – We are made out of dust, out of the ground.
- b. At Burial: earth to earth; dust to dust; ashes to ashes.
  2nd Thought: Galatians 5:17 "For the flesh lusteth against the Spirit, and the Spirit against the flesh:…"
- c. "…flesh and blood cannot inherit the kingdom of God; neither doth corruption inherit incorruption." (I Cor. 15:50).

My Divinity
I Point: John 15:16 - A chosen, ordained vessel.
- a. Acts 9:15 "…he is a chosen vessel unto me, to bear my name…"
- b. I Corinthians 1:27 "But God hath chosen the foolish things of the world to confound the wise; and God hath chosen the weak things of the world to confound the things which are mighty;"

....

My Humanity
II Point: II Corinthians 3:5 - Not sufficient of myself.
1st Thought: John 15:5 "…without me ye can do nothing."
A cast away, a withered branch, a fire brand.
Ephesians 2:1 "…dead in trespasses and sin:"
John 3:18 "…condemned already,…"
Ephesians 2:12 "…having no hope, and without God…"

My Divinity
II Point: II Corinthians 9:8 "…always having all sufficiency…"
1st Thought: II Corinthians 12:9 "…My grace is sufficient for thee: for my strength is made perfect in weakness."
- a. Ephesians 3:20 "Now unto him that is able to do exceeding abundantly above all that we ask or think,…"
- b. Philippians 4:19 "But my God shall supply all your need according to his riches in glory by Christ Jesus."

....

My Humanity
III Point: Romans 5:6-10 - An ungodly enemy, sinner, without strength.
    1st Thought: Ephesians 2:1 "...dead in trespasses and sin:"
    James 4:4 "...friendship of the world is enmity with God..."

My Divinity
III Point: Romans 5:6-10 - Justified, reconciled, saved, without condemnation.
    1st Thought: Justified, given rights again, as if you never had sinned.
    Isaiah 44:22 "I have blotted out, as a thick cloud, thy transgressions, for I have redeemed thee."
    Psalm 103:12 "As far as the east is from the west, so far hath he removed our transgressions from us."

....

My Humanity
IV Point: Romans 7:24 – A wretched old man flesh.
    1st Thought: Romans 7:24 "O wretched man that I am! who shall deliver me from the body of this death?"
    Illustration: In the days of Paul, the dead person was tied to the living murder and thus he had to die.

My Divinity
IV Point: Romans 6:4 - A new creature walking in newness of life.
    1st Thought: II Corinthians 5:17 "Therefore if any man be in Christ, he is a new creature: old things are passed away; behold, all things are become new."
    Romans 7:25 "I thank God through Jesus Christ our Lord." I might be freed from this dead body.

....

My Humanity
V Point: Judges 6:15 - The best in Father's house.
    1st Thought: Hebrew 12:16-17 - Take Esau for an example. A man in his humanity fleshly minded. Though he was the first born in the house, yet he was the last: a profane person.

My Divinity
V Point: Judges 6:14 - Mighty man of valor, to in this thy might.
    1st Thought: Take as an example Jacob of old and Gideon of old.

....

My Humanity
VI Point: Exodus 3:11 "Who am I, that I should go unto Pharaoh,..."

1st Thought: Here we have Moses in his unsaved state and in his humanity.

My Divinity
VI Point: Exodus 7:1 "...I have made thee a god to Pharaoh: and Aaron thy brother shall be thy prophet." Moses in divine power.

My Humanity
VII Point: Romans 3:23 "For all have sinned and come short of the glory of God;"

1st Thought: I Corinthians 1:29 "That no flesh should glory in his presence."

My Divinity
VII Point: II Corinthians 2:15 "For we are unto God a sweet savour of Christ..."

Colossians 1:27 "...Christ in you, the hope of glory:"

My Humanity
VIII Point: Ephesians 2:3 "...the children of wrath,..."

1st Thought: John 3:36 "...The wrath of God abideth on him."

John 3:18 "...he that believeth not is condemned already,..."

My Divinity
VIII Point: II Corinthians 6:18 - A child of God.

1st Thought: John 3:36 "He that believeth in the Son hath everlasting life:..."

John 3:18 "He that believeth on him is not condemned:..."

My Humanity
IX Point: Walking in this world. Ephesians 2:2 "...according to the prince of the power of the air, the spirit that now worketh in the children of disobedience:"

My Divinity
IX Point: Ephesians 2:4-6 - Seated in heavenly places in Christ.

1st Thought: Romans 8:16-17 Heirs; and joint-heirs with Christ.

Revelation 5:10 "And hath made us unto our God kings and priests: and we shall reign on the earth."

Serving Christ

II Corinthians 5:14-21

Text: II Corinthians 5:14 "For the love of Christ constraineth us..."

Introduction: According to our text we see that God means here, that if we have accepted Christ, we are no more our own. But we do entirely and altogether belong to our master, who gave his life for us.

The word constrains means to draw tight, to compel, to force to action, to secure by bonds, to hold back by force; to urge with power.

I Point: I Corinthians 5:14 "For the love of Christ constraineth us;..."
  a. The love of Christ constrained us to accept Him.
  b. The love of Christ constraineth us to live for Him.
  c. Matthew 6:24 "No man can sever two masters: for either he will hate the one, and love the other; or else he will hold to the one, and despise the other. Ye cannot serve God and mammon."
  d. The love of Christ commandeth us.
  Mark 8:34 "And when he had called the people unto him with his disciples also, he said unto them, Whosoever will come after me, let him deny himself, and take up his cross, and follow me."
  e. In his commandment there is this assurance.
  Matthew 16:25 "For whosoever will save his life shall lose it: and whosoever will lose his life for my sake shall find it."
  f. In our obedience there is this satisfaction.
  John 20:21 "...Peace be unto you: as my Father hath sent me, even so send I you."
  g. The love of Christ reasons with us.
  John 15:16 "Ye have not chosen me, but I have chosen you, and ordained you, that ye should go and bring forth fruit, and that your fruit, should remain: that whatsoever ye shall ask of the Father in my name, he may give it you."
  Application: We are saved to serve. We are chosen and ordained by Christ to bear the fruit of His grace. We are called upon to deny self and take up our cross and follow Christ. He is our master, we are His servant.

h. More reasoning.
Ephesians 2:8-10 "For by grace are ye saved through faith; and that not of yourselves: it is the gift of God: Not of works, lest any man should boast. For we are his workmanship, created in Christ Jesus unto good works, which God hath before ordained that we should walk in them."
Application: We are not saved by character, but by grace.
i. More reasoning.
James 2:20 "...faith without works is dead?"
Romans 6:16 "Know ye not, that to whom ye yield yourselves servants to obey, his servants ye are whom ye obey; whether of sin unto death, or of obedience unto righteousness?"
j. The love of Christ communes with us.
Matthew 26:26-28 "...Jesus took bread, and blessed it, and break it, and gave it to the disciples, and said, Take, eat; this is my body. And he took the cup, and gave thanks, and gave it to them, saying, Drink ye all of it; For this is my blood of the new testament (covenant), which is shed for many for the remission of sins."
Application: Christ wants us to be partners with Him, in life and death, in joy, and in sorrow.
In baptism we show unto the witnesses that we were buried with Him in death, and resurrected with Him in life.
Today we show that we are about His business with Him. That we are partners with the new covenant, having partaken of His life.
k. The love of Christ constraineth us to give:
1st -Ourselves - II Corinthians 8:5 "They...gave their own selves to the Lord, and unto us by the will of God."
2nd -We must give according to as the Lord blessed us.

I Corinthians 16:2 "Upon the first day of the week let every one of you lay by him in store, as God hath prospered him, that there be no gatherings when I come."
Leviticus 27:30 "And all the tithe of the land...is the LORD'S: it is holy unto the LORD."
Luke 16:10 "He that is faithful in that which is least is faithful also in much:..."

To Approve Ourselves unto God
II Corinthians 6:1-10

Theme: II Corinthians 6:4 "But in all things approving ourselves as the ministers of God,...in much patience, in afflictions, in necessities, in distresses."

Text: II Corinthians 6:3 "Giving no offence in any thing, that the ministry be not blamed:"

Introduction: I have heard the Lord speak to me on this line, "Approving ourselves as the ministers of God." I could keep busy with anything, but didn't find time to study His word. There was always something that needed to be fixed: shoes, overalls, suits, car etc., but no time for the word. Yet, I was to be His minister, surrendered in the day of salvation.

While I was starting to fix one of my old pair of shoes, though I had a new pair on hand, yet wasting my time, this was the time when the Lord spoke to me and I turned to II Corinthians 6:2-4, where I saw myself using the grace of God in vain. "(For he saith, I have heard thee in a time accepted, and in the day of salvation have I succoured thee: behold, now is the accepted time; behold, now is the day of salvation.) Giving no offence in any thing, that the ministry be not blamed: But in all things approving ourselves as the ministers of God, in much patience..." (II Corinthians 6:2-4).

I Point: To approve ourselves as His ministers in circumstances. Paul gives us here <u>Nine Circumstances</u> you may find yourself in.
a. We are to approve ourselves with meekness and submission, calmly and without discontentment.
   1. "...in afflictions,..." (II Corinthians 6:4).
      If you patiently serve the Lord, Satan will then seek to afflict you with many different afflictions:
   2. "...in necessities,..." (II Corinthians 6:4).
   3. "...in distresses,..." (II Corinthians 6:4).
   4. Yes, even to prove ourselves "in stripes," (II Corinthians 6:5).
   5. "...in imprisonments,..." (II Corinthians 6:5).
   6. "...in tumults,..." (II Corinthians 6:5).
      You will be the one looked upon as causing all the tumult, causing all the trouble in the world.
   7. "...in labours,..." (II Corinthians 6:5).
   8. "...in watchings,..." (II Corinthians 6:5).
   9. "...in fastings;" (II Corinthians 6:5).

In these different circumstances we, as His servants, must approve ourselves faithful.

II Point: <u>Nine Reactions</u> (II Corinthians 6:6-7)
1. "By pureness,…" (II Corinthians 6:6).
2. "…by knowledge,…" (II Corinthians 6:6).
3. "…by longsuffering,…" (II Corinthians 6:6).
4. "…by kindness,…" (II Corinthians 6:6).
5. "…by the Holy Ghost,…" (II Corinthians 6:6).
6. "…by love unfeigned,…" (II Corinthians 6:6).
7. "By the word of truth,…" (II Corinthians 6:7).
8. "…by the power of God,…" (II Corinthians 6:7).
9. "…by the armour of righteousness on the right hand and on the left." (II Corinthians 6:7).

III Point: <u>Nine Characters</u> in which we may present ourselves as His workers. (II Corinthians 6:8)
1. "By honour and dishonour,… (II Corinthians 6:8).
   a. God will honour you. (II Corinthians 6:8).
      "He that winneth souls is wise." (Proverbs 11:30).
   b. But the world will call you a fool.
2. "…by evil reports and good reports:…." (II Corinthians 6:8).
3. "…as deceivers, and yet true;" (II Corinthians 6:8).
   a. Two different reports will go forth from you even as of the woman in Mark's Gospel. Mark 14:3 "And being in Bethany…as he sat at meat, there came a woman having an alabaster box of ointment of spikenard very precious; and she brake the box, and poured it on his head."
   b. Some went forth telling what she had done for the Lord, while others went forth telling what she wasted.
4. "As unknown, and yet well known,…" (II Corinthians 6:9).
   a. Unknown to the fame of the world,
   b. But praise be to God, well known to Him.
5. "…as dying, and, behold we live;…" (II Corinthians 6:9).
6. "…as chastened, and not killed," (II Corinthians 6:9).
7. "As sorrowful, yet alway rejoicing;…" (II Corinthians 6:10).
8. "…as poor, yet making many rich;…" (II Corinthians 6:10).
9. "…as having nothing, and yet possessing all things." (II Corinthians 6:10).

This is the character of one approved unto God.

God's Time Is at Hand
II Corinthians 6:1-18

Text: II Corinthians 6:2 "...behold, now is the accepted time; behold, now is the day of salvation."

Introduction: We shall tonight carefully consider how much time God permits us to be without salvation.

I Point: Who needs salvation?
   a. In the natural: every one who is in a lost condition.
      1.. A person gone astray.
      ii. A person drowning.
      iii. A person attacked by someone.
      iv. A person in a burning house.
      v. A person in heavy debt.
   b. In the Spiritual: likewise everyone who is in a lost condition according to God's record of men.
      1. Isaiah 53:6 "All we like sheep have gone astray; we have turned every one to his own way;..."
      2. Psalm 14:2-3 "The LORD looked down from heaven upon the children of men, to see if there were any that did understand, and seek God. They are all gone aside, they are all together become filthy: there is none that doeth good, no, not one."
      3. Romans 3:10 "As it is written, There is none righteous, no, not one:"
      Romans 3:17-18 "And the way of peace have they not known: There is no fear of God before their eyes."
      Romans 3:23 "For all have sinned, and come short of the glory of God;"
      4. Galatians 3:22 "But the scripture hath concluded all under sin, that the promise by faith of Jesus Christ might be given to them that believe."
   c. Do we then all need salvation? Yes!

II Point: Why do all men need salvation?
a. Because of the fact that we are all in a lost condition.
b. Because of the uncertainty of life.

c. What is human life?
      1. Job 7:7 "O remember that my life is wind:..."
      2. Job 8:9 "...our days upon earth are a shadow:"
      3. Psalm 90:5 "...they are like grass which groweth up."
      4. Psalm 90:12 "So teach us to number our days, that we may apply our hearts unto wisdom."
      5. Hebrews 9:27 "And as it is appointed unto men once to die, but after this the judgment?"
      6. James 4:14 "...It is even a vapour, that appeareth for a little time, and then vanisheth away."
      7. Amos 4:12 "...prepare to meet thy God..."
   d. Physical death is the result of sin, and since all die, all have sinned.

III Point: <u>When do all men need Salvation?</u>
   a. II Corinthians 6:2 "...behold, now is the accepted time: behold, now is the day of salvation."
   b. God's time is now, today; not tomorrow, but now!

IV Point: <u>God's invitation to you</u>.
   a. Luke 14:17 "...Come; for all things are now ready."
   b. Revelation: 22:17 "And the Spirit and the bride say, Come. And let him that heareth say, Come. And let him that is athirst come. And whosoever will, let him take the water of life freely."
   c. II Corinthians 6:2 "(For he saith, I have heard thee in a time accepted, and in the day of salvation have I succoured thee: behold, now is the accepted time; behold, now is the day of salvation.)"

Separation from Sin
II Corinthians 6:11-18

Text: II Corinthians 6:17-18 "Wherefore come out from among them, and be ye separate, saith the Lord, and touch not the unclean thing; and I will receive you, And will be a Father unto you, and ye shall be my sons and daughters, saith the Lord Almighty."
It is impossible for God to bless those who are compromising with the world.

Introduction: Our text suggests absolute separation from sin and the world.
  a. I want you to notice that this is written to Christians.
  b. I want you to notice that any Christian who is not separated from sin is out of fellowship with Christ.
  c. I want you to notice that if any Christian is not free from habitual sin, he cannot please God, and God therefore calls him to come out from it.

I Point: Come out from among them.
  a. II Corinthians 6:17 "...come out from among them, saith the Lord,..."
  Come out from all your ungodly companies.
  b. Who are the ungodly companies?
  The unbelievers!
  The unbeliever is not only the infidel, but it is the person who does not believe that he or she is lost, or a sinner.
  c. God says, "For all have sinned, and come short of the glory of God;" (Romans 3:23).
  d. God says, "The heart is deceitful above all things, and desperately wicked: who can know it?" (Jeremiah 17:9).
  e. Again God says in Isaiah 64:6 "But we are all as an unclean thing, and all our righteousnesses are as filthy rags;..."
  f. Moreover we hear God say: I John 1:8 "If we say that we have no sin, we deceive ourselves, and the truth is not in us."
  g. People not believing these facts about themselves God calls unbelievers.
  Illustration: A minister once said, "I don't like the words 'being saved.' It makes a person feel as if he were lost." This "so called" minister is an unbeliever in God's sight.

II Point: <u>To what measure is God expecting us to come out?</u>
  a. II Corinthians 6:14 "Be ye not unequally yoked together with unbelievers: for what fellowship hath righteousness with unrighteousness? and what communion hath light with darkness?"
  b. That means come out in fellowship, in company, in business, in play.
  Illustration: I heard many times people say, "If so and so is a Christian, then I don't want to be one." You and I can bar the door for someone if we are not what we should be.

III Point: <u>To be separate from the Devil</u>.
  a. II Corinthians 6:15 "And what concord hath Christ with Belial? (the devil) or what part hath he that believeth with an infidel?"

IV Point: <u>Separation from idolatry.</u>
  a. What is idolatry?
  Idolatry is image worship, or any imagination in your heart.

Conclusion: Are you, my friend, separated from all these things?

God's Unspeakable Gift
II Corinthians 9:15

Text: II Corinthians 9:15 "Thanks be unto God for his unspeakable gift."

Introduction: During the Christmas season we all think much about giving. But as we think of giving and receiving, our minds and hearts go out to our heavenly Father who has given the unspeakable gift to the world.

As our text calls it, "Thanks be unto God for His unspeakable gift." (II Corinthians 9:15). Romans 8:32 "He that spared not his own Son, but delivered him up for us all, how shall he not with him also freely give us all things?"

I Point: What is this Gift?
  a. Let us notice just a few things about this, "God's unspeakable gift."
  b. The word "unspeakable" is used three times in the New Testament.
      i. II Corinthians 12:4 "How that he (Paul) was caught up into paradise, and heard unspeakable words, which it is not lawful for a man to utter.
         Application: As Paul had seen the glory of heaven, he could not find words to express the joys and glory to the saints of God.
      ii. I Peter 1:8 "Whom having not seen, ye love; in whom, though now ye see him not, yet believing, ye rejoice with joy unspeakable and full of glory:"
         This is the joy of salvation.
      iii. The third time which makes up all the times this word is used in the New Testament is our text. II Corinthians 9:15 "Thanks be unto God for his unspeakable gift."
         Application: Unspeakable means: "Not yet fully expounded." How very fitting this is of Christ. He has never been fully expounded, by any man.
  c. All I can do in explaining to you this morning, after I have cried unto God for an answer to the question, "What is this unspeakable gift?" is to say, here is God's answer: John 3:16 "For God so loved the world, that he gave his only begotten Son, that whosoever believeth in him should not perish, but have everlasting life."

- d. My answer to this question can therefore only be shouted out of my soul. The unspeakable gift is Christ Jesus, my Lord, born in Bethlehem.
- e. I John 4:9-10 "In this was manifested the love of God toward us, because that God sent his only begotten Son unto the world, that we might live through him. Herein is love, not that we loved God, but that he loved us, and sent his Son to be a propitiation for our sins."
- f. Propitiation means sacrifice.
  Romans 3:25 "Whom God hath set forth to be a propitiation (sacrifice) through faith in his blood, to declare his righteousness for the remission of sins that are past, through the forbearance of God;"

II Point: <u>What is this gift</u>?
- a. The Holy Spirit is also included in this gift. It is through the faithful Holy Spirit that we can learn to love Jesus. Oh how we thank God for the Holy Spirit.
- b. Then too, our eternal life is God's gift through Jesus Christ our Lord. I John 5:12 "He that hath the Son hath life; and he that hath not the Son of God hath not life."

Conclusion: So we find that the unspeakable gift is constituted of:
- a. God's Son.
- b. The Holy Spirit
- c. Eternal life.

Have you received this great gift of God? God wants everyone to come and receive it.

God's Grace is Sufficient
II Corinthians 12:1-10

Text: II Corinthians 12:9 "...My grace is sufficient for thee: for my strength is made perfect in weakness..."

Introduction: The reason why we have no more of God's strength is simply because we are too strong in ourselves.
1. God's glory will not mix with men's strength.
2. God's glory will not be given to men to boast.
3. Men's wisdom and men's ambition, without the knowledge and wisdom of God, cannot, and will not, glorify God.

I Point: The worldly wise man.
- a. Out of our reading, who is He?
- b. It is Saul or Paul. Acts 22:3 "I am verily a man which am a Jew, born in Tarsus, a city in Cilicia, yet brought up in this city at the feet of Gamaliel, and taught according to the perfect manner of the law of the fathers, and was zealous toward God, as ye all are this day."
    1. Saul was a man of great wisdom.
    2. Saul was a man of great authority.
    3. Saul was a man who served in the government.
    4. Saul was also out to serve the Lord Jehovah.
- c. Could the Lord use him?
  No! Indeed not. He was too wise. He was too much looked up to.
- d. Saul was a first class man in the world with much education and authority.

II Point: Saul, when he became Paul.
- a. II Corinthians 5:17 "Therefore if any man be in Christ, he is a new creature: old things are passed away; behold, all things are become new."
- b. II Corinthians 4:7 "But we have this treasure in earthen vessels, that the excellency of the power may be of God, and not of us." Paul was now a humble man, a broken man, in body and spirit. He was a man who had to look to the Lord for his daily strength and for the grace of God. He became a chosen vessel. A man whom now God could use.

III Point: <u>Paul under God's wisdom</u>.
    a. II Corinthians 12:7 "And lest I should be exalted above measure through the abundance of the revelation, there was give to me a thorn in the flesh, the messenger of Satan to buffet me, lest I should be exalted above measure."
    b. Satan was permitted to buffet him.
    c. Why must the Lord permit such things?
    Application: How often has the Lord given you a thorn in the flesh?
    d. It taught Paul to pray. (II Corinthians 12:8).
    e. My grace is sufficient for thee.
        1. Grace for a thorn.
        2. Grace for victory.
        3. Grace for ministry.
    Illustration: When the tide comes in, a little gulf that is dried up is filled. Your life is dried up? Then God will speak, "My grace is sufficient for thee...." and you are filled.
    f. II Corinthians 12:9 "...my strength is made perfect in weakness..."
    Application: You feel as if you are falling, but God says my grace is sufficient.
    You may say, "Oh Lord, I don't feel your strong grip on me." But the Lord says, "My grace is sufficient." When the Lord raised up Peter's mother-in-law He just touched her, and she rose up. His grace is sufficient.

Conclusion: Would you, my friend, like to have God's grace touch you tonight?

Examine Yourselves
II Corinthians 13:5

Topic: A believing mind, but an unsurrendered heart.

Text: II Corinthians 13:5 "Examine yourselves, whether ye be in the faith; prove your own selves..."

Introduction: These two do not work together in our text of II Corinthians 13:5. We find a timely admonition to "examine yourselves [to see] whether ye be in the faith." The importance of this self-examination lies in the fact that thousands all about us, who apparently believe, show no evidence of a change of heart.

David, the Psalmist regarded the matter of such great importance that he pleads with God to examine him to see if his heart was right. Psalm 26:2 "Examine me, O LORD, and prove me; try my reins and my heart."

I Point: A believing mind.
    a. Romans 12:16 "Be of the same mind one toward another. Mind not high things, but condescend to men of low estate. Be not wise in your own conceits."
    Application: This is how the Apostle Paul had to speak to people with a believing mind, but an unsurrendered heart.
    b. Philippians 2:3 "Let nothing be done through strife or vainglory; but in lowliness of mind let each esteem other better than themselves."
    Application: You notice these people were Christians. A believing mind can be a Christian, but yet be an unsurrendered heart.
    c. I Peter 3:8-9 "Finally, be ye all of one mind, having compassion one of another, love as brethren, be pitiful, be courteous: Not rendering evil for evil, or railing for railing: but contrariwise blessing; knowing that ye are thereunto called, that ye should inherit a blessing."
    The Apostle Peter finds it necessary here to speak to these people in this manner because of their unsurrendered hearts.
    d. Philippians 2:4-5 "Look not every man on his own things, but every man also on the things of others. Let this mind be in you, which was also in Christ Jesus:"

Application: The pattern of a surrendered mind and heart is the mind of Christ.

e. If you have not the mind of Christ you cannot glorify God. Romans 15:5-6 "Now the God of patience and consolation grant you to be likeminded one toward another according to Christ Jesus: That ye may with one mind and one mouth glorify God, even the Father of our Lord Jesus Christ."

That is a surrendered heart which creates a Christ-like mind.

Application: There is an unregenerate believing mind that, of course, has nothing to do with God. Even the devil believes and trembles. Many people believe there is a God, and are very fine folks, but are eternally lost.

II Point: <u>An unsurrendered heart.</u>
a. Jeremiah 17:9 "The heart is deceitful above all things, and desperately wicked: who can know it? I the LORD search the heart, I try the reins, even to give every man according to his ways, and according to the fruit of his doings."
b. Hebrews 10:22 "Let us draw near with a true heart in full assurance of faith, having our hearts sprinkled from an evil conscience, and our bodies washed with pure water. Let us hold fast the profession of our faith without wavering; (for he is faithful that promised;)."
Application: Let us search our hearts. Let us right here draw near with a true heart.
I wonder sometimes if our heart is always controlled by the mind of God?
c. Proverbs 23:19 "Hear thou, my son, and be wise, and guide thine heart in thy way." In what way? In the way of Christ. And only if you are guided in the way of Christ can we fulfill Luke 10:27. "And he answering said, Thou shalt love the Lord thy God with all thy heart, and with all thy soul, and with all thy strength, and with all thy mind; and thy neighbour as thyself." (Luke 10:27).

If you love the Lord God with all your heart, than you will seek Him with your whole heart, and with a surrendered heart.

Psalm 119:2 "Blessed are they that keep his testimonies, and that seek him with the whole heart."

Joshua 22:5 "...serve him with all your heart and with all your soul."

Application: If you will seek the Lord. If you will cleave unto him, and walk in his ways, then you will serve him with rejoicing and gladness.

d. Ephesians 3:17 "That Christ may dwell in your hearts by faith; that ye, being rooted and grounded in love."
Application: Christ cannot dwell in an unsurrendered heart. But if you are rooted and grounded in Him, He then will dwell in you.
e. Colossians 3:15 "And let the peace of God rule in our hearts, to the which also ye are called in one body; and be ye thankful."
f. And the climax of all this exhortation is according to Philippians 4:7. "And the peace of God, which passeth all understanding, shall keep your hearts and minds through Christ Jesus."

Conclusion: Oh, beloved, if you realize this teaching, then your prayer will be as David of old: "Create in me a clean heart, O God; and renew a right spirit within me." (Psalm 51:10).

Sermon Outlines from the Book of Galatians

Christ - According to Scripture

Galatians 4:4-18

Theme: Christ's coming into the world according to the scripture.

Text: Galatians 4:4 "But when the fulness of the time was come, God sent forth his Son, made of a woman, made under the law."

I Point: <u>Scripture prophecy</u>.
   a. Micah 5:2 "But thou, Beth-lehem Ephratah, though thou be little among the thousands of Judah, yet out of thee shall he come forth unto me that is to be ruler in Israel; whose goings forth have been from of old, from everlasting."
   b. John 7:42 "Hath not the scripture said, That Christ cometh of the seed of David, and out to the town of Bethlehem, where David was?"
   c. Jeremiah 23:5-6 "Behold, the days come, saith the LORD, that I will raise unto David a righteous Branch, and a King shall reign and prosper, and shall execute judgment and justice in the earth. In his days Judah shall be saved, and Israel shall dwell safely: and this is his name whereby he shall be called "THE LORD OUR RIGHTEOUSNESS."
   d. Galatians 4:4 "But when the fulness of the time was come, God sent forth his Son, made of a woman, made under the law."

II Point: <u>If Christ were not born according to the scripture, What then?</u>
   a. If Christ were not born through the line of David, He could not be your Saviour. Luke 2:4 "And Joseph also went up from Galilee, out of the city of Nazareth, into Judaea, unto the city of David, which is called Bethlehem; (because he was of the house and lineage of David:)."
   b. If Christ were not born in Bethlehem, He could not be your Saviour.
   c. If Christ were not born of the virgin, Mary, He could not be your Saviour.
   d. If the Christ child would not have been persecuted of Herod the king as He was, He could not have been your Saviour. Or if Herod had not killed all the children because of the birth of Christ, He could not have been your Saviour.

Matthew 2:17-18 "Then was fulfilled that which was spoken by Jeremy the prophet, saying, In Rama was there a voice heard, lamentation, and weeping, and great mourning, Rachel weeping for her children, and would not be comforted, because they are not."
   e. If Christ had been born at any other date or any other year, He could not have been your Saviour. Galatians 4:4 "But when the fulness of the time was come, God sent forth his Son, made of a woman, made under the law."
   f. He, Christ, had to be born at the fulness of time according to the scriptures. Matthew 2:6 "And thou Bethlehem, in the land of Juda, art not the least among the princes of Juda: for out of thee shall come a Governor, that shall rule my people Israel."

III Point: <u>Christ had to live and die according to the scripture</u>.

   a. If Christ had not died on the cross, He could not have been your Saviour.
   b. If Christ had died in Gethsemane, He could not have been your Saviour. Christ had to live and die on the cross according to the scriptures.

IV Point: <u>If Christ had not risen from the grave, as He did, He could not have been your Saviour</u>.

   a. Romans 10:9 "That if thou shalt confess with thy mouth the Lord Jesus, and shalt believe in thine heart that God hath raised him from the dead, thou shalt be saved."

Conclusion:
a. We know that Christ was born according to scripture.
b. We know He lived according to scripture.
c. We know He died according to scripture.
d. We know He rose again according to scripture.
e. And you will have to be saved according to scripture.
f. Or you will be damned according to scripture.

The Three Christian Characters
Galatians 5:16-6:1-10

Theme: The three Christian characters against which there is no law.

Text: Galatians 5:22-23 "But the fruit of the Spirit is love, joy, peace, longsuffering, gentleness, goodness, faith, Meekness, temperance: against such there is no law."

Introduction: God is the lawgiver and indeed very strict. Any one not complying with His laws is sure to suffer. But there are characters against which there is no law.
1. Inward
2. Outward
3. Upward

I Point: <u>Inward</u>

  a. Galatians 5:22 - Love, joy, and peace, against this possession there is not law.
  b. These are <u>inward</u> possessions of a true Christian.
   1. <u>Love</u> - There can be no law against love. (True love) John 3:16 "For God so loved the world, that he gave his only begotten Son, that whosoever believeth in him should not perish, but have everlasting life."
   2. <u>Joy</u> - This is also without law. No one can rob you of the joy in Christ.
   3. <u>Peace</u> – There is no law against peace in your soul. Peace that passes understanding.

   Application: Romans 8:35-39 "Who shall separate us from the love of Christ?..."

   Illustration: The world may take away your life, but it cannot take away your peace.

II Point: <u>Outward</u>

  a. <u>Longsuffering</u>: - A gift of the Spirit.
     Naturally many times we would fly off the handle, but God gives longsuffering.
  b. <u>Gentleness</u>: - A gift of the Spirit.
     In some people you can feel the gentleness of God in their life.

    c.   <u>Goodness</u> – A gift of the spirit.
There is no law against goodness. The world does not always receive your goodness. But God will reward you for your goodness at the judgment seat of Christ. There is no law or restriction against goodness.
Matthew 5:9."Blessed are the peacemakers: for they shall be called the children of God."

III Point: <u>Upward</u>

    a.   <u>Faith</u>
There is no law against faith.
This is an upward expression toward God.
To have immovable faith in the Lord is a gift of the Spirit.

    b.   <u>Meekness</u> – It is a gift of the Spirit to be meek.
Moses was meek because he had an upward look toward God.
No law on earth can restrict you from an upward look to God.

    c.   <u>Temperance</u> – A gift of the Spirit.
Christian life requires temperance.
Application: In the last days when trials are very great, God says, "...look up, and lift up your heads; for your redemption draweth nigh." (Luke 21:28).

Illustration: When you are locked in, just look up to God.

Sermon Outlines from the Book of Ephesians

How to Pray
Ephesians 6:1-24

Text: Ephesians 6:18 "Praying always with all prayer and supplication in the Spirit, and watching thereunto with all perseverance and supplication for all saints."

Introduction: Today, I would like to take you through six points on prayer.
- 1st - The importance of prayer.
- 2nd - Prayer unto God.
- 3rd - Obeying and praying.
- 4th - Praying in the name of Jesus.
- 5th - Praying in the Spirit.
- 6th - Always praying.

I Point: <u>The importance of prayer</u>.
- a. Ephesians 6:18 "Praying always..."
  Application: That means, you must pray, pray, pray. You must put all your energy, and all your heart into prayer. How seldom do we pray things through.

 # 1. <u>Why must I always pray?</u>
  i. Because there is a devil.
  ii. He is coming.
  iii. He is mighty.
  iv. He never rests.
  v. He is ever plotting the downfall of the child of God.
  vi. If the child of God relaxes in prayer, the devil will succeed in ensnaring him.
- a. Ephesians 6:12 "For we wrestle not against flesh and blood, but against principalities, against powers, against the rulers of the darkness of this world, against spiritual wickedness in high places."
- f. I Peter 5:8 "Be sober, be vigilant; because your adversary the devil, as a roaring lion, walketh about, seeking whom he may devour:"

 # 2. <u>Reason for constant prayer</u>.
- a. Because this is God's appointed way for obtaining things.
- b. James 4:2 "...ye have not, because ye ask not."
  Illustration: "Why is it?" Many Christians ask, "Why am I making so little progress in my Christian life? It is because you "neglect to pray." God says, "Ye have not, because ye ask not." (James 4:2).

3. Reason for constant prayer.
   a. Because those men, whom God set for us as an example and pattern, regarding prayer, show us that it is the most important business in their lives.
   b. Paul: Romans 1:9 "For God is my witness, whom I serve with my spirit in the gospel of his Son, that without ceasing I make mention of you always in my prayers;"
   c. The Twelve Disciples: Acts 6:4 "But we will give ourselves continually to prayer, and to the ministry of the word."

4. Reason for constant prayer.
   a. Because prayer was one of the most important part in the earthly life of our Lord.
   b. Mark 1:35 "And in the morning, rising up a great while before day, he went out, and departed into a solitary place, and there prayed."
   c. Luke 6:12 "And it came to pass in those days, that he went out into a mountain to pray, and continued all night in prayer to God."

5. Reason for constant prayer.
   a. Because prayer is, even now, the most important ministry of our risen Lord.
   b. Hebrews 7:25 "Wherefore he is able also to save them to the uttermost that come unto God by him, seeing he ever liveth to make intercession for them."
   c. Romans 8:34 "Who is he that condemneth? It is Christ Jesus that died, yea rather, that is risen again, who is even at the right hand of God, who also maketh intercession for us."
   d. Prayer then is yet the most principal occupation of our risen LORD.
   e. Therefore, brother and sister, take time to pray and take plenty of it.
   f. Is there joy in such prayer?
      1. Someone may say, "I cannot find sufficient interest or want to pray."
      Application: Did you really give yourself over to prayer?
   *Application: There are few to none who ever get saved unless someone had prayed for that soul.

g. It is through prayer if we ever will see a revival at all.
      1. It was so in the days of Knox.
      2. It was so in the days of Wesley and Whitfield.
      3. It was so in the days of Finney.
      4. It was so in the days of Brainerd.
      5. And it will be so in our days if you and I start praying so.

II Point: <u>Prayer unto God</u>.
   a. Acts 12:5 "...prayer was made without ceasing of the church unto God for him [Peter]."
   b. Very much of "so-called" prayer, both public and private, is not unto God.
   c. We must have a definite and vivid realization that God is bending over us and listening as we pray.
      1. Psalm 86:1 "Bow down thine ear, O LORD, hear me: for I am poor and needy."
      2. Hebrews 5:7 "Who in the days of his flesh, (Christ) when he had offered up prayers and supplications with strong crying and tears..."
      3. Romans 15:30 "...strive together with me in your prayers..."
         The prayer that prevails with God is the prayer into which we put our whole soul and heart.
      4. United prayer. Acts 17:5 "...prayer was made without ceasing of the church unto God..."
      5. Matthew 18:19 "...if two of you shall agree on earth as touching any thing that they shall ask, it shall be done for them of the Father which is in heaven."

III Point: <u>Obeying and praying</u>.
   a. I John 3:22 "And whatsoever we ask, we receive of him, because we keep his commandments, and do those things that are pleasing in his sight."
   b. Constantly this question among Christians comes up, "Is it sin to go to the theatre, dance, to smoke and drink?" The answer is: "Pray about it and then follow the still small voice leading you into all truth."

IV Point: <u>Praying in the name of Jesus</u>.
   a. John 14:13 "And whatsoever ye shall ask in my name, that will I do, that the Father may be glorified in the Son."

    b. I John 5:14 "And this is the confidence that we have in him, that, if we ask any thing according to his will, he heareth us:"

V Point: <u>Praying in the Spirit</u>.
    a. Romans 8:26 "Likewise the spirit also helpeth our infirmities: for we know not what we should pray for as we ought: but the Spirit itself maketh intercession for us with groanings which cannot be uttered."
Ephesians 6:18 "Praying always with all prayer and supplication in the Spirit…"
    b. To run heedlessly into God's presences is foolishness.

VI Point: <u>Always praying and not fainting</u>.
    a. Luke 18:1 "…men ought always to pray, and not to faint;"
    b. Application: Don't believe it if someone tells you it is unbelief on your part to pray twice or more for one thing. It is not! It is faith!
    c. Illustration: George Muller prayed every day for two men for over 50 years.

Conclusion: Ephesians 6:18 "Praying always with all prayer and supplication in the Spirit, and watching thereunto with all perseverance and supplication of all saints;"

Spiritual Warfare

Ephesians 6:10-20

Theme: Satan's line of attack and God's line of defense.

Introduction: The Christian life includes spiritual warfare with the powers of darkness. It is interesting to observe that all above us, and over us, and under us, the enemy is in action and in attack.

I Point: Satan's line of attack.
- a. Skeptical: In Genesis 3:1-4 - It began.
  1. The first attach was to create doubt.
  2. Genesis 3:4 "And the serpent said unto the woman, Ye shall not surely die:"
     Creating the question: "Hath God really spoken?"
  3. Present day attack. Acts 20:29 "For I know this, that after my departing shall grievous wolves enter in among you, not sparing the flock."

- b. Heretical: One that denies the validity or authority of the scripture. Heretical: against the Son, denying His deity and His atonement at Calvary.
  1. II Peter 2:1 "But there were false prophets also among the people, even as there shall be false teachers among you, who privily shall bring in damnable heresies, even denying the Lord that bought them and bring upon themselves swift destruction."
  2. Application: We have many different cults, even in our town right here.

- c. Fanatical: Against the Holy Spirit, denying His functioning power, as well as substituting those counterfeits, the very manifestation of which brands them of satanic origin and control.
  1. I John 4:1 "BELOVED, believe not every spirit, but try the spirits whether they are of God: because many false prophets are gone out into the world."
  2. They want you to become fanatical. Remember Ephesians 2:1 "And you hath he quickened, who were dead in trespasses and sins:"

II Point: God's line of defense.
   a. The truth – John 17:17 "Sanctify them through thy truth: thy word is truth."
   b. The full truth - I John 5:10 "He that believeth on the Son of God hath the witness in himself: he that believeth not God hath made him a liar; because he believeth not the record that God gave his Son."
   c. I John 5:12 "He that hath the Son hath life; and he that hath not the Son of God hath not life."
   d. Nothing but the truth.
      1. Accept no substitute for the Word of God.
      2. Application: All the doctrines of men and teachings of human conception are but grass in comparison to the Word of God.

Satan's Defeat

Ephesians 6:10-18

Introduction: No man can defeat Satan alone, for he is mightier than any man.

I Point: The greatest guards against Satan's devices.
1. Humility.
2. Unselfishness.
3. Patience in affliction.
4. Slow to anger.
5. A forgiving spirit.

These five things are splendid aids to fight the devil, but they by themselves are not enough to lay him low.

But they do keep him from taking advantage of us. These are negative protections. What we need is the positive fortification, combined with these negative protections to fight this spiritual warfare.

a. Submission to God is the first positive protection.
James 4:7 "Submit yourselves therefore to God. Resist the devil, and he will flee from you."

Application: The world is filled with people who seek to defeat the devil only by the negative weapons of our warfare.

Illustration: Take these two! Peter and Judas, they both denied Christ. The one after denying His Lord went out in repentance and submission. The other went out and hung himself. He was sorry for himself, but not repentant.
See the difference?
1. One was humble and filled with submission.
2. The other was humiliated and filled with remorse.

Illustration: Paul defeated Satan when he discovered a thorn in his flesh, the massager of Satan to buffet him, by submitting it to God.
II Corinthians 11:8-9 "For this thing I besought the Lord thrice, that it might depart from me. And he said unto me, My grace is sufficient for thee: for my strength is made perfect in weakness..."

I Peter 5:8-9 – Simon Peter calls our attention to the fact that we must resist Satan in the faith.

Illustration: It is not enough just to make up our minds to turn over a new leaf, start doing better, or quit doing something bad. No! That is not enough. We must submit ourselves to God and resist the devil by being sober, vigilant and having faith in God.

This is an everyday constant battle of "resisting steadfast in faith." Here are the armours of God you must put on. Ephesians 6:11-17 "Put on the whole armour of God, that ye may be able to stand against the wiles of the devil."

Ephesians 6:12 "For we wrestle not against flesh and blood, but:
1. "…against principalities,…"
2. "…against powers,…"
3. "…against rules of the darkness of this world,…"
4. "…against spiritual wickedness in high places."

Ephesians 6:13 "Wherefore take unto you the whole armour of God that ye may be able to withstand in the evil day, and having done all, to stand."

<u>Six Positive Protections: Ephesians 6:14-17.</u>
1. Ephesians 6:14 "Stand therefore, having your loins girt about with <u>truth</u>,…"
2. Ephesians 6:14 "…having on the <u>breastplate of righteousness</u>;…"
3. Ephesians 6:15 "And your feet shod with the preparation of the <u>gospel of peace</u>;"
4. Ephesians 6:16 "Above all, taking the <u>shield of faith</u>…"
5. Ephesians 6:17 "And take the <u>helmet of salvation</u>…"
6. Ephesians 6:17 "…and the <u>sword of the Spirit</u>, which is the word of God."

Conclusion: These are the armour of God available to us in order to fight and defeat Satan. Couple these six positive armours of God with the five negative aids of humility, unselfishness, patience in affliction, slow to anger, and a forgiving spirit and you will be able to defeat Satan.

Sermon Outlines from the Book of Philippians

Christ is All
Philippians 1:1-26

Text: Philippians 1:21 "For to me to live is Christ, and to die is gain."

Introduction: Christ alone and His approval was life to Paul.

I Point: Life to Paul.
   a. It was Christ.
   b. Philippians 1:3-5 - Paul's link with the Philippian believers was fellowship in Christ.
   c. Philippians 1:6-8 - The victory for all the churches was Christ.
   d. Philippians 1:8-11 - His confidence for the welfare of the churches was Christ.

II Point: Suffering to Paul.
   a. It was with Christ.
   b. Philippians 1:20 "According to my earnest expectation and my hope, that in nothing I shall be ashamed, but that with all boldness, as always, so now also Christ shall be magnified in my body, whether it be by life, or by death."

III Point: Death to Paul.
   a. Philippians 1:21 "For to me to live is Christ, and to die is gain."
   Application: It was true of Paul, but is it true of you and I?
   Illustration: Living consists of our union with the Lord Jesus Christ.
   b. Paul sang in prison.
   c. Paul praised the Lord with chains on his hands.
   d. Paul gave counsel and advice to others when the boat was sinking.
   e. We hear Paul preaching and singing as he marched to his death chained to a Roman soldier.
   Application: Paul's choice was not a choice between two evils, but rather a choice between two bests.
       i. To live is Christ.
       ii. To die is Christ.

The later (to die) he said is far better, but for him to live in his body was better for the people.

Philippians 1:23-24 "For I am in a strait betwixt two, having a desire to depart, and to be with Christ; which is far better: Nevertheless to abide in the flesh is more needful for you."

IV Point: <u>What is Christ to you?</u>
 a. You will find what Christ was to Paul as you read the Book of Acts and Paul's Epistles.
    1. In Acts – Christ his Saviour.
    2. In Romans - I am ready to preach; I am a debtor; I am a bond slave to Christ.
    3. In I and II Corinthians – Christ is all in all.
    4. In Galatians – It is the power of Christ.
    5. In Ephesians – It is the believer's position in Christ.
    6. In Philippians – It is the knowledge of Christ.
    7. In Colossians – It is Christ in you.
    8. In I & II Thessalonians – It is the coming of Christ.
    9. In I & II Timothy – It is the ministry of Christ, and Christ the judge in that day, and the Crown of Life.
    10. In Titus - It is the hope of Christ.
    11. In Philemon – It is the prisoner of Christ.

Conclusion: To Paul, Christ was all his life. He had no end in view, but Christ. His life was not preaching; it was not His work for missions; nor was it his personal evangelism. Christ alone and His approval was life for Paul.

Christ wants to be all and all to His own now. He should be the root, the stem, the vine, the branches, the twigs, and the fruit in one's life.

Unity in Christ
Philippians 1:1-30

Introduction: Unity is exceedingly essential:
1. In worship and service.
2. In suffering.
3. In humility.
4. In purpose.

I Point: <u>Unity in worship and service</u>.
- a. Philippians 1:3-5 – Paul speaks of unity in service.
  Philippians 1:5 "For your fellowship in the gospel from the first day until now;"
- b. What stirred his heart was the fellowship in soul winning.
  1. It was not in the service of a church as we know of.
  2. It was not in athletics.
  3. It was not in building programs.
  4. It was not in church cleanup campaigns.
  5. But, it was in soul winning.
- c. We notice that he rejoiced over the sweet union.
  Philippians 1:7 "...ye all are partakers of my grace."
  They forgave one another.
  Philippians 4:2 - They were patient and helped one another.

II Point: <u>Unity in sufferings</u>.
- a. Philippians 1:14 "And many of the brethren in the Lord, waxing confident by my bonds, are much more bold to speak the word without fear."
  Application: Many of the most precious experiences in this world come through suffering. The world was strengthened and made better because of the suffering of some of God's saints. Some of the most precious books we have in our libraries have been written in prison cells, such as: The Book of Revelation by the Apostle John on the isle of Patmos; John Bunyan's Pilgrim's Progress; Sir Walter Raleigh's World History was also written in prison.
- b. The next fragrance of unity in suffering is "striving together."
  1. Philippians 1:27 "...that ye stand fast in one spirit, with one mind striving together for the faith of the gospel:"
  Illustration: Games such as baseball, football, and the like, must be in unity, or there is defeat. Striving together is not all fun and games; it many times is suffering together in pain.

III Point: <u>Unity in humility</u>.

a. Philippians 2:1-4 - Is a call to humility.
b. Philippians 2:1 – The Lord's people are told to be humble enough to let the consolation of Christ mend their broken hearts.
c. The Lord's people are asked to think with one accord. Philippians 2:2 "...having the same love, being of one accord, of one mind."
d. Philippians 2:3 "Let nothing be done through strife or vainglory; but in lowliness of mind let each esteem other better than themselves."
e. Philippians 2:4 "Look not every man on his own things, but every man also on the things of others."
f. Humility will reign where there is love for others. What is life in this world? It is unity, unity, unity. It is not how much a person possesses, nor how much authority one has; it is unity.

IV Point: <u>Unity of purpose</u>.

a. What is our purpose in all of this?
b. Philippians 1:21 "For to me to live is Christ, and to die is gain."
Many Christians are like the tumbleweed; they will go with the wind.
Oh, that we might be true yokefellows one with another.

Illustration: In the olden days, the boss would take the yoke; then call for the ox by name. The ox would come and put his head under the yoke. Then the boss would call for the next ox by name, and he would come and put his head under the yoke and they would work together in unity.

Psalm 133:1 "Behold, how good and how pleasant it is for brethren to dwell together in unity!"

Fellowship in Christ
Philippians 2:1-11

Introduction: Fellowship is a unity of hearts, minds, hopes and aims. Without fellowship we will be dry, dead, and cold. And we will not have the comfort of love that Apostle Paul speaks about here, which is the result of fellowship.

Love at first sight is not to be depended upon, it must come through the avenue of fellowship; otherwise, the love revealed is without comfort. Love cannot be conveyed to any one by just words. It must come through actions, such as we find in unity and fellowship.

I Point: Fellowship.
  a. Fellowship is the oil that makes all the fitted parts operate smoothly.
  b. Paul seemed to like the word "fellowship" for he uses it very often in this little Epistle of Philippians.
  c. Paul realized that without fellowship among Christians there will be no sweet communion together in Christ.
  d. Paul speaks of the fellowship in the gospel.
    Philippians 1:5 "For your fellowship in the gospel from the first day unto now;"
    Application: You tell me you would like to see a revival. I would say, alright! We'll see how you will fellowship in the gospel, such as: Sunday services, prayer meetings, young people's programs, Youth for Christ rallies, mission circle meetings.
    Or perhaps it is just like my little youngsters who come to me and say, "Daddy, I love you!" I say in return, "Okay, we'll see how you act next time I tell you to do something."

  Love is sacrifice, not words. God so loved that He gave. He fellowshipped with the people to prove His love.
  If you say you love your pastor, I will say, "We shall see how much you will fellowship with me."

II Point: <u>Sweet Fellowship</u>.
- a. Sweet fellowship means confidence in one another, and respect for one another.
- b. Sweet fellowship is this: When you can share your joy and also your sorrow with one another; to laugh and to weep with one another.

    Romans 5:5 "And hope maketh not ashamed; because the love of God is shed abroad in our hearts by the Holy Ghost which is given unto us."

    John 15:17 "These things I command you, that ye love one another."

    Many of us will need to confess our own disobedience in not loving one another before His love can truly fill our hearts.
- c. Paul reminded the Corinthian Church of the fellowship as in I Corinthians 1:9 "God is faithful, by whom ye were called unto the fellowship of his Son Jesus Christ our Lord."
- d. The Apostle Paul wanted to have complete fellowship with Christ.
    1. Philippians 3:10 "That I may know him, and the power of his resurrection, and the fellowship of his sufferings, being made conformable unto his death;"

        Paul wanted to feel the beating, the plucking of his beard, the lashing, the thorns, the nails. He wanted to be like Christ.
    2. We sometimes sing the song, "I would be like Jesus." Would you?

        You cannot be like Jesus unless you have fellowship with Him.

        Fellowship means union, communion, sweet attachment. It means giving and taking of a loving heart.

<u>Conclusion</u>:

If this fellowship exists in our hearts then the next theme of the Apostle Paul fits right into our lives.
"Rejoicing in Christ."

Rejoicing in Christ
Philippians 3:1-14

Introduction: The Apostle Paul always found a reason to rejoice in Christ.
1. In Philippians 1:4 - He rejoices in prayer.
2. Philippians 1:18 - He rejoices over the fact that Christ is being preached.
3. Philippians 1:25 - He rejoices over the faith the Philippians have in Christ.
4. Philippians 1:26 - He looks forward to more abundant joy.
5. Philippians 1:28-30 - He rejoices for the privilege of suffering for Christ and asks them all to rejoice with him.
6. Philippians 2:1 – Reveals unto us that Paul rejoiced greatly over the unity and fellowship with the saints.
7. Philippians 2:16 – Paul indicates that his joy was increased by the growth of the church of God.

I Point: <u>Rejoicing in Prayer</u>.
   a. Philippians 1:4 "Always in every prayer of mine for you all making request with joy."
   b. What gave Paul this joy and rejoicing over the church at Philippi? (Answer) Philippians 1:5 "For your fellowship in the gospel from the first day until now;"
   Prayer is grievous where there is no fellowship, but it becomes very sweet and attractive where there is fellowship.
   The greatest thing in life is growth. From childhood we look forward to growth. And where there is unity and fellowship there is growth: spiritually, prayerfully, and in number.
   A doctor said 80% of all physical ailments are spiritual ailments. And they are mainly because of the lack of joy in the Lord. (Saved and unsaved alike.)

II Point: <u>Rejoicing over faith</u>.
   a. Paul brings to our attention the fact that the Philippian Christians were happy Christians.
   Philippians 1:23-26 – Paul was in strait betwixt two. He would like to have been with Jesus; but, also to be with the Philippian Church to see their rejoicing in Christ.
   Philippians 1:27 "...that ye stand fast in one spirit, with one mind striving together for the faith of the gospel:"

- b. Philippians 2:1-4 - Paul tells them that if they would like to make him very happy as he always wants to be, they then should be of one mind, and of one heart in the things of the Lord.
  That indeed brings great joy to any preacher.

III Point: <u>Looking forward to a more abundant joy.</u>
- a. Philippians 1:26 - That is in his absence and in their presence.
  So far they were absent from each other, but now he looked forward to being together with them.
- b. Philippians 1:29 "For unto you it is given in the behalf of Christ, not only to believe on him, but also to suffer for his sake;" To the Apostle Paul the greatest joy there was in this life was to be like Jesus, to suffer like Him, and for His sake.
  It is when we have joy in the sufferings for Christ that we touch the hem of His garment.
  A mother had two unsaved sons. She went to the preacher about it, and he said, "Have you ever wept over them?"

IV Point: <u>Rejoicing in humility.</u>
- a. Philippians 3:1 "Finally, my brethren, rejoice in the Lord..." There he calls them to forget their surroundings, their persecutions, their oppositions, and local quarrels, and to be a singing happy group of Christians.
- b. Having himself abased he sees Christ exalted in him. Philippians 4:12 "I know both how to be abased, and I know how to abound..."
  Philippians 3:8 "...I count all things but loss for the excellency of the knowledge of Christ Jesus my Lord: for whom I have suffered the loss of all things, and do count them but dung, that I may win Christ."

Conclusion: A woman was asked, "Do you know Jesus? Do you love Him?" She answered, "You can't know Him and not love Him!"

That I May Know Him

Philippians 3:1-16

Text: Philippians 3:10 "That I may know him, and the power of his resurrection, and the fellowship of his sufferings, being made conformable unto his death;"

Introduction: The Lord has laid down in this verse not only the determination of Paul to know Him, but He tells us how to begin. In order to know Christ you have to start at the back end of this verse.

I Point: Philippians 3:10 "...being made conformable to His death."
- a. There is no possible way you and I can know Jesus until we have completely taken our stand at the cross.
- b. I must rest in His atonement on the cross for my salvation. Illustration: I am dependent on Him just as you are dependent on that pew to hold you up.
- c. I must identify myself with the death of Jesus on the cross to the extent, that as if, that death was my death in Christ.
- d. Illustration: This is the only time the word "conformable" is used in the testament, as if God would point out to you and to me that this act cannot be duplicated anywhere else. Application: The dictionary says this about conformable, "having the same dip."
- e. At the cross I must see Him and myself being crucified. Galatians 2:20 "I am crucified with Christ: nevertheless I live; yet not I, but Christ liveth in me: and the life which I now live in the flesh I live by the faith of the Son of God, who loved me, and gave himself for me."
  1. Christ died for us.
  2. He was made sin for us.
  3. And if you and I look to that cross we must say and believe and trust that the Lord Jesus Christ is our death.
  4. We identify ourselves with Him in His death.

-
  - f. Illustration: Leon Tucker gave an illustration several years ago: He said that the cross is God's burned out place. The judgment had struck at the cross. You and I standing there can watch the fire burn around us, but it cannot get to us.
  Application: Two objects cannot stand in the same place at the same time. It must be either sin or Christ. And if you want to stand there you must take the place of Christ.
    1. To be made conformable with Christ is not just a profession, nor is it just a verbal confession. It is a transformation.
  - g. Illustration: I can go into a strange group of people and speak on the conformity of Christ. I see there a group within the group whose faces are lit up. The rest have not heard what I said. Their eyes do not see. Their hearts have not understood.
  - h. In order to know Jesus Christ we must first be made conformable bodily to His death on the cross. I see that, every time a man or woman gets down on their knees and accepts Jesus Christ as their personal Savior. There is a transformation that makes that person different than the rest.
  That does not happen if he just goes down to the altar or stands before the people.

II Point: <u>Philippians 3:10 "…and the fellowship of his suffering…"</u>
  - a. I believe Paul is talking about the same thing here that he is talking about in Galatians 2:20. "I am crucified with Christ: nevertheless I live; yet not I, but Christ liveth in me: and the life which I now live in the flesh I live by the faith of the Son of God, who loved me, and gave himself for me."
  - b. When you went to the cross of Jesus Christ and became conformable to His death, there was no suffering. He did all the suffering there. I come "Just as I am without one plea, but that Thy blood was shed for me." After you and I are Christians, being made conformable to Christ's death, that is where the suffering for a Christian begins.
  - c. You and I never get to know Jesus Christ until we begin to suffer, and step out and follow Him. Jesus suffered without the gate. Let us therefore go forth unto Him bearing his reproach.

- d. You just step into some circle of your worldly friends and start to tell them what Jesus Christ is to you. Some will laugh. Some will ridicule. Some, of course being polite, will be silent until you leave. Then they will say, "This poor fellow is losing his mind."
- e. Or you just try to gather a group of friends at your home for a prayer meeting. How many will you get out? Lost people, and people who have lost out with the Lord, have no fellowship of His suffering.
- f. Suppose the Lord Jesus were sitting here and I were here as His friend and you would turn Him out. Could I stay here? "No!"
- g. Or suppose a friend and I were here and you would order my friend out. Would I stay here? Not on your life!
- h. I like to think of it on this way. I am being made conformable unto His death and have fellowship with His suffering. If any one dares to turn me out, the Lord will then go out too. He is in fellowship with my suffering, if I am with His.

III Point: Philippians 3:10 "... and the power of his resurrection."
- a. I cannot know the power of His resurrection until I have had a death.
- b. You never know what it is to have a thing come back to you until you gave it up.
- c. How are you going to know what it is to be raised from the dead, until you die.
- d. You must come to the place where you are willing to die with Him.
- e. Do you think it didn't cost the Lord Jesus Christ something? It did, and it will cost you something, too.
- f. To know Him, and power of His resurrection, it costs. It cost plenty.
- g. Don't look for anything good that doesn't cost you something.
- h. We have too many people who would like to be a Christian, but they don't want to pay the price of be a Christian.
- i. In order to be made conformable to His death, and to have the fellowship of His suffering, and the power of His resurrection, it will cost.

The Power of His Resurrection
Philippians 3:7-14

Text: Philippians 1:10 "That ye may approve things that are excellent; that ye may be sincere and without offence till the day of Christ;"

Introduction: There are six different resurrection powers before us which I would like to relate to you folks at this time.

The Apostle Paul declares that everything in the world is accounted by him as loss, compared to the knowledge of Christ and the power of His resurrection. In the Old Testament God speaks often of His power as the power by which He brought Israel up out of Egypt. But in the New Testament His power is spoken of as the power by which He raised Christ from the dead. There is, according to God's Holy Word, wonderful power in the resurrection.

I Point: <u>The power of the resurrecting faith</u>.
- a. Romans 4:17 "(As it is written, I have made thee a father of many nations,)..."
  Romans 4:19-20 "And being not weak in faith, he considered not his own body now dead, when he was about an hundred years old, neither yet the deadness of Sarah's womb. He staggered not at the promises of God..."
  Application: It was through this faith that Abraham's old dead body was able to produce the generation, as the stars in the heavens.
- b. Hebrews 11:17-19 "By faith Abraham, when he was tried, offered up Isaac: and he that had received the promises offered up his only begotten son. Of whom it was said, That in Isaac shall thy seed be called: Accounting that God was able to raise him up, even from the dead; from whence also he received him in a figure."
- c. Abraham believed that God was able to raise up Isaac from the dead. Christ Jesus our Lord says, Abraham "...rejoiced to see my day:..." (John 8:56).
- d. Loving faith is resurrection faith.
  Romans 10:9-10 "That if thou shalt confess with thy mouth the Lord Jesus, and shalt believe in thine heart that God hath raised him from the dead, thou shalt be saved. For with the heart man believeth unto righteousness; and with the month confession is made unto salvation."

Application: There are many folks today who profess to be believers, and have a dead faith. Your faith is vain if you are yet in your sins. A person not believing in the resurrection of Christ, his faith will end at the grave. Oh, that I may know the power of the resurrection.

II Point: <u>The power of resurrection assurance</u>.
- a. Romans 4:25 "Who was delivered for our offences, and was raised again for our justification."
  Application: If Christ had only died we would have no assurance that God had accepted His atoning death on Calvary. But when He arose from the dead God declared by His resurrection that all believers in Christ were justified.
- b. I Peter 1:3 "Blessed be the God and Father of our Lord Jesus Christ, which according to His abundant mercy hath begotten us again unto a lively hope by the resurrection of Jesus Christ from the dead."
- c. The Apostle Paul in I Corinthians 15:55 shouts it out, "O death, where is thy sting? O grave, where is thy victory?"
- d. There is likewise assurance in the resurrection to all unsaved, that they will be judged. We read in Acts 17:31 "Because he hath appointed a day, in the which he will judge the world in righteousness by that man whom he hath ordained; whereof he hath given assurance unto all men, in that he hast raised him from the dead."

III Point: <u>The power of the resurrection in grace and victory</u>.
- a. Acts 4:33 "And with great power gave the apostles witness of the resurrection of the Lord Jesus: and great grace was upon them all."
  Application: The resurrection is powerful in bringing great grace upon your life.
  Victory over sin and flesh comes to those who count that "...we have been planted together in the likeness of his death, we shall be also in the likeness of his resurrection:" (Romans 6:5).
- b. Romans 8:11 – Declares that we have the same power for victory that raised up Jesus Christ from the dead.
  Romans 8:11 "But if the Spirit of him that raised up Jesus from the dead dwell in you, he that raised up Christ from the dead shall also quicken your mortal bodies by His Spirit that dwelleth in you."
- c. Application: Real victory then, is resurrection victory.

IV Point: <u>Resurrection power in witnessing</u>.
- a. When the apostles were choosing one to take Judas' place, they said it, "...must one be ordained to be a witness with us of his resurrection." (Acts 1:22).
  Application: No witness of Jesus Christ can be powerful who leaves out the resurrection.
  It is the Holy Spirit that witnesses through us, and unless we are willing to have His witness of the resurrection, He will not witness at all.
- b. When Paul preached to the philosophers in Athens he spoke to them of the resurrection of Christ. Acts 17:31 "Because he hath appointed a day, in the which he will judge the world in righteousness by that man whom he hath ordained; whereof he hath given assurance unto all men, in that he hath raised him from the dead."
  Application: There is great power in the testimony of His resurrection.

V Point: <u>The power of resurrection service</u>.
- a. Romans 7:4 "Wherefore, my brethren, ye also are become dead to the law by the body of Christ; that ye should be married to another, even to him who is raised from the dead, that we should bring forth fruit unto God."
  Application: No fruit is accepted by God unless it comes by the power of His resurrection.

VI Point: <u>Power of resurrecting position</u>.
- a. Ephesian 2:4-6 "But God, who is rich in mercy, for his great love wherewith he loved us, Even when we were dead in sins, hath quickened us together with Christ (by grace ye are saved:) And hath raised us up together, and made us sit together in heavenly places in Christ Jesus."
  Application: Every Christian should take this resurrection position with His living Lord by faith. We need, as His children, to take our resurrection position seriously and live in its power daily.

Conclusion: Do you know the power of His resurrection?

Sermon Outlines from the Book of Colossians

Christ
Colossians 3:1-17

Theme: Christ is the light of the world.

Text: Colossians 3:11 "...Christ is all, and in all."

Introduction: There are 5 points before us that I would like to bring to your attention which circle around Christ.
1. Christ is our hope. (I Timothy 1:1)
2. Christ is our peace. (Ephesians 2:14)
3. Christ is our life. (Colossians 3:4)
4. Christ is our joy. (I Peter 1:8)
5. Christ is our all. (Colossians 3:11)

The Holy Bible richly abounds with exaltation of Christ the eternal Son of God. But among all the many exaltations written of Christ by the Holy Spirit I believe these five are of the most precious, for they show unto us the very life and light of Christ.

I Point: Christ is our hope.
a. I Timothy 1:1 "PAUL, an apostle of Jesus Christ by the commandment of God our Saviour, and Lord Jesus Christ, which is our hope;"
  1. Application: When was it in your life that there seemed to be no hope, and then you fled to Christ, who is, and was, and proved himself to be your hope? For He is.
  2. Illustration: The hope of Psalm 31:24. "Be of good courage, and he shall strengthen your heart, all ye that hope in the LORD."
  3. David had this hope.
  Psalm 16:9 "Therefore my heart is glad, and my glory rejoiceth: my flesh also shall rest in hope."
  4. And Abraham had this hope as per Romans 4:18 "Who against hope believed in hope, that he might become the father of many nations; according to that which was spoken, So shall thy seed be."

II Point: Christ is our peace.
a. Ephesians 2:14 "For he is our peace, who hath made both one, [Jew and Gentile] and hath broken down the middle wall of partition between us;"
Application: The world looks for peace, but as long as they will leave out the Prince of Peace, there will be no peace.

- b. Isaiah 53:5 "But he was wounded for our transgressions, he was bruised for our iniquities: the chastisement of our peace was upon him; and with his stripes we are healed."
- c. But to those who have rejected the Prince of Peace, Isaiah 57:21 says "There is no peace, saith my God, to the wicked." And again Isaiah 48:22 "There is no peace, saith the LORD, unto the wicked."
- d. The Apostle Paul puts the right emphasis on what we call peace. Romans 14:19 "Let us therefore follow after the things which make for peace, and things wherewith one may edify another."

III Point: <u>Christ is our life</u>.
- a. Colossians 3:4 "When Christ, who is our life, shall appear, then shall ye also appear with him in glory."
- b. Application: Life and light are very closely connected.
- c. Illustration: All things that live must come to the light. For it gives life as in plants and grass. It cleanses; it also darkens, and then light gives sight. One light supersedes the other. Likewise, an ordinary life is superseded by life abundant in Christ.
- d. John 1:4 "In him was life; and the life was the light of men."

IV Point: <u>Christ is our joy.</u>
- a. I Peter 1:8 "Whom having not seen, ye love; in whom, though now ye see him not, yet believing, ye rejoice with joy unspeakable and full of glory:"
- b. Application: Joy is hard to explain. Some people have joy. Romans 14:17 "For the kingdom of God is not meat and drink; but righteousness, and peace, and joy in the Holy Ghost."
- c. The world wonders where is the joy in Christian life? But the very fact that there was joy in heaven at your conversion sets loose a trail of joy that passes all understanding.

V Point: <u>Christ is our all</u>.
- a. Colossians 3:11 "...Christ is all, and in all."

Conclusion:
Psalm 34:1 "I WILL bless the LORD at all times: his praise shall continually be in my mouth."

Sermon Outlines from the Book of I Thessalonians

The Resurrections
I Thessalonians 4:13-18

Introduction: Last Sunday we had the study of the material nature and the spiritual nature of man.

And we came to the place where we were convinced, according to scripture, that the material body remains in the grave, and the spirit goes on to its respective place. If a Christian, their spirit goes to paradise; if not a Christian, their spirit goes to hades, or hell, (not the final place Gehenna).

Through scripture it was also proved that the saved have now conscious bliss; whereas, the unsaved have now conscious torment. The proof is Luke 16:19-31 - The rich man and Lazarus.

I Point: <u>Will the righteous remain in paradise for all eternity</u>?
   a. The resurrection.
      Some people disbelieve the resurrection.
      1st argument – No body remains.
      2nd argument – Destruction of the body by fire.
      3rd argument – Destruction of the body by beast.

      Application: All these excuses that man may make will not change or alter the fact one bit.
      Luke 1:37 "For with God nothing shall be impossible."

      The infallible word of God declares that the dead will be resurrected, so we need not be concerned in the lest how the resurrected body will be provided.

   b. The resurrection of the body is taught in the Old Testament.
      Job 19:26 "And though after my skin worms destroy this body, yet in my flesh shall I see God:"
      Daniel 12:2 "And many of them that sleep in the dust of the earth shall awake, some to everlasting life, and some to shame and everlasting contempt."
   c. The resurrection of the body was taught by Christ himself.
      John 5:28-29 "Marvel not at this: for the hour is coming, in the which all that are in the graves shall hear his voice, And shall come forth; they that have done good, unto the

resurrection of life; and they that have done evil, unto the resurrection of damnation."

Here we have Jesus, himself, teaching the resurrection of the righteous and unrighteous.

    d. The same was taught by the Apostle Paul.

Acts 24:15 "...there shall be a resurrection of the dead, both of the just and unjust."

Application: Do not get confused. There are two resurrections, but at different times.

All shall be resurrected. I Corinthians 15:23 "But every man in his own order:…."

Here the word "order" is a military word: meaning rank or group.

Paul puts them in order:

    1st Resurrection - I Corinthians 15:23 "...Christ the Firstfruits;..." This resurrection was over 2000 years ago.

    2nd Resurrection - I Corinthians 15:23 "...afterward they that are Christ's at his coming." (The saved).

    3rd Resurrection - I Corinthians 15:24 "Then cometh the end,…" a 1000 years later. (The unsaved). Revelation 20:5 "But the rest of the dead lived not again until the thousand years were finished…"

II Point: When will the first resurrection take place?

    a. At the second coming of Christ, when Christ descends from heaven, "...the dead in Christ shall rise first: Then we which are alive and remain shall be caught up together with them in the clouds, to meet the Lord in the air:…" (I Thessalonians 4:13-17).

Application: That seems very logical. For the Spirit of the dead in Christ come with Him. If we who are alive would go first, then we would meet our loved ones who went on before us, without their bodies.

    b. The living ones, who will be changed, will not feel the sting and pain of death. This is just for those who have died already and have enjoyed the presents of Christ for some time.

I Corinthians 15:55 "O death, where is thy sting? O grave, where is thy victory?"

III Point: <u>Where will the saved then be?</u>
   a. We shall ever be with the Lord.
      Romans 8:1 "There is therefore now no condemnation to them which are in Christ Jesus, who walk not after the flesh, but after the Spirit."
      The sins of the believer were judged in Christ.
   b. II Corinthians 5:10 "For we must all appear before the judgment seat of Christ; that every one may receive the things done in his body, according to that he hath done, whether it be good or bad."
      Application: This is for rewards, not for judgment of saved or lost.
      Illustration: The Greek word "judgment seat" is (Bema) award; it has to do only with those who are saved.

IV Point: <u>Manor of rewards</u> – There are Five Crowns.
1. The crown of life. (James 1:12)
2. The crown of glory. (I Peter 5:4)
3. The crown of rejoicing. (I Thessalonians 2:19)
4. The crown of righteousness. (II Timothy 4:8)
5. The crown of incorruptible. (I Corinthians 9:25)

1. James 1:12 "Blessed is the man that endureth temptation: for when he is tried, he shall receive the <u>crown of life</u>,..." It is the martyr's crown, for those faithful, even unto death."
2. I Peter 5:4 "And when the chief Shepherd shall appear, ye shall receive a <u>crown of glory</u>." It is the Shepherd's crown for those who feed the flock of God.
3. I Thessalonians 2:19 "For what is our hope, or joy, or <u>crown of rejoicing</u>?..." It is the soul winner's crown.
4. II Timothy 4:8 "Henceforth there is laid up for me a <u>crown of righteousness</u>;..." It is for those who love and look for Christ's appearing.
5. I Corinthians 9:25 "Now they do it to obtain a corruptible crown; but we an <u>incorruptible [crown]</u>." It is for those who disciplined their bodies and showed self-control, striving to live a holy and godly life.

*The Five Crowns are expanded upon further in The Christian's Crowns, page 409.

Sermon Outlines from the Book of II Timothy

A Mother's Prayer
II Timothy 1:1-13

Text: II Timothy 1:5 "When I call to remembrance the unfeigned faith that is in thee, which dwelt first in thy grandmother Lois, and thy mother Eunice; and I am persuaded that in thee also."

Introduction: We shall at this time look into the length and breadth that a mother's prayer will reach.

I Point: From how far back will God answer a mother's prayer?
  a. II Timothy 1:5 - "...and thy mother Eunice;..." Our text suggest from his mother's days.
  b. We could go still farther back.
  c. II Timothy 1:5 "...the unfeigned faith...which first dwelt in thy grandmother Lois,..."

II Point: The Present, or mother's days.
  a. Thy mother Eunice.
  b. Timothy, this great preacher, was what he was because of his mother's and grandmother's prayers.
  Illustration: Many times we hear that expression, "I am what I am, because of my praying mother."
  c. The greatest blessing a child can have in this world is praying parents.
  I am a minister of the gospel today because of my praying mother.
  d. How many a boy in the arm forces was protected through all the war because of a praying mother?
  e. The victory of those still alive from war is not to be contributed to the dictators or leaders of our land, but to the ones who have prevailed in prayer before God.
  f. The most blessed crown there will be in glory will be to a praying mother.
  g. Whereas, on the other hand, the most dreadful condemnation will be to a mother who will have her own children with her in hell, condemning her for ever because she prayed not.

III Point: Past prayers of mothers.
  a. How many times do we read of men coming to Christ at the last point of life because of their praying mother?
  Illustration: A man last his arm, and in the hospital he found the New Testament his mother had hid in his bag. Then not only did he himself come to the Lord because of it, but also a dying boy next to him.

IV Point: What is an ideal Mother?
  a. I Samuel 1:1-28 -Hannah of old. She first prayed for a child. Then she gave him back to the Lord, and stood with him in the ministry of the Lord all her life in faithful prayer.
  b. And she will share eternity with Samuel, her son, crowned with many crowns.

God's Divine Rule

II Timothy 1:1-14

Text: Proverbs 22:6 "Train up a child in the way he should go: and when he is old, he will not depart from it."

Introduction: We want first to look into the divine rules God has for parents. Then next into the respect He has unto the generations to come, for the prayers of the parents and grandparents.

I Point: <u>God's divine rule</u>.
   a. God has a divine rule for everything. His entire creation has a divine rule.
   b. He has a divine rule for men. He brings under this rule the length of our life.
   c. He has a divine rule for parents.
   Deuteronomy 6:6-7 "And these words, which I command thee this day, shall be in thine heart: And thou shalt teach them diligently unto thy children, and shalt talk of them when thou sittest in thine house, and when thou walkest by the way, and when thou liest down, and when thou risest up."
   Application: Yet we find homes, and even Christian homes, where fathers and mothers never talk to their children about the Lord. In fact they have no family prayer time with them. And in some homes they don't even say grace at the table.
   d. Of Abraham, God spoke these words: Genesis 18:19 "For I know him, that he will command his children and his household after him, and they shall keep the way of the LORD..."
   e. Proverbs 22:6 "Train up a child in the way he should go: and when he is old, he will not depart from it." This is God's divine rule.

II Point: <u>God's respect for the prayer of a Christian mother and father.</u>
   a. II Timothy 1:5 "When I call to remembrance the unfeigned faith that is in thee, which dwelt first in thy grandmother Lois, and thy mother Eunice; and I am persuaded that in thee also."

Application: We find throughout the entire Bible mighty men, and you can trace it back to the prayers of their mother. Take the life of Samuel. He was what he was, because of Hannah his mother who prayed.

Take the life of our today men of God. It usually is because of a praying mother.

Yes, God has great respect to the prayers of a mother.

   b. I have told you of the prayers of my mother, and how her prayers made me what I am today. (Read the autobiography of Mark Houseman *Under the Red Star*.)

III Point: <u>In contrast, take the unfortunate one's who had not a praying mother.</u>
- a. Let us take those wicked kings of old. Their mothers had been the cause of their downfall.
- b. Oh that mother's may see their responsibility before God to their family.

Sermon Outlines from the Book of Titus

To Be a Pattern
Titus 2:1-10

Text: Titus 2:7 "In all things shewing thyself a pattern of good works: in doctrine shewing uncorruptness, gravity, sincerity,"

Introduction: God wants His people to be a pattern. God is interested in his creation to make it a pattern.

    i. God wants young folks to be a pattern.
    ii. God wants parents to be a pattern.
    iii. In order to be a pattern we must "Study [the Word] to shew thyself approved unto God, a workman that needeth not to be ashamed, rightly dividing the word of truth." (II Timothy 2:15).

I Point: How God forms His patterns.
    a. The care of a Christian mother.
    b. The study of God's word in a Christian seminary.
    Illustration: Science tells us that a fiery Opal was nothing more than a handful of sand. God placed it in the bowels of the earth and applied great heat from beneath and a stupendous weight from above. And when men find it, it is a beautiful Opal.
    c. An amethyst, to begin with, is nothing more than a handful of clay.
    d. A diamond is nothing more than a handful of black carbon.

How it is done? We don't know, but we do know that the Lord can take a useless fellow, or an old drunkard, or perhaps a sinful woman, and transform them into a life that will someday adorn the crown of Jesus Christ.

Illustration: Dr. Robert S. Lee has called attention to the fact that God takes oxygen and hydrogen, both of them are odorless, tasteless and colorless, and combines them with carbon which is insoluble black and tasteless. And the result of this combination is beautiful sweet white sugar.

Application: How is it done? Take the blood of Jesus Christ and apply it on a black sinner, and God says that he shall be whiter than snow and a sweet smelling savour unto the Lord.

II Point: <u>God requests confidence and faith</u>.

    a.   Illustration: A father, who was the fire chief in the city, brought his little girl to kindergarten. He looked at the structure, and then he said to his little girl, "Should fire break out in this place please don't run out, just sit down on this chair and I will come get you." A fire did break out, and her father did come and get her.

Conclusion:
God has a plan.
God has a purpose.
God has a design.
God has the means to transform your life.

All he asks of you is just yieldedness to Him.

Salvation Brought

Titus 2:11-15

Text: Titus 2:11 "For the grace of God that bringeth salvation hath appeared to all men."

I point: <u>Salvation brought</u>.
   a. Titus 2:11 "For the grace of God that brought salvation hath appeared to all men."
   b. God knows the shortness of men's life.
      1. Psalm 90:5-6 "...they are like grass..."
      2. Job 7:7 "...my life is wind..."
      3. Job 8:9 "...our days upon the earth are a shadow:"
      4. James 4:14 "...It is even a vapour."

II Point: <u>God teaches us</u>.
   a. Titus 2:12 - Teaches us to:
      1. Deny ungodliness.
      2. Deny worldly lusts.
      3. Live Soberly.
      4. Righteousness.
      5. Godliness.

III Point: <u>God's goal</u>
   a. Titus 2:13 "Looking for that blessed hope, and the glorious appearing of the great God and our Saviour Jesus Christ."

IV Point: <u>What He has done for us</u>?
   a. Gave Himself.
   b. Redeemed us.
   c. Purified us.
   d. He wants us to live for Him.

Conclusion: Proverbs 14:34 "Righteousness exalteth a nation: but sin is a reproach to any people."

Psalm 111:10 "The fear of the LORD is the beginning of wisdom: a good understanding have all they that do his commandments: his praise endureth for ever."

Sermon Outlines from the Book of Hebrews

The Priestly Service of Christ – The office
Hebrew 5:1-10

Text: Hebrews 5:1 "For every high priest taken from among men is ordained for men in things pertaining to God, that he may offer both gifts and sacrifice for sins:"

Introduction: The Priestly service of Christ is something very wonderful. Without it no man could be saved.

The Office is a three-fold service.
1. It is an offering.
2. It is an intercession.
3. It is a throne of judgment.

I Point: The conditions that were to be fulfilled in order that Christ might become God's Priest.
- a. Hebrews 5:1 – He had to be taken from among men. It behoved God to become man.
- b. Hebrews 5:1 – He had to be ordained. No man can ordain God. The lower has to be ordained of the higher. Christ had to be appointed or ordained of men to represent men.
- c. Hebrews 5:4 "And no man taketh this honour unto himself, but he that is called of God..." He had to be called of God.
- d. He had to serve in things pertaining to God.
- e. He had to offer gifts and sacrifices for sin.

II Points: Christ fulfilled all these conditions.
- a. Hebrews 2:14-16 – He had to take on Him the nature of man. The seed of Abraham.
- b. Hebrews 3:2, Hebrews 5:6, Hebrews 7:15, 16, and 24 - He was appointed after the order of Melchisedec.
- c. Hebrews 5:5 – He glorified not Himself.
- d. Hebrews 2:17 - He served in things pertaining to God.
- e. Hebrews 8:3-6, Hebrews 9:11-14 – He secured eternal redemption by the sacrifice of Himself.

III Point: Christ the King Priest.
- a. Hebrews 7:17 - He was priest not after the order of Aaron, but after the order of Melchisedec, meaning our eternal High Priest.
- b. Hebrews 5:6 "As he saith also in another place, Thou art a priest for ever after the order of Melchisedec."

   c. Genesis 14:18-20, Hebrews 7:2 – Christ is a High Priest after the order of Melchisedec. And also the King of Salem and King of Peace.

IV Point: <u>The Priestly service of Christ therefore is divided into three parts and looks from the cross to the throne.</u>
   a. Hebrews 9:25-26 – His offering at the cross.
   b. Hebrews 9:11-12 & 24, Hebrews 10:12 - His intercession at the throne of God.
   c. Hebrews 9:28, Hebrews 10:11-1 - His coming again to his own throne.
   d. Matthew 25:31-32 "When the Son of man shall come in his glory, and all the holy angels with him, then shall he sit upon the throne of his glory: And before him shall be gathered all nations: and he shall separate them one from another, as a shepherd divideth his sheep from the goats:"

Conclusion: Are you, my friend, ready to stand before the throne of Christ?

*This is Part I of the Priestly Service of Christ:
  Part I – Office - Hebrews 5:1-10, page 391.
  Part II – Offering - Hebrews 9: 6-28, page 393.
  Part III – Intercession - Hebrews 7:25, page 396.
  Part IV – The Second Coming - Psalm 110, page 119.

The Priestly Service of Christ - The Offering
Hebrews 9:6-28

Introduction: Last time we had for our discussion on His office as Priest and King after the order of Melchisedec. Today we shall talk about His offering.

There are 5 things we shall look at:
1. The time.
2. The conditions.
3. The place.
4. The manner.
5. The Result.

I Point: <u>The Time</u>.
- a. Hebrews 9:26 "...but now once in the end of the world hath he appeared to put away sin by the sacrifice of himself."
  Application: What do we mean by the end of the world?
  Answer: The last week in Daniel (Chapter 9) or the last 2000 years before the millennium.
- b. Romans 5:6 "For when we were yet without strength, in due time Christ died for the ungodly."
  Application: In spite of the fact that it was the end of the ages, we were yet without strength.
  The coming of Christ was due.
  The offering was due.
  The price was due.
  It was at the right time that Christ should come and die.
- c. Galatians 4:4-5 "But when <u>the fulness of the time</u> was come, God sent forth his Son, made of a woman, made under the law, To redeem them that were under the law, that we might receive the adaption of sons."
  Application: The time was full. Every device of man had been tried. Every law, including God's laws, was exhausted; but, man could not be brought into sonship with God.

II Point: <u>The Conditions</u>.
- a. Romans 5:6 "For when we were yet without strength, in due time Christ died for the ungodly."
  Application: There was not a man found fit to redeem himself or to redeem others.
- b. Romans 5:8 "But God commandeth his love toward us, in that, <u>while we were yet sinners</u>, Christ died for us." No one had excess to the throne of God.

   c. Romans 5:10 "For it, when we were enemies, we were reconciled to God by the death of his Son..."
   Application: That is the condition that God saw man.

III Point: <u>The Place</u>.
   a. Did God choose the nicest place? No! He chose the basest place. And probably the most wicked place.
   Luke 9:51 "And it came to pass, when the time was come that he should be received up, he stedfastly set his face to go to Jerusalem,"

   Luke 13:34 "O Jerusalem, Jerusalem, which killest the prophets, and stonest them that are sent unto thee, how often would I have gathered thy children together, as a hen doth gather her brood under her wings, and ye would not!"

   Revelation 11:8 "And their dead bodies (The two witnesses) shall lie in the street of the great city, which spiritually is called Sodom and Egypt, where also our Lord was crucified."
   b. Hebrews 13:12 "Wherefore Jesus also, that he might sanctify the people with his own blood, suffered without the gate."
   Application: The place appointed for His offering was upon <u>the cross at Calvary</u>.
   c. John 19:17-18 "And he bearing his cross went forth into a place called the place of the skull, which is called in the Hebrew Golgotha: Where they crucified him,..."
   Philippians 2:7-8, Colossians 1:20, Hebrews 13:10-12.

IV Point: <u>The Manner</u>.
   a. Hebrews 10:7 "Then said I, Lo, I come (in the volume of the book it is written of me,) to do thy will, O God."
   b. <u>Substitutional</u>.
   II Corinthians 5:21 "For he hath made him to be sin for us, who knew no sin; that we might be made the righteousness of God in him."
   I Peter 3:18 "For Christ also hath once suffered for sins, the just for the unjust, that he might bring us to God..."
   c. <u>Without spot</u>.
   I Peter 1:19 - We are redeemed "...with the precious blood of Christ, as of a lamb without blemish and without spot:"

Hebrews 9:14 "How much more shall the blood of Christ, who through the eternal Spirit offered himself without spot to God, purge your conscience from dead works to serve the living God?"
- d. Acceptable, as according to Philippians 2:8-11 (Read).
- e. Final, John 19:30 "...It is finished: and he bowed his head and gave up the ghost."

V Point: The Result.
- a. Psalm 103:12 "As far as the east is from the west, so far hath he removed our transgressions from us."
- b. Forgiven - Hebrews 10:17 "And their sins and iniquities will I remember no more."
- c. Sanctified - Hebrews 10:10 "By the which will we are sanctified through the offering of the body of Jesus Christ once for all."
- d. Perfected – Hebrews 10:14 "For by one offering he hath perfected for ever them that are sanctified."
- e. Glorified - II Corinthians 3:18 - "But we all, with open face beholding as in a glass the glory of the Lord, are changed into the same image from glory to glory, even as by the Spirit of the Lord."
  II Thessalonians 1:10 "...(because our testimony among you was believed) in that day."

Conclusion: If Christ has done all this for you, what have you done for Him?

Romans 12:1 "I BESEECH you therefore, brethren, by the mercies of God, that ye present your bodies a living sacrifice, holy, acceptable unto God, which is your reasonable service."

*This is Part II of the Priestly Service of Christ:
  Part I – Office - Hebrews 5:1-10, page 391.
  Part II – Offering - Hebrews 9: 6-28, page 393.
  Part III – Intercession - Hebrews 7:25, page 396.
  Part IV – The Second Coming - Psalm 110, page 119.

The Priestly Service of Christ – The Intercession
Hebrews 7:25

Introduction: Last Sunday we saw the Priestly Service of Christ as the offering for mankind. Today we shall see him as the intercession for mankind.
1. The place of intercession.
2. For whom His is the intercession.
3. The basis of intercession.
4. The special purpose of intercession.

I Point: The place of intercession.
- a. The Holy of Holies or heaven. Hebrews 9:3 "...the Holiest of all;"
  Application: The sanctuary in the tabernacle is just an allegory, or just symbolically of the place of intercession of Christ in heaven.
- b. Hebrews 9:8 "...the way into the holiest of all was not yet made manifest..."
- c. Here we have Christ as an high priest by His own suffering. Hebrews 9:12 "...having obtained eternal redemption for us." He set down as intercessor.
- d. Hebrews 7:25 "Wherefore he is able also to save them to the uttermost that come unto God by him, seeing he ever liveth to make intercession for them."
- e. Hebrews 9:24 "For Christ is not entered into the holy places made with hands, which are the figures of the true; but into heaven itself, now to appear in the presence of God for us:"

II Point: For whom?
- a. Hebrews 9:24 "...now to appear in the presence of God for us:"
  Not for the unsaved, but for His own. It is the Holy Spirit that convicts men of sin, of righteousness, and judgment. But it is Christ that intercedes for His own.
- b. Hebrews 7:25 "Wherefore he is able also to save them to the uttermost that come unto God by him, seeing he ever liveth to make intercession for them."
- c. John 17:9-10 "I pray for them: I pray not for the world, but for them which thou hast given me: for they are thine. And all mine are thine, and thine are mine; and I am glorified in them."

III Point: <u>The basis of the plea.</u>
 a. Hebrews 9:12 "...by <u>his own blood</u> he entered in once into the holy place, having obtained eternal redemption for us."
 b. Exodus 12:13 "...when I see the blood, I will pass over you..."
 c. I John 1:7 "...the blood of Jesus Christ his son cleanseth us from all sin."
 d. The finished work of Christ. John 17:18 "As thou hast sent me into the world, even so have I also sent them into the world."

IV Point: <u>The special purposes of the plea.</u>
 a. <u>To sustain life</u>.
 Hebrews 9:24 "...to appear in the presence of God for us."
 Romans 8:34 "Who is he that condemneth? It is Christ that died, yea rather, that is risen again, who is even at the right hand of God, who also maketh intercession for us."
 I John 2:1 "My little children..."
 Hebrews 7:25 "Wherefore he is able also to save them to the uttermost that come unto God by him, seeing he ever liveth to make intercession for them."
 b. <u>To give cleansing</u>.
 I John 1:9 "If we confess our sins, he is faithful and just to forgive us our sins, and to cleanse us from all unrighteousness."
 c. <u>To give grace</u>.
 Hebrews 4:15-16 – Read. "...that we may obtain mercy, and find grace to help in time of need." (Hebrews 4:16).
 d. <u>To secure victory</u>.
 Hebrews 2:18 "For in that he himself hath suffered being tempted, he is able to succour them that are tempted." (Succour means to assist and support in times of hardship and distress.)

*This is Part III of the Priestly Service of Christ:
 Part I – Office - Hebrews 5:1-10, page 391.
 Part II – Offering - Hebrews 9: 6-28, page 393.
 Part III – Intercession - Hebrews 7:25, page 396.
 Part IV – The Second Coming - Psalm 110, page 119.

Christ our Deliverer
Hebrews 9:24-28

Text: Hebrews 9:27 "And as it is appointed unto men once to die, but after this the judgment:"

Introduction: We want to deal with this wonderful deliverance in the past, present and future.

I Point: <u>Atonement – Past.</u>
   a. Colossians 1:13 "Who hath delivered us from the power of darkness, and hath translated us into the kingdom of his dear Son:"
   b. I Thessalonians 1:10 "And to wait for his Son from heaven, whom he raised from the dead, even Jesus, which delivered us from the wrath to come."
   c. Ephesians 1:3-8 (read) "In whom we have redemption through his blood, the forgiveness of sins, according to the riches of his grace;" (Ephesians 1:7).
   d. Colossians 2:13 "And you, being dead in your sins...hath he quickened together with him, having forgiven you all trespasses;"
   e. Matthew 1:21 "And she shall bring forth a son, and thou shalt call his name JESUS: for he shall save his people from their sins."
   Application: The Past! Just look in the past and see your sins.
   Some of us who have tasted sin appreciate our salvation more.

II Point: <u>Atonement and advocacy- Present.</u>
   a. II Timothy 3:11 "...what persecutions I endured: but out of them all the Lord delivered me."
   b. II Timothy 4:17 "Notwithstanding the Lord stood with me, and strengthened me; that by me the preaching might be fully known, and that all the Gentiles might hear; and I was delivered out of the mouth of the lion."
   c. II Peter 2:9 "The Lord knoweth how to deliver the godly out of temptations,..."
   d. I John 1:7 "...the blood of Jesus Christ his Son cleanseth us from all sin."(In cleansing).

- e. I John 2:1 "...we have an advocate with the Father, Jesus Christ the righteous:"
  Application: In obedience to the indwelling spirit of God we have power over sin.
- f. Revelation: 12:11 "And they overcame him by the blood of the Lamb, and by the word of their testimony; and they loved not their lives unto the death."

III Point: <u>Christ - our final deliverer – Yet in the Future</u>.
- a. Philippians 3:20-21 "For our conversation [citizenship] is in heaven; from whence also we look for the Saviour, the Lord Jesus Christ: Who shall change our vile body, that it may be fashioned like unto his glorious body, according to the working whereby he is able even to subdue all things unto himself."
- b. John 14:3 "And if I go and prepare a place for you, I will come again, and receive you unto myself; that where I am, there ye may be also.
- c. John 17:22 "And the glory which thou gavest me I have given them; that they may be one, even as we are one:"
- d. Titus 2:13 "Looking for that blessed hope, and the glorious appearing of the great God and our Saviour Jesus Christ;"
- e. I John 3:2 "Beloved, now are we the sons of God, and it doth not yet appear what we shall be: but we know that, when he shall appear, we shall be like him; for we shall see him as he is."

Conclusion:

The final deliverance from penalty of sins has to do with the first coming of Jesus Christ. - <u>Past</u>.

Deliverance from the power of sin has to do with His present intercession. – <u>Present</u>.

Deliverance from the presence of sin has to do with the second coming of Jesus Christ. – <u>Future</u>.

True Faith

Hebrews 11:1-7

Theme: True faith in the midst of Spiritual declension.

Text: Hebrews 11:7 "By faith Noah, being warned of God of things not seen as yet, moved with fear, prepared an ark to the saving of his house; by the which he condemned the world, and became heir of the righteousness which is by faith."

I Point: <u>Under what circumstance had Noah this faith</u>?
- a. Spiritual death all around him.
- b. A valley of dry bones.
- c. Hebrews 11:1 "Now faith is the substance of things hoped for, the evidence of things not seen."

II Point: <u>The nature of faith</u>.
- a. Noah - Hebrews 11:7 "...moved with fear..."
  Application: Does our fear of God move us to action?
- b. A two-fold fear.
  1. Fear toward salvation.
  2. Fear toward service.

III Point: <u>The manifestation of faith</u>.
- a. Noah - Hebrews 11:7 "...prepared an ark..."
- b. He was moved to action for God.

IV Point: <u>The result of faith</u>.
- a. Hebrews 11:7 "...to the saving of his house;..."(family).
- b. Hebrews 11:7 "...by the which he condemned the world,..."

V Point: <u>The reward of faith</u>.
- a. Noah - Hebrews 11:7 "...became heir of the righteousness which is by faith."
- b. Application: As the woman with the alabaster box in Mark 14:9 "Verily I say unto you, Wheresoever this gospel shall be preached throughout the whole world, this also that she hath done shall be spoken of for a memorial of her."

The Christian Walk
Hebrews 12:1-2

Text: "Wherefore seeing we also are compassed about with so great a cloud of witnesses, let us lay aside every weight, and the sin which doth so easily beset us, and let us run with patience the race that is set before us."

Introduction: There are four distinct points here to be dealt with.
1. Witnesses: Hebrews 12:1 "WHEREFORE seeing we also are compassed about with so great a cloud of witnesses,…"
2. Lay aside: Hebrews 12:1 "…let us lay aside every weight, and the sin which doth so easily beset us,…"
3. Run with patience: Hebrews 12:1 "…let us run with patience the race that is set before us."
4. Keep your eyes on the goal: Hebrews 12:2 "Looking unto Jesus the author and finisher of our faith;…"

I Point: We are compassed about with witnesses.
1. **First Witness** - God Himself.
    a. Psalm 33:13 "The LORD looketh from heaven; he beholdeth all the sons of men."
    b. Psalm 139:1-2 "O Lord, thou hast searched me, and known me. Thou knowest my downsitting and mine uprising, thou understandest my thoughts afar off."
    c. Revelation 19:12 - God, whose eyes are like unto a flame of fire, has focused them upon us.

2. **Second Witness** – The angelic Host.
    a. II Kings 6:15-16 "And when the servant of the man of God was risen early, and gone forth, behold, an host compassed…And he answered, Fear not: for they that be with us are more than they that be with them."
    b. Numbers 22:27 "And when the ass saw the angel of the LORD, she fell down under Balaam:…"

3. **Third Witness** – Satan himself.
    a. I Peter 5:8 "Be sober, be vigilant; because your adversary the devil, as a roaring lion, walketh about, seeking whom he may devour:"
    b. Job 1:8 "And the LORD said unto Satan, Hast thou considered my servant Job, that there is none like him in the earth, a perfect and an upright man, one that feareth God, and escheweth evil?"

4. **Fourth Witness** – Men (people around you watch you closely indeed.)
   Illustration: A business man said to a preacher, "Would you like to know who is a Christian is your congregation?" The preacher said, "Yes." The business man answered, "Just ask the store owners in your town."
   Illustration: There is a race, a course with people all around us focusing their eyes upon the racers, to see how they run the course.

II Point:
1. Lay Aside.
   a. Hebrews 12:1 "...let us lay aside every weight, and the sin which doth so easily beset us..."
   b. Every person has a different kind of trial. Just as our faces differ, so do our trials.
      Illustration: How do the men that run the race "lay aside?" They simply strip off their clothes and put on a racing suit.

III Point:
1. Run with Patience.
   a. Hebrews 12:1 "...let us run with patience the race that is set before us,"
      Illustration: Men who run the race patiently wait for the signal to start.

IV Point:
1. Keep your eyes on the goal – Jesus Christ.
   a. Hebrews 12:2 "Looking unto Jesus the author and finisher of our faith;..."
      Illustration: The greatest inspiration for the race is the sight of the goal.

Conclusion: Paul said, "I press toward the mark for the prize of the high calling of God in Christ Jesus." (Philippians 3:14).
II Timothy 4:7 "I have fought a good fight, I have finished my course, I have kept the faith:"

Looking
Hebrews 12:1-3

Text: Hebrews 12:2 "Looking unto Jesus the author and finisher of our faith;..."

Introduction: There are four different looks 1 would like to present at this time.

I Point: <u>Looking for salvation</u>.
    a. Read – Numbers 21:7-8 "...when he looketh upon it, shall live." (Numbers 2:8).
    b. You may say this is in the Old Testament. But let's look at John 3:14 "And as Moses lifted up the serpent in the wilderness, even so must the Son of man be lifted up:"
    c. The people in Numbers 21:7-8 saw themselves guilty, and looked. Will you, my friend, look?

II Point: <u>Looking for an example</u>.
    a. Hebrews 12:2 "Looking unto Jesus the author and finisher of our faith;..."
    b. Where not to look:
        i. Look not to your church.
        ii. Look not to your pastor.
        iii. Look not to your parents.
        iv. Look not to your hypocrites.
        v. Look not to yourself.

III Point: <u>Looking for Sanctification</u>.
    a. II Corinthians 3:18 "But we all, with open face beholding as in a glass the glory of the Lord, are changed into the same image from glory to glory, even as by the Spirit of the Lord."
        i. When Moses was in the presence of Christ his face shone.
        ii. When Stephen was in the presence of Jesus his face shone like an angel.
        iii. When a person is in prayer with the Lord his face shines.

IV Point: <u>Looking for His coming</u>.
    a. Titus 2:13 "Looking for that blessed hope, and the glorious appearing of the great God and our Saviour Jesus Christ;"
        1. Are you looking for His coming?
        2. When you look for someone you get ready to meet him.

Conclusion: Are you ready to meet the Lord?

Sermon Outlines from the Book of James

What Is Your Life
James 4:12-17

Text: James 4:14 "...For what is your life? It is even a vapour, that appeareth for a little time, and then vanisheth away."

I Point: <u>What is your life?</u>
 a. James 4:14 "...It is even a vapour..."
 b. Job 8:9 "...our days upon earth are a shadow:"
 Application:
 1. We are here on the earth to develop into the life to come.
 2. Illustration: Like a child in the womb of its mother, so are we on the earth to develop into life.
 3. According to our figuring it is years and time, but to God a 1000 years are but as yesterday.
 Psalm 90:10 "The days of our years are threescore years and ten; and if by reason of strength they be fourscore years, yet is their strength labour and sorrow; for it is soon cut off, and we fly away."

II Point: <u>What have you accomplished?</u>
 a. As for your destiny, it is here and then sealed.
 Hebrews 9:27 "And as it is appointed unto men once to die, but after this the judgment:"
 b. God's way of looking is Psalm 90:12 "So teach us to number our days, that we may apply our hearts unto wisdom."
 Application: Proverbs 9:10 "The fear of the LORD is the beginning of wisdom:..."
 c. Jeremiah 8:9 "The wise men are ashamed, they are dismayed and taken: lo, they have rejected the word of the LORD; and what wisdom is in them?"

II Point: <u>Your responsibility</u>
 a. II Corinthians 6:2 "...I have heard thee in a time accepted, and in the day of salvation have I succoured thee;..."
 John 3:7 "Marvel not that I say unto thee, Ye must be born again."
 b. John 3:3 "...Except a man be born again, he cannot see the kingdom of God."
 II Corinthians 6:2 "...behold, now is the accepted time; behold, now is the day of salvation."

Prevailing Prayer
James 5:16

Text: James 5:16 "...The effectual fervent prayer of a righteous man availeth much."

Introduction: Charles G. Finney (1792-1875) was an American Presbyterian minister and leader in the Second Great Awakening in the United States. He has been called the Father of Modern Revivalism. One is struck with the fact that in the life of Finney, every revival began in prayer. The greater the sin or opposition, the more Finney prayed.

I Point: <u>What is prevailing prayer?</u>
   a. For prayer to be effectual it must be for a definite objective. Elias [Elijah] James 5:17 "...prayed earnestly that it might not rain:...
   b. Prayer must be in accord with the will of God.
I John 5:14 "And this is the confidence that we have in him, that, if we ask any thing according to his will, he hearth us:"
Romans 8:26-27 "Likewise the Spirit also helpeth our infirmities: for we know not what we should pray for as we ought; but the Spirit itself maketh intercession for us with groanings which cannot be uttered. And he that searcheth the heart knoweth what is the mind of the Spirit, because he maketh intercession for the saints according to the will of God."
Mark 3:35 "For whosoever shall do the will of God, the same is my brother, and my sister, and mother."
Application: Is it God's will that His Church should be cleansed and awakened to life in Christ and service for the lost?
If so, then let us get right with God ourselves.

II Point: <u>Prayer for the glory of God.</u>
   a. No effectual prayer can be made unless it is for the glory of God. Ephesians 3:16-17 "That he would grant you, according to the riches of his glory, to be strengthened with might by his Spirit in the inner man; That Christ may dwell in your hearts by faith; that ye, being rooted and grounded in love."

III Point: Prayer through the intercession of the Holy Spirit.
  a. Romans 8:27 "And he that searcheth the hearts knoweth what is the mind of the Spirit, because he maketh intercession for the saints according to the will of God."
  b. A Spirit led prayer is persevering.
     Genesis 32:26 "...I will not let thee go, except thou bless me."
  c. A Spirit led prayer is a prayer of faith.
     James 1:6 "But let him ask in faith, nothing wavering. For he that wavereth is like a wave of the sea driven with the wind and tossed."
     Mark 11:24 "Therefore I say unto you, What things soever ye desire, when ye pray, believe that ye receive them, and ye shall have them."
     I John 5:14 "And this is the confidence that we have in him, that, if we ask any thing according to his will, he heareth us:"

Conclusion: Let us pray with prevailing prayer for revival.

Sermon Outlines from the Book of II Peter

The Christian's Crowns

II Peter 1:1-9

Text: II Peter 1:4 "Whereby are given unto us exceeding great and precious promises:..."

Introduction: Among the exceeding great and precious promises referred to in II Peter 1:4, it is interesting to find that faithfulness in its varied form is to be rewarded by our Lord in a very special way.

There are five different crowns, and we should note carefully their respective names and the purpose for which they are bestowed.

1. The Crown of Life - (James 1:12).
2. The Crown of Righteousness - (II Thessalonians 4:8).
3. The Crown of Rejoicing - (I Thessalonians 2:19).
4. The Incorruptible Crown - (I Corinthians 9:25).
5. The Crown of Glory - (I Peter 5:4).

I Point: <u>The Crown of Life</u>.

a. James 1:12 "Blessed is the man that endureth temptation: for when he is tried, he shall receive the crown of life, which the Lord hath promised to them that love him."

b. First, I want you to notice that the reward here spoken of is to come in the life after this life, during which he is tempted, tried, and suffered, even unto death.

c. In the letter to the church at Smyrna, we notice the Holy Spirit writing to them. Revelation 2:10 "...be thou faithful unto death, and I will give thee a crown of life."

Application: Many times we look for a crown in this life. But that is wrong. Do not look for rewards here, but for trials, temptations, misunderstandings and mistreat-ments; for pain, for agony, and the death of the body. That is your reward here.

II Point: <u>The Crown of Righteousness</u>.

    a. II Timothy 4:8 "Henceforth there is laid up for me a crown of righteousness, which the Lord, the righteous judge, shall give me at that day: and not to me only, but unto all them also that love his appearing."

    b. This crown is given at "That Day." Oh, but would we not like to have it now, so that all the people could see we are righteous. But there shall be no glory given to the flesh. You are not righteous until you see Him and shall be made righteous through Him.

    c. But we can here recognize the righteous by their blessed hope, as per Titus 2:13 "Looking for that blessed hope, and the glorious appearing of the great God and our Saviour Jesus Christ;"

This crown of righteousness will be given to those who look for and love His appearing.

III Point: <u>The Crown of Rejoicing</u>.

    a. I Thessalonians 2:19 "For what is our hope, or joy, or crown of rejoicing?..."

    b. There is a crown of rejoicing bestowed upon the saints even here in this present life, and that is the joy of soul winning. But you notice that completeness of this joy will be at His coming when we will lay our trophies at His feet.

    c. The crown of rejoicing is when we shall there meet once again.

Illustration: One's life here might be like the violin of the concert player. In the midst of the beautiful music the string snapped, but the concert player did not quit, nor did he let on that anything was wrong. He finished the concert and there was great rejoicing.

IV Point: <u>The Incorruptible Crown</u>.

    a. I Corinthians 9:25 "And every man that striveth for the mastery is temperate in all things. Now they do it to obtain a corruptible crown; but we an incorruptible."

    This crown is a rewarding crown for good works and a temperate life.

    b. But you have to be first enlisted into the race to run for this incorruptible crown.

    Illustration: A man sold all that he had and went out to find diamonds. But he was not temperate, neither was he prosperous. Because of great disappointment, he took his own life in the stream. After his death, the most beautiful diamonds were found in that very stream.

V Points: <u>The Crown of Glory</u>.

    a. I Peter 5:4 "And when the chief Shepherd shall appear, ye shall receive a crown of glory that fadeth not away."

    b. The crown of glory is a special reward for those who faithfully feed the flock of God. That does not mean just the preacher, but all those that feed the flock.

    c. Revelation 3:11 has a warning to all. "Behold, I come quickly: hold that fast which thou hast, that no man take thy crown." (Revelation 3:11). That is: Suddenly! Therefore hold that fast which thou hast.

Conclusion: Are you looking forward to "That Day" when you will be crowned?

Sermon Outlines from the Book of I John

A Fourfold Attitude Towards Sin
I John 1:1-2:3

Text: I John 1:8 "If we say that we have no sin, we deceive ourselves, and the truth is not in us."

Introduction:
    1st – Denying the fact of being a sinner.
    2nd – Confessing sin.
    3rd – Victory over sin.
    4th – Repeating or falling back into sin.

I Point: <u>Denying the fact of being a sinner</u>.
- a. I John 1:8 "If we say that we have no sin, we deceive ourselves, and the truth is not in us."
  The possession of a sinful nature.
  Application: It is common among people to deny this fact. They say:
  1. I have a divine spark.
  2. Adams sins are not mine.
  3. I am not a sinner.
  4. I am not as bad as you think.
  5. I do the best I can.
- b. The Committal of a sinful act.
  Application: It is common among people to hide sin.
  1. Deny what you've done.
  2. It is not to bad what I have done.
  3. Look at Mr. so and so; he sins more than I do.
- c. What is the result of these, your self-justifications?
  I John 1:8 "If we say that we have no sin, we deceive ourselves, and the truth is not in us."
  1. Self-deception
  2. Heaping on more sin.
  3. We question God's statement. I John 1:7 "...the blood of Jesus Christ his Son cleanseth us from all sin." We ourselves try to justify ourselves, when God says it takes the blood of Christ.
  4. We make God a liar. He says we are sinners.
     I John 1:10 "If we say that we have not sinned, we made him a liar, and his word is not in us."
  5. I John 1:8 "...the truth is not in us.

II Point: <u>Confessing sin</u>.
1st step in confession.
- a. I John 1:9 "If we confess our sins..."
- b. In other words – renouncing and forsaking sin.
- c. Or you hate the sin so much that you quit doing it.
  Repentance is no sooner repentance until you have confessed and quit it.

Illustration: A little boy always prayed before he stole, "Lord forgive me if I steal again." Then he goes ahead and steals. That is not repentance.

2nd Step in Confession.
- a. After you have confessed your sin, you must believe that God has forgiven you.
- b. In other words, we must accept God's declaration when He says, I John 1:9 "...he is faithful and just to forgive us our sins, and to cleanse us from all unrighteousness."

III Point: Victory over sin.
- a. I John 2:1 – Victory is possible.
- b. I John 2:14 – "...the word of God abideth in you..."
  Application: If you will live in the word of God day by day. (Daily morning devotions)
- c. I John 4:4 "...greater is he that is in you, than he that is the world."

IV Point: Repeating or falling back into sin.
- a. It indeed is possible.
- b. Just quit reading God's word and you took one giant step backward.
  Illustration: Someone has said:
  1. If I don't read the Bible one day I notice it.
  2. If I don't read the Bible two days my wife notices it.
  3. If I don't read the Bible for one week all my neighbors will notice it.
- c. I John 2:1 "...If any man sin, we have an advocate with the Father, Jesus Christ the righteous:"
  Illustration: Christ is there interceding for us who are saved.
  Therefore the Holy Spirit will convict you of sin.
- d. What to do.
  1. Recognize the advocacy.
  2. Recognize the provision made for it.
     I John 1:7 "But if we walk in the light, as he is in the light, we have fellowship one with another, and the blood of Jesus Christ his Son cleanseth us from all sin."
  3. Confess your fault and be cleansed. I John 1:9. "...he is faithful and just to forgive us our sins, and to cleanse us from all unrighteousness."

Conclusion: Hebrews 2:3 "How shall we escape, if we neglect so great salvation;..." If you will meet God on His word, He will meet you upon His promises.

How to Promote a Revival
I John 2:15-17

Theme: Sins of Commission.

I Point: <u>Why we have not revival.</u>
- a. <u>Worldly-mindedness.</u>
  1. I John 2:15 "Love not the world, neither the things that are in the world…"
  2. James 4:3 "Ye ask, and receive not, because ye ask amiss, that ye may consume it upon your lusts."
- b. <u>Pride.</u>
  - 2.. I Peter 5:5 "…God resisteth the proud, and giveth grace to the humble."
- c. <u>Envy.</u>
  1. James 4:11 "Speak not evil one of another, brethren."
  2. Ephesians 4:31 "Let all bitterness, and wrath, and anger, and clamour, and evil speaking, be put away from you, with all malice;"
  3. Romans 14:10 "But why dost thou judge thy brethren? or why dost thou set at naught thy brethren? for we shall all stand before the judgment seat of Christ."
- d. <u>Censoriousness.</u> (Blaming or finding fault).
  1. James 3:6 "And the tongue is a fire, a world of iniquity; so is the tongue among our members, that it defileth the whole body, and seteth on fire the course of nature; and it is set on fire of hell."
  2. I Peter 2:1 "Wherefore laying aside all malice, and all guile, and hypocrisies, and envies, and all evil speakings."
- e. <u>Levity.</u>
  1. Ephesians 5:18 "And be not drunk with wine, wherein is excess; but be filled with the Spirit;"
- f. <u>Robbing God</u>
  1. Malachi 1:7 "Ye offer polluted bread upon mine altar;…" and Malachi 3:8-10
- g. <u>Bad Temper</u>.
  1. God will not look you over for medals, degrees and diplomas, but for scars.

The Sin Question
I John 3:1-24

1. **What is sin?**
   "To sin, err, to miss the mark, an error, offence, trespass." (Webster's Dictionary).
   I John 3:4 "...sin is the transgression of the law."
   Romans 14:23 "...for whatsoever is not of faith is sin."
2. **Who is the originator of sin?**
   Ezekiel 28:14 - Satan, the anointed cherub. A perfect creation fell because of pride.
3. **When did sin originate?**
   I John 3:8 "He that committeth sin is of the devil; for the devil sinneth from the beginning..."
   Genesis 3:1 - Doubt by Satan.
   Genesis 3:4 - Lie by Satan.
   Genesis 3:6 - Unbelief by Satan.
   Genesis 3:7 – Disobedience, sin and death by Satan.
   Genesis 3:8 - Lost to God.
   Genesis 5:3 - Man in Adam's likeness.
4. **Are all sinners?**
   Romans 3:9 "...we have before proved both Jews and Gentiles, that they are all under sin;"
   Romans 3:12 "They are all gone out of the way, they are all together become unprofitable; there is none that doeth good, no, not one."
   Romans 3:19 "...all the world may became guilty before God."
5. **What are the effects of sin?**
   Ezekiel 18:4 "...the soul that sinneth, it shall die."
   Ecclesiastes 9:18 "...one sinner destroyeth much good."
   James 1:15 "Then when lust hath conceived, it bringeth forth sin: and sin, when it is finisher, bringeth forth death."
6. **The unbeliever's sin.**
   Matthew 12:36 "...they shall give account thereof in the day of judgment."
   Habakkuk 1:13 "Thou art of purer eyes than to behold evil, and canst not look on iniquity:"
   Hebrews 9:27 "And as it is appointed unto men once to die, but after this the judgment:"
   John 8:24 "...if ye believe not that I am he, ye shall die in your sins..."

7. **The believer's sins.**
   <u>Where they were.</u>
   Isaiah 53:6 "...the LORD hath laid on him the iniquity of us all."
   II Corinthians 5:21 "For he hath made him to be sin for us, who knew no sin; that we might be made the righteousness of God in him."
   I Peter 2:24 "Who his own self bare our sins in his own body on the tree, that we, being dead to sins, should live unto righteousness: by whose stripes ye were healed."
   Hebrews 1:3 "Who being the brightness of his glory, and the express image of his person, and upholding all things by the word of his power, when he had by himself purged our sins, sat down on the right hand of the Majesty on high;"

   <u>Where they are.</u>
   Isaiah 38:17 "...thou hast cast all my sins behind thy back."
   Isaiah 44:22 "I have blotted out, as a thick cloud, thy transgressions, and, as a cloud, thy sins: return unto me; for I have redeemed thee."
   Psalm 103:12 "As far as the east is from the west, so far hath he removed our transgression from us."
   Micah 7:19 "...thou wilt cast all their sin into the depths of the sea."
   Colossians 2:13 "And you, being dead in your sins...hath he quickened together with him, having forgiven you all trespasses;"
   Hebrews 10:17 "And their sins and iniquities will I remember no more."

Propitiation for Our Sins
I John 4:1-21

Text: I John 4:10 "Herein is love, not that we loved God, but that he loved us, and sent his Son to be the propitiation for our sins."

Introduction: Four different "not's" will be discussed.
1. Not that we loved God.
2. Not the righteous, but sinners.
3. Not by works of righteousness.
4. Not I, but Christ.

I Point: <u>Not that we loved God.</u>
    a. I John 4:10 "...but that he loved us,..."
    b. What a good thing this is. For if it was by our loving Him, what a poor chance we would have.
       Application: You tell me; how much do you love God?
       It is His love that conceived the plan of salvation.

II Point: <u>Not the righteous, but sinners.</u>
    a. No merit entitles us to salvation. We are none of us good enough.
       Romans 3:10 "As it is written, There is none righteous, no, not one:"
       Matthew 9:13 "...I am not come to call the righteous, but sinners to repentance."
       1. The thief on the cross.
       2. The Apostle Paul calling himself the chief of sinners.
       3. The cruel jailer in Acts 16:25-34.
       4. The Samaritan woman. (John chapter 4).
    b. Romans 5:6 "For when we were yet without strength, in due time Christ died for the ungodly."
       He died for you and me.

III Point: <u>Not by works of righteousness.</u>
    a. Titus 3:5 "Not by works of righteous which we have done, but according to his mercy he saved us, by the washing of regeneration, and renewing of the Holy Ghost;"
    b. Ephesians 2:9. "Not of works, lest any man should boast."
       Not by works of righteousness which we have done such as: baptism, confirmation, Holy Communion, or joining a church, etc.
    c. Not by religious works such as: living morally, church work, giving, doing good, etc.

d. It is not that God is not pleased with such type of works, but they will not suffice to save us.
  e. Only one work counts: Only the finished work of Christ, can avail for salvation.

IV Point: <u>"Not I, but Christ."</u>
  a. Galatians 2:20 "I am crucified with Christ: nevertheless I live; yet not I, but Christ liveth in me: and the life which I now live in the flesh I live by the faith of the Son of God, who loved me, and gave himself for me."
  b. This reveals the true secret. Salvation is not from myself. Salvation is of the Lord.
    1. Christ in me for life and holiness.
    2. Christ with me for peace and service.

Conclusion: Colossians 1:27 "...Christ in you, the hope of glory:"

Sermon Outlines from the Book of Revelation

What God Sees in the Churches
Revelation 3:1-22

Introduction: Revelation 2:29 "He that hath an ear, let him hear..." This is repeated again and again, after each message to each of these seven churches, so that they are without an excuse before God.

You may say, "Let him hear what?
Answer: Rev. 2:29 "...what the Spirit saith unto the churches."

I Point: Revelation 2:1-7 - The message to the Church at Ephesus.
  a. Good works.
  b. Hard labour.
  c. Long patience.
  d. Hating of evil.
  e. Standing for the truth.
     Application: Well, what could be said or seen against this church? Surly it is good?
     God says, Revelation 2:4 "Nevertheless I have somewhat against thee, because thou hast left thy first love."
  1. **Compromise!!**
     Revelation: 2:5 "Remember therefore from whence thou art fallen and repent,..."
  2. Do you think there could be a lesson for us in this message of the Spirit to the church of Ephesus?
  3. The lesson is: Do not compromise with the world.

II Point: Revelation 2:8-11 -The message to the Church at Smyrna.
  a. Good works.
  b. Tribulation.
  c. Poverty.
     Application: God sees them rich, and promises to them a crown of life if they be faithful unto death.
  1. He also sees those who are just carrying the name, but in their hearts they are blasphemers.
  2. However He says, Revelation 2:10 "Fear none of those things which thou shalt suffer:..."
  3. Isaiah 41:10 "Fear thou not; for I am with thee: be not dismayed; for I am thy God: I will strengthen thee; yea, I will help thee; yea, I will uphold thee with the right hand of my righteousness."

III Point: Revelation 2:12-17 - Message to the Church at Pergamos.
    a.   Good works.
    b.   Holding fast His name.
         Application: But she is compromising with the lust of the world.
    c.   Revelation 2:16 "Repent, or else I will come unto thee quickly, and will fight against them with the sword of my mouth."

IV Point: Revelation 2:18-29 - Message to the Church at Thyatira.
    a.   Good works.
    b.   Charity.
    c.   But immorality.
         God says, Revelation 2:22 "Behold, I will cast her into a bed, and them that commit adultery with her into great tribulation, except they repent of our deeds."

V Point: Revelation 3:1-6 - Message to the Church at Sardis.
    a.   Has a name as a Church of Christ, but is dead.
         Application: What a picture of our today's churches.
         1.   Fundamental, but dead.
         2.   Sound, but saints asleep.
    b.   Revelation 3:4 - Yet, there are a few, alive even at Sardis.

VI Point: Revelation 3: 7-13 - Message to the Church of Philadelphia.
    a.   Revelation 3:8 "I know thy works: behold, I have set before thee an open door, and no man can shut it;..."
         Application: Revelation 3:10 - This is the church that He (the Lord) will keep out of tribulation. They shall meet Him in the air. They shall be taken up. Why? Because they had a heart for the lost, and an open door for the gospel.

VII Point: Revelation 3:14-19 - Message to the Church of Laodicea.
    a.   Revelation 3:15 "I know thy works, that thou art neither cold nor hot:..." You just exist. Are you a Christian? Sure, but that is all. You have no care, no love for others, and God says, "...I will spue thee out of my mouth." (Revelation 3:16).
    b.   Self-exaltation. Revelation 3:17 - boasting, proud, rich in their own eyes, but poor in Spirit.
         Illustration: A man who has everything around him, but nothing upward.

Witnesses Concerning Christ
Revelation 5:1-14

Theme: Witnesses concerning Christ as the Son of God.
Text: Revelation 5:11-14.

Introduction: John 20:31 "But these are written, that ye might believe that Jesus is the Christ, the Son of God; and that believing ye might have life through his name." The best way we may know that anything is true is by witnesses. Truth is always certified by faithful witnesses.

1st Witness: John the Baptist.
　John 1:34 "And I saw, and bare record that this is the Son of God."

2nd Witness: The voice from heaven.
　Matthew 3:17 "And lo a voice from heaven, saying, This is my beloved Son, in whom I am well pleased."

3rd Witness: Nathanael when he met Jesus.
　John 1:49 "Nathanael answered and saith unto him, Rabbi; thou art the Son of God; thou art the King of Israel."

4th Witness: The unclean spirits:
　Mark 3:11 "And unclean spirits, when they saw him, fell down before him, and cried, saying, Thou art the Son of God."

5th Witness: The people who saw Him.
　Matthew 14:33 "Then they that were in the ship came and worshipped him, saying, Of a truth thou art the Son of God."

6th Witness: Jesus Himself
　Mark 14:61-63 "...the high priest asked him, and said unto him, Art thou the Christ, the Son of the Blessed? And Jesus said, I am: and ye shall see the Son of man sitting on the right hand of power, and coming in the clouds of heaven. Then the high priest rent his clothes, and saith, What need we any farther witnesses?"

7th Witness: All the heavenly host.
　Revelation 5:11-13 "And I beheld, and I heard the voice of many angels round about the throne and the beasts and the elders: and the number of them was ten thousand times ten thousand, and thousands of thousands; Saying with a loud voice, Worthy is the Lamb that was slain to receive power, and riches, and wisdom, and strength, and honour, and glory, and blessing."

Conclusion: Here we have seven witnesses. These are only a very few. Do you believe they spoke the truth? If so, will you join them in witnessing for Christ?

Romans 10:9 "That if thou shalt confess with thy mouth the Lord Jesus, and shalt believe in thine heart that God hath raised him from the dead, thou shalt be saved."

Matthew 10:32 "Whosoever therefore shall confess me before men, him will I confess also before my Father which is in heaven."

I John 4:2 "Hereby know ye the Spirit of God: Every spirit that confesseth that Jesus Christ is come in the flesh is of God:"

Philippians 2:11 "And that every tongue should confess that Jesus Christ is Lord, to the glory of God the Father."

The Final and Last Resurrection
Revelation 20:11-15

Introduction: Last Sunday we saw the final heaven, and we saw the beauty of heaven brought out in I Corinthians 2:9 "...Eye hath not seen, nor ear heard, neither have entered into the heart of man, the things which God hath prepared for them that love him."

I Point: The Present Hell.
Or the abode of departed unsaved Spirits.
  a. The word hell is not a popular word to preach on. People will say God is too good; He is too just to send men to hell. Some say it is a medieval age doctrine.
  b. But the Bible more frequently speaks of the wrath of God than of the love of God. The love of God is mentioned 28 times. The wrath of God is mentioned 61 times. Christ speaks more often of punishment than of heavenly joy.

II Point: The present and future hell distinguished.
  a. Last Sunday we made clear distinction between the present heaven (The Bride), and the future heaven (New Jerusalem).
  b. Now let us distinguish between the present hell and the hell of the future.
   i. The Present Hell, "Hades."
      That is the place Luke 16:22-33 speaks about.
   ii. The Future Hell, "Gehenna." Christ said in Matthew 23:33 "Ye serpents, ye generation of vipers, how can ye escape the damnation of hell?" (Gehenna)
   iii. Tartarus Hell: The place where the fallen angels are.
      II Peter 2:4 "For if God spared not the angels that sinned, but cast them down to hell, (Tartarus) and delivered them into chains of darkness, to be reserved unto judgment;" also Jude 1:6 "And the angels which kept not their first estate, but left their own habitation, he hath reserved in everlasting chains under darkness unto the judgment of the great day."
   iv. The Present Hell "Hades" of Luke 16:24 is very clearly pictured as being a flame. Luke 16:24 "...I am tormented in this flame."
      Mark 9:43 "...the fire that never shall be quenched:"

III Point: <u>The resurrection of the wicked</u>.
  a. Just as the righteous will not remain in paradise to spend eternity in a disembodied state; so, neither will the wicked remain in "Hades" in a disembodied state.
  b. Revelation: 20:13 "And the sea gave up the dead which were in it; and death and hell (Hades) delivered up the dead which were in them:…"
  Application: That means that the graves gave up the body, and so did the sea. And hades "Hell" delivered up the spirits in it. And these wicked ones again stand before God in their three unison – body, soul, and spirit.
  Illustration: There will be no desire for them to rise. But they must appear before the judgment in their body.
  c. They stand before the Great White Throne Judgment.
  Not to see whether or not they are eternally lost. They know they are eternally lost. But this is a judgment of the body as well as of the spirit.
  There will be degrees of punishment. (Luke 12:47-48).
  There we notice that death and hades or (Hell) will be cast into the lake of fire; or as in the Hebrew (Tophet), or as in the Greek (Gehenna). It is called this in the New Testament 12 times. Then the words Lake of Fire are used 5 times to describe Gehenna or Tophet.
  d. Second death. It is when the body, which is raised mortal and corruptible, will die the second time, and the spirit that is the life of that soul will be in torment forever in the lake of fire.

Conclusion: Revelation 20:15 "And whosoever was not found written in the book of life was cast into the lake of fire."
Revelation 21:8 "But the fearful, and unbelieving, and the abominable, and murderers, and whoremongers, and sorcerers, and idolaters, and all liars, shall have their part in the lake which burneth with fire and brimstone: which is the second death."
Revelation 20:12 "And I saw the dead, small and great, stand before God, and the books are opened: and another book was opened, which is the book of life: and the dead were judged out of those things which were written in the books according to their works."
According to Luke 12:47-48, there are degrees of punishment, and the dead shall be judged according to their works. All those who deserve the first degree of punishment are recorded there. Also there are those whose lives were so good and moral that they could plead that they were just, but whose names failed to appear in the

book of life. Matthew 7:22-24 "Many will say to me in that day, Lord, Lord, have we not prophesied in thy name? and in thy name have cast out devils? and in thy name done many wonderful works? And then will I profess unto them, I never knew you: depart from me, ye that work iniquity." These also were cast into the lake of fire.

Isaiah 30:33 "For Tophet is ordained of old; yea, for the king it is prepared; he hath made it deep and large: the pile thereof is fire and much wood; the breath of the LORD, like a stream of brimstone, doth kindle it."

The lake of fire burns with brimstone (sulfur). The dictionary says brimstone is a blue flame with suffocating odor.

<u>Bible verses that refers to the lake of fire.</u>
1. Matthew 3:12 "...But he will burn up the chaff with unquenchable fire."
2. Matthew 5:22 "...whosoever shall say, Thou fool, shall be in danger of hell fire."
3. Matthew 5:29 "...and not that thy whole body should be cast into hell."
4. Matthew 10:28 "...fear him which is able to destroy both soul and body in hell."
5. Matthew 13:42 "And shall cast them into a furnace of fire: there shall be wailing and gnashing of teeth."
6. Matthew 18:8-9 "...rather than having two hands or two feet [or two eyes] to be cast into hell fire."
7. Matthew 23:15 "...ye make him twofold more the child of hell than yourselves."
8. Matthew 23:33 "Ye serpents, ye generation of vipers, how can ye escape the damnation of hell?"
9. Matthew 25:46 "And these shall go away into everlasting punishment:..."
10. Mark 9:44 "...Where their worm dieth not, and the fire is not quenched."
11. Luke 12:5 "...Fear him, which after he hath killed hath power to cast into hell;..."
12. Revelation 20:15 "And whosoever was not found written in the book of life was cast into the lake of fire."
13. Revelation 21:8 "But the fearful, and unbelieving, and the abominable, and murderers, and whoremongers, and sorcerers, and idolaters, and all liars, shall have their part in the lake which burneth with fire and brimstone: which is the second death."

The Great White Throne
Revelation 20:11-15

I Point: <u>Judgment - Who is the judge?</u>
    a. Revelation 20:12 – God the Father is the judge.
    b. I Timothy 2:5 – Tells us that today we have a meditator or intercessor between man and God the Father, even Christ.
    c. But in those days there shall be no mediator.

II Point: <u>Who is to be judged</u>?
    a. II Peter 3:7 "But the heavens and the earth, which are now, by the same word are kept in store, reserved unto fire against the day of judgment and perdition of ungodly men."
    b. Revelation 20:12 – All the wicked died small and great, good and bad. All such whose names were not found in the book of life.
    c. The supreme question in that day will be, "Is your name written in the book of life?"
    d. Revelation 21:27 "And there shall in no wise enter into it any thing that defileth, neither whatsoever worketh abomination, or maketh a lie: but they which are written in the Lamb's book of Life."
    e. The wicked will not be judged. They are already condemned. John 3:18 "...he that believeth not is condemned already..."
    f. They are judged not to see whether or not they are entitled to eternal life, but to determine their degree of punishment. Luke 12:47-48 "And that servant, which knew his lord's will, and prepared not himself, neither did according to his will, shall be beaten with many stripes. But he that knew not, and did commit things worthy of stripes, shall be beaten with few stripes..."
    g. There is no escape.
    h. Revelation 20:11 – The earth fled away, and sky also. No more footholds on the old earth (world).

III Point: <u>What is to be the final and just judgment?</u>
    a. Revelation 21:8 - Lake of Fire, burning with fire and brimstone.
    b. Revelation 20:14 – The second death for the body, but eternal dying for the spirit.
    c. Mark 9:48 "Where their worm dieth not, and the fire is not quenched."

    d. Matthew 25:41 "...Depart from me, ye cursed, into everlasting fire,..."
    e. Matthew 25:46 "And these shall go away into everlasting punishment:...."
    f. Matthew 13:41-42 "The Son of man shall send forth his angels, and they shall gather out of his kingdom all things that offend, and them which do iniquity; And shall cast them into a furnace of fire: there shall be wailing and gnashing of teeth."

IV Point: <u>Will this be eternal?</u>
    a. If heaven is to be eternal then hell is to be eternal. One demands the other. And if Satan ever gets out again he will try the same thing over.
    b. If hell were not eternal why was Christ's supreme sacrifice on Calvary made? If souls would ever have a chance to get free from hell, then Christ died in vain. He paid too great a price.
    c. Here are Christ's own words. Matthew 25:46 "And these (the wicked) shall go away into everlasting punishment: but the righteous unto life eternal."
    These words everlasting and eternal are one and the same word, translated from the word, (Aionios) which is also used for the existence of God. And if that does not mean eternal then we must also believe that heaven and God will someday end and be blotted out. But if it means that God is eternal, then that means heaven and hell are eternal.

V Point: <u>For ever and ever</u>.
    a. What do we understand by the expression for ever and ever?
    b. Revelation 14:11 "And the smoke of their torment ascended up for ever and ever: and they have no rest day or night..."

Conclusion:
Revelation 20:10 "And the devil that deceived them was cast into the lake of fire and brimstone, where the beast and false prophet are, and shall be tormented day and night for ever and ever."

Jesus said, Revelation 1:18 "I am he that liveth, and was dead; and, behold, I am alive for evermore, Amen; and have the keys of hell and of death."

Whom Do You Expect to See in Heaven?

Revelation 21:1-17

Text: Revelation: 21:27 "And there shall in no wise enter into it any thing that defileth, neither whatsoever worketh abomination, or maketh a lie: but they which are written in the Lamb's Book of life."

Introduction: There are so many people that hope to get into heaven, but they don't know what company they will have there. If you really find out you might not even like to be there.

I Point: <u>Population of Heaven</u>.
   a. Of course you only hope to meet those that belong to a church. Is that right???
   b. Or those who have done the very best they could.
   c. Perhaps only those who are greatly respected in the world - the big shots.
   d. Or perhaps only those who belong to a nice society, drive a nice car, and have a nice home.
   e. Or perhaps it is the preachers only and the choir singers that will be there.
   f. Or perhaps it is only your particular church.
   g. Or perhaps it is only those who can say I had never yet quarreled with my neighbor.
   h. What do you think? Who do you think you will find there?

II Point: <u>Who will be there</u>?
   a. Matthew 21:31 "...Verily I say unto you, That the publicans and the harlots go into the kingdom of God before you."

   b. Heaven will be populated with murders, harlots, thieves, liars, ugly ones, and the poor and beggars.

   c. Here is the company among which we found Jesus when He was on earth. Mark 2:16-17 "And when the scribes and Pharisees saw him eat with publicans and sinners, they said unto his disciples, How is it that he eateth and drinketh with publicans and sinners? When Jesus heard it, he saith unto them, They that are whole have no need of the physician, but they that are sick: I came not to call the righteous, but sinners to repentance."

d. All these, regardless of what sort they are that have heard His call and came out, they shall be in Heaven.
  Revelation: 7:14 "These are they which...have washed their robes, and made them white in the blood of the Lamb."
  Revelation 21:27 "And there shall in no wise enter into it any thing that defileth, neither whatsoever worketh abomination, or maketh a lie: but they which are written in the Lamb's book of life."

If you hope to be there you must be washed, "Born again:"
  a. Isaiah 1:18 "Come now, and let us reason together, saith the LORD: though your sins be as scarlet, they shall be as white as snow; though they be red like crimson, they shall be as wool."
  b. I John 1:9 "If we confess our sins, he is faithful and just to forgive us our sins, and to cleanse us from all unrighteousness."
  c. I John 1:7 "But if we walk in the light, as he is in the light, we have fellowship one with another, and the blood of Jesus Christ his Son cleanseth us from all sin."
  d. John 3:7 "...Ye must be born again."

III Point: <u>The population of hell</u>.
  a. The first one everybody will see in hell will be the preachers who preached a lie. The blind leading the blind. Matthew 15:14 "...And if the blind lead the blind, both shall fall into the ditch."
  The reason why he will be first noticed is because everybody will point their finger at him and say you preached a lie.
  b. There will be "so called" Christians there.
  c. There will be good church workers there.
  d. There will be people who sang in the choir there.
  e. There will be murderers there with blood still dripping from their hands.
  f. There will be the blasphemers.
  g. There will be harlots with their rotten old bodies burning in hell.
  h. And yes, there will be loving fathers and mothers there, pointed out by their children who will say, "You told me a lie."

Revelation 21:8 "But the fearful, and unbelieving, and the abominable, and murderers, and whoremongers, and sorcerers, and idolaters, and all liars, shall have their part in the lake which burneth with fire and brimstone: which is the second death."

Why shall these be found in Hell?
   a. Not because of their sin. Isaiah 1:18 "...though your sins be as scarlet, they shall be as white as snow;..."
   b. But simply because of their rejection of Christ.

      1. Mark 16:16 "...he that believeth not shall be damned."
      2. John 3:18 "...he that believeth not is condemned already..."
      3. John 3:36 "...he that believeth not the Son shall not see life; but the wrath of God abideth on him."
      4. Hebrews 2:3 "How shall we escape, if we neglect so great salvation;"

Conclusion:
Will you be, tonight, a child of the King of Kings?

The Final Heaven
Revelation 21:1-8

Text: Revelation 21:1 "And I saw a new heaven..."

Introduction: Last Sunday we had the glorified resurrected bodies. We noticed the substance these bodies are made of, and the actions these bodies could perform. As well as the liberty we shall enjoy when in a glorified body. Today I would like to take up the eternal abode of the righteous.

I Point: <u>The Present Heaven</u>.
  a. Paradise. This is the third heaven, or the present heaven.
  b. In the presence of Christ, but disembodied. But Paul said which is far better, even now.
  c. We learned last time that they will not always be there. But will receive their bodies at the second coming of Christ.

II Point: <u>No saint has yet entered the final heaven</u>.
  a. We must clearly distinguish between the present heaven and the eternal final heaven.
  b. There is a wrong impression given to the believers as to the present and final heaven. Your loved ones who trusted in Christ are not yet in the final heaven.

III Point: <u>The Final Heaven</u>.

  Here are references to the final heaven.
  a. Hebrews 11:16 "...he hath prepared for them a city."
  b. Heaven is spoken of as a city. Hebrews 11:10 "...which hath foundations, whose builder and maker is God."
  c. Hebrews 13:14 "For here have we no continuing city, but we seek one to come."
  d. The city is described as the New Jerusalem.
     Revelation 21:16 "And the city lieth foursquare."
  e. This city in itself is not the entire heaven.
  f. This heavenly city is a prepared place for a prepared people, as per John 14:2-3 "I go to prepare a place for you...that where I am, there ye may be also."

IV Point: <u>The final heaven as a country</u>.

    a. Hebrews 11:14 "...they seek a country."
   Hebrews 11:16 – "...they desire a better country, that is, an heavenly: [country]."

    b. I Peter 1:3-5 - Peter refers to heaven as a place where believers have an inheritance awaiting them.

    c. Paul exclaims, I Corinthians 2:9 "...Eye hath not seen, nor ear heard, neither hath entered into the heart of man, the things which God hath prepared for them that love him."

V Point: <u>The description of heavenly Jerusalem.</u>

    a. We notice here Revelation 21:2 "...I, John, saw the holy city, the New Jerusalem coming down from God out of heaven,..." He describes it as a city having its own light – which is Jesus. And as a stone most precious as per Revelation 21:1-27.

    b. Revelation 21:27 "And there shall in no wise enter into it any thing that defileth, neither whatsoever worketh abomination, or maketh a lie:..."

    c. Jesus said, John 3:3 "...Except a man be born again, he cannot see the kingdom of God."
   Application: If this is to be the place which Christ has prepared for his saints, the new heaven, then it can only be a New Jerusalem; for the country of Jerusalem cannot embrace all the redeemed.

       Revelation 21:16 - The size of this city, the New Jerusalem, is 12,000 furlong foursquare, or 1,500 miles foursquare, or 22,500 miles long and the broad one mile high.

Conclusion: Are you looking forward to the New Jerusalem?

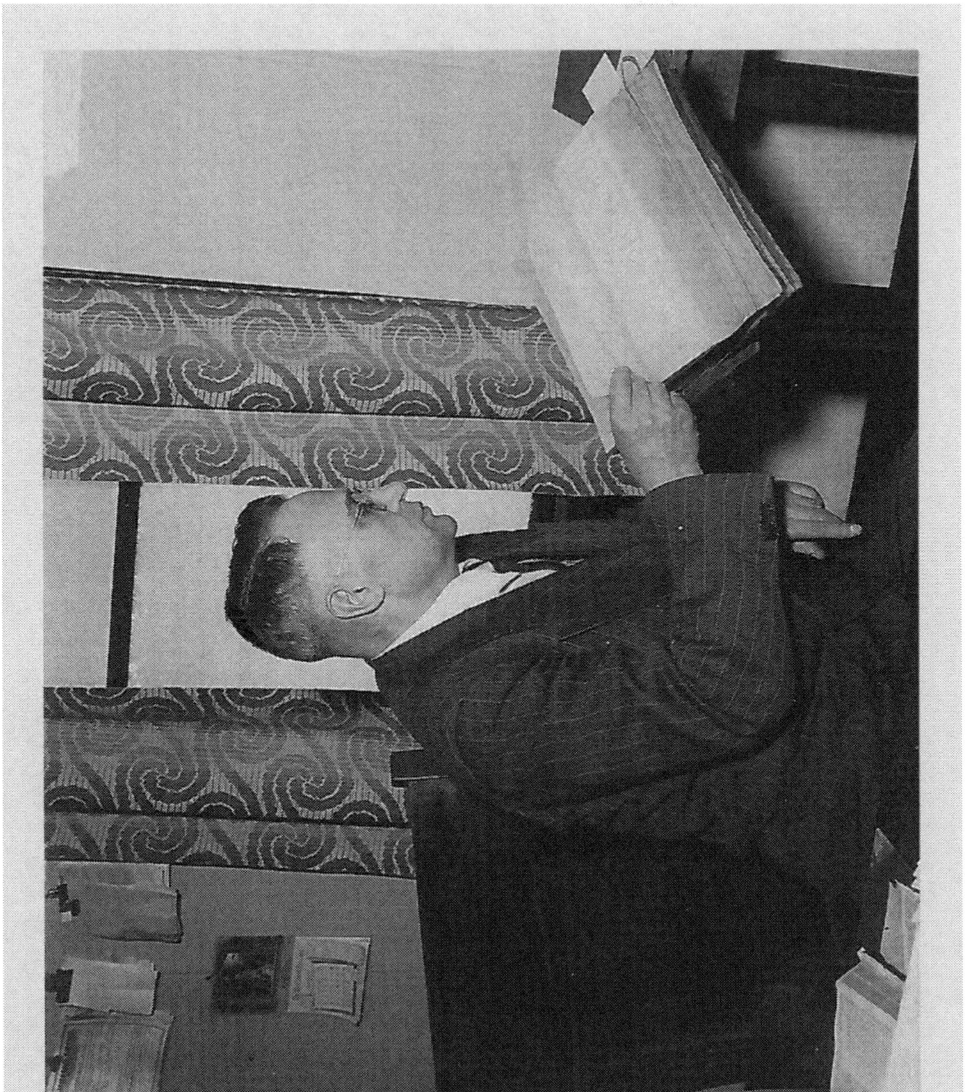

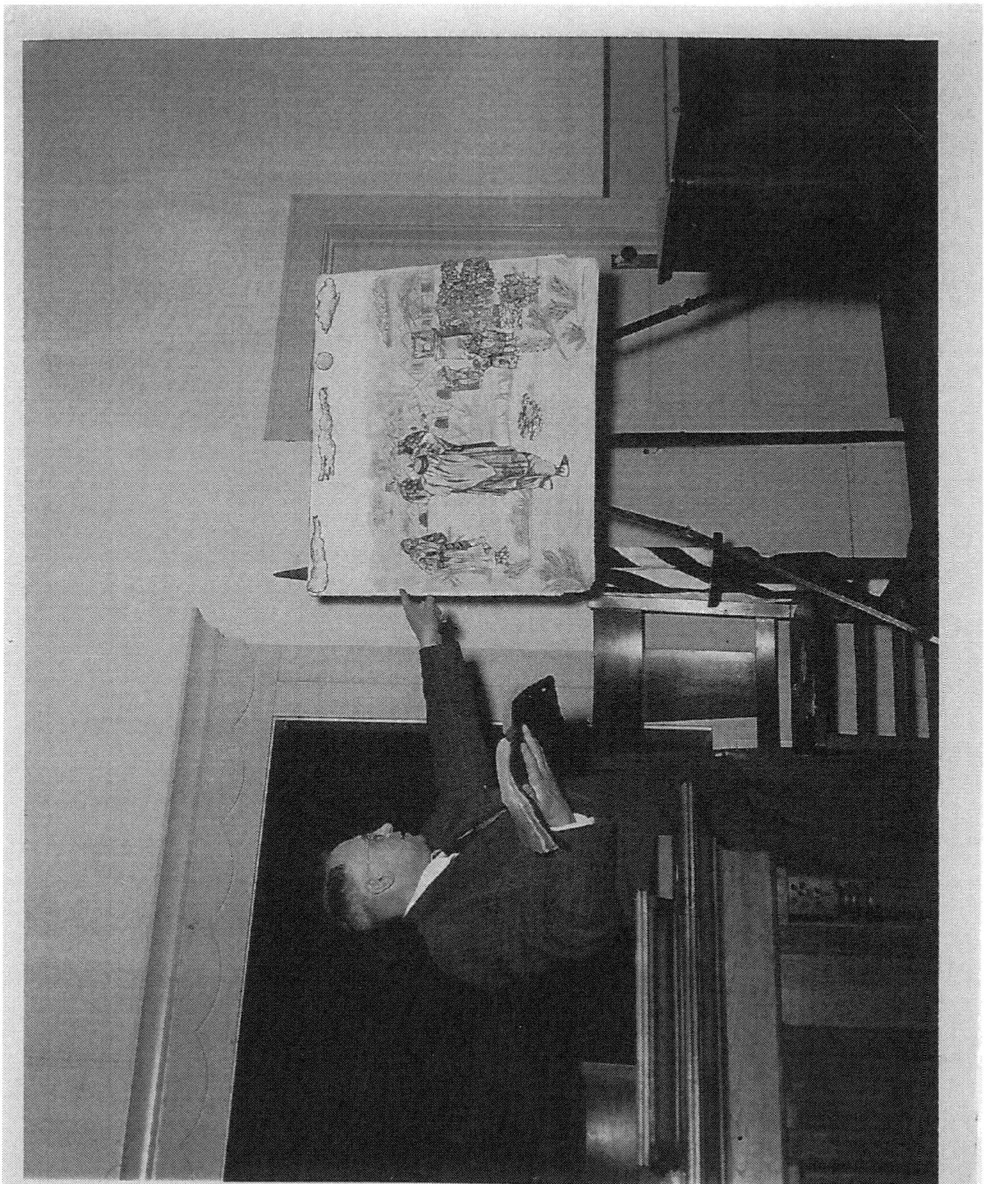

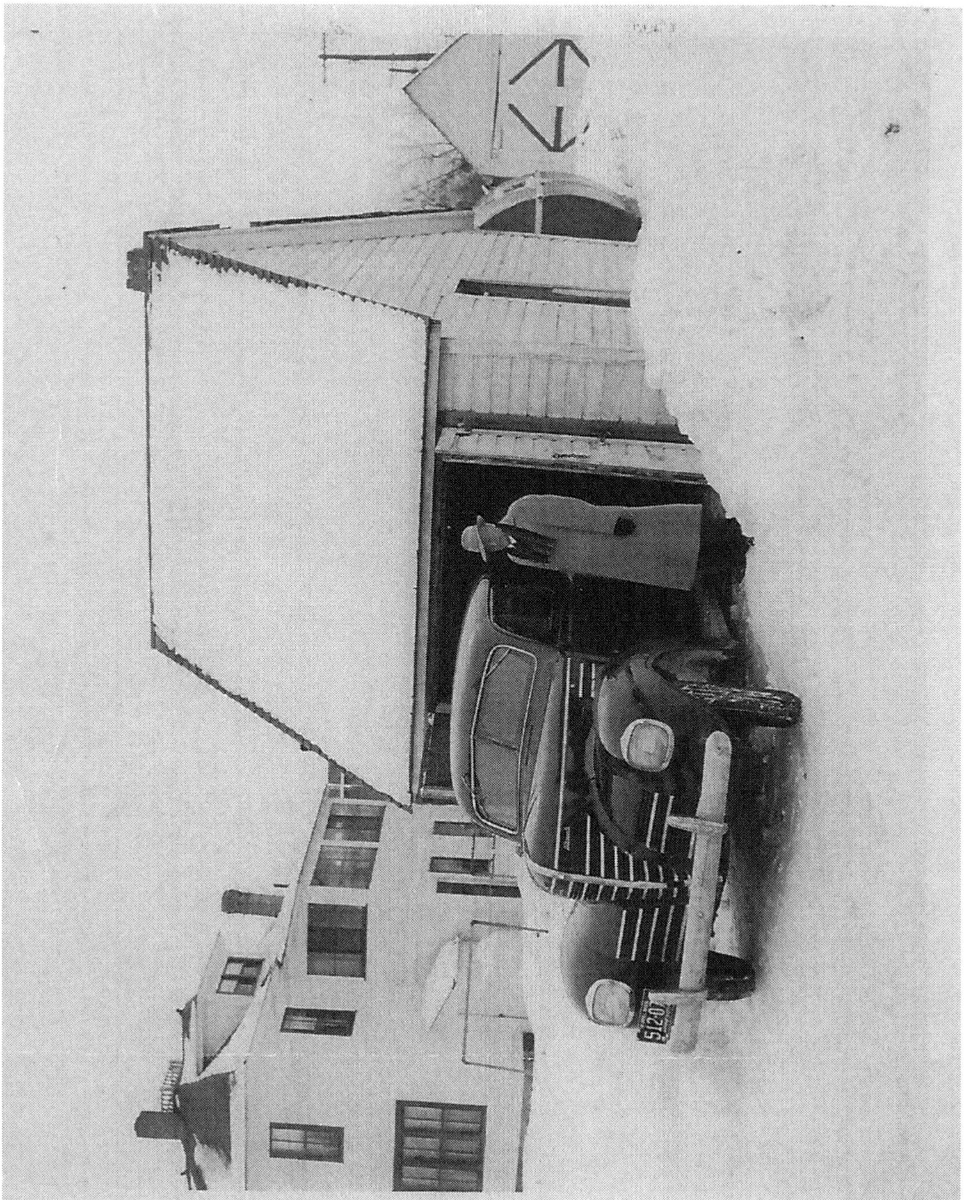

Quotes of Mark Houseman

"The blessed part of Christian life is to overcome trials and to triumph over difficulties."

"God will not look you over for medals, degrees and diplomas, but for scars."

"God will never permit temptation to come upon you, unless He can trust you to be faithful."

"The idea that it takes something very peculiar to promote a revival is unscriptural. The churches have been trying now everything: picture shows, music, programs and feasting. But there is one thing they have not done. They have not returned from their backsliding. The Church has not returned to its knees."

"True Christianity is made up of an empty cross, an empty tomb, and a glorified risen Saviour sitting at the right hand of God."

"Faith without testing is the same as muscles with exercise."

"There is no trouble too big, no humiliation too deep, no suffering too severe, no love too strong, no labour too hard, and no expense too great, if it is spent in the effort to win a soul."

"God expects that the gospel should go out from us as living water goes out from the fountain."

"God's price demands not a creed, not a church, not a method, but a life unto death."

"It is when we have joy in the sufferings for Christ that we touch the hem of His garment."

"To be made conformable with Christ is not just a profession, nor is it just a verbal confession, it is a transformation."

Made in the USA
Columbia, SC
24 February 2019